For Amanda, David and Olivia

Contents

Foreword

Jonathan Simon[1]

Wrongful Convictions, Miscarriages of Justice, and the Path to a Better Politics of Criminal Justice

As I write this, the execution of a death row inmate, Troy Davis, by the State of Georgia in the United States continues to draw media attention and expressions of outrage from around the world. The outcry over Davis' execution, the latest of more than one thousand since the resumption of capital punishment in 1977, is a testament not to opposition to capital punishment (most executions draw little comment), but lingering doubt over Davis' guilt. Convicted of shooting an Atlanta police officer to death more than twenty years ago, Davis maintained his innocence from the start. Davis' claim has been bolstered in recent years by the fact that a number of eye-witnesses recanted their testimony and blamed heavy police coercion for their original testimony. His cause was taken up by a large number of prominent public figures, not only traditional death penalty opponents, but also a former Director of the Federal Bureau of Investigation and a conservative former Member of Congress from Georgia. In 2010 the US Supreme Court ordered a lower court to conduct a hearing into Davis' innocence claims. Despite the fact that the court failed to find sufficient reason to overturn the verdict, doubt continued up to the moment of Davis' execution, with the George Board of Pardons (which has the power to commute a sentence) apparently splitting 3–2, and final temporary stay by the Supreme Court.

Twenty years ago, in the early 1990s, as death sentences and support for the death penalty surged, a small cluster of US lawyers and journalists began to promote a public awareness that potentially many US prisoners, including on death row, were wrongfully convicted; victims of heavy-handed police tactics, junk science experts in forensic identification of crime-scene evidence, incompetent defense lawyers and unprincipled prosecutors (all compounded by 'death qualified' juries who brought something less than a presumption of innocence to their work). As new DNA technology made it possible to re-examine biological evidence from even decades-

---

[1]Adrian A. Kragen Professor of Law, UC Berkeley.

old cases, lawyers succeeded in reopening cases and winning the release of prisoners. These victories created powerful media events. Few things (except violent crimes themselves) compete in drama and televisibility with the story of a person wrongly locked in prison for decades under threat of execution. The images of middle-aged men, both softened by age and hardened by prison into a dignified but non-threatening solidity, walk-ing into the embrace of siblings and adult children who had kept their faith alive for years, touched an American public supposedly unified behind a common sense as victims of a high-crime society and support for harsh and unremitting punishment.

Like most criminologists and socio-legal scholars at the time, I per-sonally failed to see much importance in these developments. Alarmed by the growth of mass incarceration since the start of my graduate studies in the early 1980s, I was primarily concerned with understanding why Americans were so committed to excessively punishing the guilty (com-pared to historic norms). If some of those convictions were tainted by pro-cedural failures, even if in some cases that meant that a factually innocent person was being punished, that was at worst a poignant but small result of the same intemperate turn in penality. Today it is clear that this could not have been more wrong. The work of overturning long finalized con-victions in court, and collating a growing list of 'high risk' police and pros-ecutorial factors that can lead to wrongful convictions, has produced what Michel Foucault would have called a 'power/knowledge' formation in which legal actions, were producing 'truth effects,' which were in turn producing new opportunities for action. The action has even moved, albeit slowly, into legislatures, long the engines of excessive punishment, which began to debate recommendations to outlaw poor forensic practices and to estab-lish clearer legal pathways to challenge suspicious evidence.

Today there is widespread agreement among observers that the issue of wrongful convictions is responsible for a significant drop in public support for the death penalty in the United States, along with substantial declines in the number of death sentences sought by prosecutors and handed down by jurors. The spotlight shown on problematic police investigations and the lack of prosecutorial oversight has also opened a new vulnerability to the broader apparatus of excessive punishment. For decades, under the slogan of 'war on crime,' enhancing the power of police and shielding them from judicial oversight, has been seen as synonymous with protect-ing the public from violent crime. Wrongful convictions raise the poss-ibility or even probability that the actual perpetrator remains at large and possibly still active criminally, an inference that places 'tough on crime' policies disastrously out of joint with creating public safety.

While there is no empirical evidence yet that this injury to the logic of the war on crime is weakening public support for long prison sentences and the weakening of legal due process procedures, comparable to that detected in support for capital punishment, it may be occurring. Prison populations are dropping in many states and some have even begun sentencing reforms and while these developments are attributable to a number of factors, including long-term declines in crime rates and hard fiscal times, these effects would likely be far more limited had the knowledge/power spiral of wrongful convictions not begun to undermine the politics of punitive populism.

Most of the work by criminologists and socio-legal scholars on this topic has focused on documenting the frequency of wrongful convictions and classifying and analyzing the practices which produce it. In the UK, a stronger critical criminology tradition has also produced a discussion of the structures of power and inequality that cause justice processes to fail (or to succeed at some other, perniciously motivated project of race or class control). In effect, this scholarship extends that basic knowledge/power spiral of litigation and journalism around wrongful convictions with a focus on policy solutions or political critiques.

Michael Naughton's *Rethinking Miscarriages of Justice: Beyond the Tip of the Iceberg*, first published in 2007, made knowledge/power effects of wrongful convictions itself the subject on the inquiry in a central way. Rather than investigate the factual predicates of wrongful convictions or trace the pattern of discriminations inscribed in the operation of criminal justice and manifest in these miscarriages of justice, Naughton examined the consequences of how wrongful convictions were being problematized in both popular and criminological discourse and explored how those effects might be expanded considerably by problematizing them in different ways and in different fields.

As the title suggests, the first and most important move is reframing (and renaming) the problem from the presence of factually innocent people in prison (one possible meaning of wrongful conviction) to a problem of all people who are in prison (or subject to other criminal penalties) because of a procedural failure of justice, whether they are factually guilty or innocent. This is a move well justified in at least two senses. First, the legal system is simply not constituted to produce either factual guilt or innocence. To prioritize those external events, like DNA, or confessions, which can bring strong evidence of such a status into the legal process, is to render invisible a vastly larger multitude of individuals whose cases do not involve such evidence. Second, because the substantive harms of wrongful conviction, both to the individual involved and to the integrity and legitimacy of the legal system are largely the same. Troy Davis' case is a good example of this. There was no definitive evidence proving his innocence, and he was executed after a court in an extraordinary procedure ordered by the Supreme Court failed to find him innocent. Yet many features of the police investigation of his case, including coercive tactics used against witnesses reveal the kind of practices associated with the war on crime that both denies rights and undermines the reliability and thus the crime control mission of the law.

As Naughton documents, examining miscarriages of justice in this broader sense immediately and radically rescales and distributes the field. Much of the discussion of wrongful conviction has focused solely on those released from prison by virtue of extraordinary court actions (through a habeas petition in the US or a referral by the Criminal Cases Review Commission), and often by the introduction of new evidence in the form of DNA, witness recantations, or a confession by another person, a class that consists of a relatively tiny portion of criminal cases. The miscarriages of justice framework brings in all cases where a conviction has been reversed by a court, including the through the routine appellate process; a class of cases that number in the thousands in the UK and the tens of thousands in the US on an annual basis.

The potential power/knowledge effects of problematizing miscarriages of justice can be expanded further by broadening the legal context of miscarriage of justice to human rights (especially in the UK where the Human Rights Act and the European Convention on Human Rights open important channels for legal and political claims to be raised, but increasingly in the US as well) and by exploring the range of harms created by such miscarriages that lie beyond the continuing incarceration of those wrongfully convicted. Indeed this is the kind of expansion of which will be necessary if the knowledge/power effects produced by the emergence of wrongful convictions is going to help to produce a broad transformation of the way criminal justice is used to govern contemporary societies.

In this regard *Miscarriages of Justice* anticipates Ian Loader and Richard Sparks' recent call[2] for criminologists to abandon the effort to wish away the public and political influence on criminal justice in favor of an effort to contribute toward a 'better politics' of crime. With its focus on how the framing of wrongful conviction acts to shape the ways government itself is problematized, the Miscarriages of Justice is an effort to turn criminology and socio-legal studies from how criminal justice governs the

---

[2]Ian Loader and Richard Sparks, *Public Criminology?* (Routledge 2010).

population (an important topic on which much ink has been spilled), towards the possibility of counter flows of knowledge and the surveillance of government by the governed, a topic on which very little has been said and which makes this an important read well beyond criminology and socio-legal studies.

List of Tables

Preface

The issue of miscarriages of justice has always been a constant pressing social concern, not least for the obvious harm caused to the victims. At the same time, the possibility that innocent people have been wrongly convicted of serious crimes has resulted in some of the most progressive changes to the criminal justice system in attempts to prevent their occurrence in the future. The case of Adolf Beck led to the establishment of the Court of Criminal Appeal in 1907; the Confait Affair resulted in the Royal Commission on Criminal Procedure and the introduction of formal guidelines on police investigations under the Police and Criminal Evidence Act (1984); the Guildford Four, the Birmingham Six, and other less well publicised cases, led to the Royal Commission on Criminal Justice and the establishment of the Criminal Cases Review Commission; more recently, the cases of Sally Clark and Angela Cannings have raised significant questions about the limits of forensic expert witness evidence.

This signalled to me the validity of a process for introducing changes to the criminal justice system (that may equally apply to other areas of society, too), described by Michel Foucault as 'governmentality', interpreted here as introducing a new relationship between governed and government in post-sovereign, rule of law societies, under which government needs a mandate from the governed in the form of tangible evidence of real cases that the criminal justice system is in need of corrective intervention. In contrast to existing analyses, I read this as placing a certain onus on the governed in the realm of criminal justice: we must proactively unearth 'errors' with the existing criminal justice system arrangements that cause apparent harm to the governed; we must strive to achieve successful appeals as evidence of such claims, transforming our voices on such causes of harm into powerful forms of counter discourse; we must attempt to cause public crises of confidence in aspects of the criminal justice system as a prerequisite to corrective intervention by government.

Although not the direct topic of this book, the Innocence Network UK and the University of Bristol Innocence Project were founded to link up this dual concern with the wrongful conviction and imprisonment of the innocent and an aspiration to effect changes to the criminal justice system. The hope is to create a machine for unearthing 'errors' with the criminal justice system, evidenced by successful appeals, to prevent and/or reduce wrongful convictions and the harm that they cause, not only to direct victims, but secondary victims and, even, society as a whole. However, as this book makes clear, this does not mean that we should somehow abandon concerns with miscarriages of justice that derive from technical breaches of due process in favour of a narrower concern with the wrongful conviction and/or imprisonment of the innocent. On the contrary, the theoretical perspective constructed in what follows emphasises the extent to which the legitimacy of the criminal justice system depends on a rigid compliance with due process which underpins the relationship between governed and government in the processes of governmentality. Moreover, on a more empirical level, the work of The Innocence Project, a non-profit legal clinic affiliated with the Benjamin N. Cardozo School of Law at Yeshiva University, New York, reaffirms the need for vigilance on the conventional causes of miscarriages of justice. Since it was established in 1992, almost 200 cases have led to exonerations through DNA testing, some of which were of men and women on death row. Perhaps surprisingly, however, The Innocence Project has found that eyewitness misidentification is the single greatest cause of the wrongful conviction of the innocent in the US, playing a role in 75 per cent of convictions overturned through DNA testing; that in more than 25 per cent of the DNA exoneration cases, factually innocent defendants made incriminating statements, delivered outright confessions or pleaded guilty to crimes that they did not commit; and, that in more than 15 per cent of cases of wrongful conviction overturned by DNA testing, an informant or 'jailhouse snitch' testified against the innocent defendant. As such, we must demand adherence to due process, precisely to protect against the wrongful conviction and imprisonment of the innocent.

Defining key terms is an important first step for any sociological enquiry, providing coherence to the analysis and the premises from which it may proceed. As will be seen, this is an urgent task for the study of miscarriages of justice and the wrongful conviction/imprisonment of the innocent, which is in dire need of definitional clarity and methodological consistency. More specifically, the starting point for this book is a radical redefinition of miscarriages of justice, separating how they are understood and practised by the criminal justice system from public discourses that see miscarriages of justice in terms of the wrongful conviction of the innocent. From this platform, a systematic engagement with, and analysis of, the various 'voices' and 'audiences' that mediate the miscarriages of justice problem is undertaken.

Informed and inspired by a novel interpretation of Foucault's theses on power, knowledge and governmentality and the zemiological approach ('zemia' a Greek word meaning 'harm' or 'damage'), I have sought to highlight the limits of the entire criminal justice process and to challenge the dominant discourses in all spheres – media, campaigning, practitioner, academic and governmental – that see miscarriages of justice as rare and exceptional cases of wrongful imprisonment. This exposes miscarriages of justice as mundane features of the criminal justice system, opening up a scale of miscarriages of justice that has not hitherto been subjected to critical appraisal. It reveals the limitations of all previous attempts to reform the criminal justice system to prevent miscarriages of justice. It presents a new perspective on the extensive range and different forms of harm that befall victims of miscarriages of justice and wrongful convictions.

On a more practical level, the available sources for this book were extremely limited. Whilst there is a surfeit of newspaper articles on miscarriages of justice and a growing bank of biographical accounts from victims in high profile cases, there is a dearth of academic literature on any of my main research questions. To account for this, a constructive data analysis approach is adopted to provide information and illustrations for the various analyses that are offered, derived from official statistics, academic literature, newspapers, appeal court judgements and relevant websites. As such, this book is not a review of existing literature on miscarriages of justice. On the contrary, the overall attempt here is to contribute to new ways of thinking about and acting upon miscarriages of justice. It is an attempt to contribute to the production of more effective forms of counter discourse that might, truly, prevent miscarriages of justice from occurring and the extensive range of harmful consequences that they cause. It is to seek to disturb the dominant discourse on miscarriages of justice, replacing it with a new 'regime of truth' that more appropriately portrays the scale of the problem and the damage that they cause.

Finally, there are a number of people that I would like to acknowledge for the part that they have each played in helping to shape my thoughts on these matters. Firstly, thanks to Gregor McLennan and Tom Osborne, the supervisors of the doctoral thesis upon which the book is based, for ongoing support, without which this work would, certainly, have been the poorer; to Ruth Levitas and Paddy Hillyard who also had a hand in the doctoral thesis and/or work since; to Julie Price, Aneurin Morgan Lewis and Mike O' Brien, Innocence Network UK colleagues; to the members of the University of Bristol Innocence Project, especially Gabe

Tan, who also provided invaluable assistance in compiling the index; and, to friends and other colleagues from the wider miscarriage of justice community including Bernard Naughton, Hazel Kierle, Andrew Green, John McManus, Paddy Joe Hill, Paul Blackburn, Kevin Kerrigan, Allan Jamieson, Dennis Eady, Robert Schehr and Bob Woffinden. The usual caveat applies, of course, any error or mistakes are my own.

Michael Naughton

Introduction

The Royal Commission on Criminal Justice (1993) (RCCJ) spells out an authoritative vision of criminal justice that fits well with popular sentiment:

> All law-abiding citizens have a common interest in a system of criminal justice in which the risks of the innocent being convicted...are as low as human fallibility allows...mistaken verdicts can and do sometimes occur and our task [when such occasions arise] is to recommend changes to our system of criminal justice which will make them less likely in the future...The widely publicised miscarriages of justice which have occurred in recent years have created a need to restore public confidence in the criminal justice system (Royal Commission on Criminal Justice, 1993: 2–6).[1]

The task of the legal system from this view is that it should acquit the innocent in criminal trials and, if it is apparent that it is failing in that task, should be quickly brought into line with its intended purpose. From this perspective, it is, perhaps, unsurprising, then, that the public *belief* that the criminal justice system is responsible for convicting an innocent victim has been at the heart of some of the most far-reaching changes of the criminal justice system in the shape of professed safeguards to prevent miscarriages of justice and to restore public confidence that it is operating as it is thought it should.

A recent example of a legislative change to the criminal justice system to prevent possible miscarriages of justice to the innocent flowed from the RCCJ, which was, primarily, established in response to the public crisis of confidence following the successful appeals of the Guildford Four (see Conlon, 1990; May, 1994), the Maguire Seven (see

Kee, 1986) and the Birmingham Six[2] (see Mullin, 1986), all of whom were convicted for crimes related to Irish Republican Army (IRA) bombings in the 1970s.[3] These cases exemplified, among other things,[4] an apparent reluctance by successive Home Secretaries to return potentially meritorious cases in which the public believed the cases of innocent victims of miscarriages of justice back to the Court of Appeal (Criminal Division) (CACD) for political, as opposed to legal, reasons. In resolving the public crisis of confidence in the cases of the Guildford Four, Birmingham Six, and so on, one of the most significant amendments spawned by the RCCJ was the Criminal Appeal Act (1995), which took away the power of referral from the Home Secretary and established the Criminal Cases Review Commission (CCRC), an independent public body with the task of investigating alleged or suspected miscarriages of justice that have already been through the appeals system and have not succeeded (for details, see Criminal Cases Review Commission, 2006).

It is interesting to note, however, that although the CCRC was established in response to a public crisis of confidence based on cases in which innocent victims were *believed* to be unable to overturn their wrongful convictions through the existing post-appeal mechanisms, it is subordinated by statute to the appeal courts, only referring applications if it is felt that there is a 'real possibility' that the case will be overturned (Criminal Appeal Act, 1995: s. 13(1)a). As will become evident, in this sense, the CCRC is not so much concerned with the possible wrongful conviction of the innocent as it is with breaches of due process and, therefore, 'technical' miscarriages of justice. So, too, are a range of other significant changes of the criminal justice system in response to perceived miscarriages of justice to victims believed to be factually innocent that will be detailed below. To be sure, the criminal justice system's notion of a miscarriage of justice does not correspond with popular thoughts as they relate to concerns about the possible wrongful conviction of the innocent. Instead, the official test of a miscarriage of justice relates to prevailing procedures of due process, not whether appellants are innocent.

From this perspective, it is also interesting to note that both popular (deriving from the public and political spheres) and legal discourses alike have excluded from their critical gaze the overwhelming majority of 'low profile' miscarriages of justice that are overturned each and every day in the CACD and the Crown Court from already established causes and/or harmful consequences to these victims of miscarriages of justice in favour of concerns with victims in post-appeal cases which display new causes or raise new concerns. As such, existing approaches, therefore, are extremely restricted in terms of calculating the number of victims of miscarriages of justice, as evidenced by successful appeal, that are also affected by the problem, as well as the different kinds of harm that miscarriages of justice cause.

Finally, the changes to the criminal justice system that have been introduced in response to calls to eliminate miscarriages of justice really do nothing to reduce them or the harm caused to victims in any meaningful way. To stay with the same example, the CCRC sits at the end of the criminal justice process. It is a post-appeal, and very much an extra-judicial remedy for qualifying applicants which has no real power to stop miscarriages of justice from occurring. As will be shown, the same is true of all previous changes to the criminal justice system in response to perceived miscarriages of justice which have not prevented miscarriages of justice from occurring. Instead, the changes in the law have served to create and consolidate the existing system, reinforcing the idea that additional routes to the appeal courts or variations to forms of punishment is sufficient to deal with the problem of miscarriages of justice. This signals significant limitations for all previous attempts to *prevent* miscarriages of justice from occurring and the harmful consequences that they engender.

The aim of the book

Against this background, the overall aim of this book is to provide a more adequate sociological depiction of:

- the distinction between popular (public and political) discourses on miscarriages of justice as they relate to beliefs that innocent victims are wrongly convicted and what the criminal justice system deems to be a miscarriage of justice;
- the scale of miscarriages of justice in England and Wales;
- the extensive forms of harm that miscarriages of justice engender to primary and secondary victims; and, therefore,
- the limits of all previous changes to the criminal justice system to prevent miscarriages of justice from occurring.

In the absence of any properly established literature in this area, I want to begin to map a new terrain for miscarriages of justice as a field of empirical enquiry and as an activity of counter-discourse. I want to show that miscarriages of justice as popularly understood are not synonymous with legal definitions. Moreover, I want to reveal that miscarriages of justice as understood from the perspective of the legal system are not the exception to the rule but, rather, they are a routine and, even, mundane feature of the criminal justice process. It will be argued, further, that the changes to the criminal justice system in response to public crises of confidence act, not in any way to prevent miscarriages of justice but, rather, to provide a recognition of the particular cause of miscarriage of justice and the procedural means through which such miscarriages can be overturned. This does not *prevent* miscarriages of justice. Quite the opposite, it *creates* (in the Foucauldian sense) the conditions necessary for miscarriages of justice to be officially *produced*, bringing them to light.

To these ends, the book firstly explores arguments about the meaning, scale and causes of miscarriages of justice and calls for a pragmatic revision of definitions of miscarriages of justice to include all successful appeals against criminal conviction. Simultaneously, this brings into focus a corresponding scale of victims of miscarriages of justice that has not previously been sufficiently acknowledged or subjected to appropriate critical appraisal.

The analysis then turns to the primary 'voices' – from the spheres of government, victim support/campaigning and academia – that have been constructed and deployed in the discursive interplay aimed at the supposed reform of the criminal justice system for the elimination of miscarriages of justice. In addition, two further analyses are offered which cover human rights and the zemiological perspective, which adopts an innovative, holistic approach to the harmful consequences of social and legal phenomena. This analysis presents a new counterdiscursive voice on miscarriages of justice that may more effectively participate in the negotiation of the problem.

Following Collini (1991: 3) I use the metaphor of 'voice' as opposed to the more usual terminology of 'thought', 'views' or 'theories' of a particular author because it more adequately captures the 'identity', in the broadest sense, which a particular participator in the dialogue and/or negotiation of miscarriages of justice seeks to present. At the same time, a notion of voice draws attention to the characteristic patterns of forms of 'discourse'/'counter-discourse' (again in the Foucauldian sense) that reveal the relation between individual commentators in the various domains and the 'audiences' to which they are addressed and hope to activate.[5] The attempt here is to show that, because they are rooted in an extremely limited definition of miscarriages of justice as exceptional events, and a corresponding perception of the scale of miscarriages of justice as rare and small scale, all existing voices against miscarriages of justice have themselves been limited in their remit and impact. Consequently, not only do existing voices tend to concentrate on a narrow view of the legal plane (i.e. some successful appeals) at the expense of the moral consequences and social harm of miscarriages of justice (i.e. all successful appeals), the form and extent to which they have participated in the changes to the criminal justice system that have been achieved have also been extremely limited. The exceptionalism displayed in the terrain of miscarriages of justice, which is often geared to the exposure of alarming and outrageous individual moral wrongs, paradoxically serves only to minimise the sense that there is something systematically and mundanely alarming about the operation of the criminal justice system. Exceptionalism, in fact, makes it relatively easy to restore an adequate 'legal equilibrium' once the apparent cause of the miscarriage of justice that the exceptional cases exemplify have been adjusted for. However, my own more 'mundane' voice constructed and deployed here actually leads to a fuller and deeper sense of the moral consequences which accompany the operations of the criminal justice process.

In this sense, there is a theoretical dimension to the book of considerable importance for the available critical voices or counter-discourses against miscarriages of justice, which have generally been over-concerned with what Foucault described as a 'sovereign' view of power. Put another way, oppositional counter-discourses have tended to be caught up in 'conspiracy' accounts of the causes and harmful consequences of miscarriages of justice and their remedy. Consequently, the counter-strategies that have been devised and/or deployed have been rather moralistic and negative in nature, as if nothing can be achieved by discursive contestation other than a legitimisation of the system or form of power to which critics stand totally opposed. Ironically, this severely diminishes the potential force of critical counter-discourse against miscarriages of justice. As Foucault's researches demonstrated, forms of power are not just about the brutal domination of the weaker by the stronger, whether measured in physical or economic terms. They are also about the interplay of forms of knowledge (discourse) and their counter-discursive opposition that are *productive* and/or *constitutive* of forms of social reality and human conduct:

> We should admit...that power produces knowledge (and not simply by encouraging it because it serves power or by applying it because it is useful); that power and knowledge directly imply one another;

that there is no power relation without the correlative constitution of a field of knowledge, nor any knowledge that does not presuppose and constitute at the same time power relations (Foucault, 1977: 27).

Accordingly, the various existing counter-discursive voices do, of course, need to be heard and appreciated for the contribution to the depictions of miscarriages of justice that they make and the critiques of the criminal justice system that they have produced. I am, emphatically, not saying that existing voices are in any way wrong or unwarranted. Rather, because existing voices against miscarriages of justice are grounded in exceptionalist definitions and understandings of miscarriages of justice, they are simply very limited in terms of the scale of miscarriages of justice that can be conceived and calculated. At the same time, in being almost entirely orientated towards unearthing new causes and/or harmful consequences of miscarriages of justice, existing voices against miscarriages of justice have not undertaken analyses of the wider harmful implications of the current scale of successful appeals against criminal conviction. Finally, existing voices do not deliver an adequate understanding of power, of discourse and its counter-discursive opposition, or of the constitutive character of the exercise of power in the realm of criminal justice and the limits of previous changes to the criminal justice system. To attend to this, the analyses in the various chapters of this book together contribute to a new account of the forms of power and harm inhabiting the terrain of miscarriages of justice, seeking to encourage an array of anti-discursive voices of miscarriages of justice that are not currently articulated.

Theoretical lens

Whilst I do not see this as a primarily theoretical book, and certainly not as a book that only theoretically minded readers will be interested in, the empirical and discursive analyses that stand as its main content do have a theoretical rationale that is quite important to me, and which comes to the forefront at various points in the argument. To be sure, and as may already be apparent, the theoretical lens through which this book attempts to make sense of miscarriages of justice and the changes to the criminal justice system to eliminate or reduce their occurrence is a conceptual framework comprised of three central tenets present in Foucault's work:

- exercises of power are intrinsically about relations of power/ knowledge which determine the 'regimes of truth' that govern how we think and act upon social problems, such as miscarriages of justice. A little like labelling theory, if definitions of miscarriages of justice are rethought to include all successful appeals, new ways of thinking about and acting on miscarriages of justice will come forward.
- modern societies are managed or governed in an altogether different way from sovereign forms of society that they have come to replace and in which power was arbitrarily exercised over subjects required to obey. Rather, governmental rationality or 'governmentality' in what I term 'rule of law' societies operates as a system of social management with the purported aim of fostering the wellbeing of the population to which it is mandated responsibility for. Governmentality is about *relations of power* between government and governed, whereby legitimate government acts must be mandated by the governed.
- the governed, therefore, need to challenge the truths that we live by, the existing regimes of truth, to reveal subjugated discourses that bring to light evidence from members of the population/the governed of situations and occurrences that detract from public wellbeing. This was not sufficiently developed by Foucault, but under certain circumstances, when the conditions are right, such forms of counter-discourse have the necessary forcefulness to inform forms of counter-discourse and move us to a different regime of truth. This new regime must, also, however, be subjected to rigorous critique as part of the on-going governmentality project.

For my purposes here, then, power in governmentality society can be understood as the negotiated interplay of discourse and its counter-discursive opposition. The form of this negotiated outcome then constitutes (*produces*) a new regime of truth, and new forms of 'social reality'. As this relates specifically to the issue of the existing regime of truth on miscarriages of justice, it will be shown that due to a definitional blind spot all eyes have been focused on successful appeals that derive from just one possible route, as opposed to wider analyses that take account, also, of the various other routes that determine criminal appeals. Consequently, thousands of successful appeals that are overturned each year in England and Wales by routine and mundane criminal appeal mechanisms, and the corresponding number of victims that are affected by 'justice in error' have been, equally, severely neglected. These subjugated voices need to be heard for what they have to say about the limitations of the existing criminal justice system and, by implication, the limitations of governmentality to protect us from 'errors of justice' and the harm that they cause.

On the face of it, an attempt to analyse the moral consequences of miscarriages of justice as evidenced by official statistics on successful appeals against criminal conviction from a Foucauldian-inspired perspective might seem unpromising or even contradictory. It is not uncommon for Foucault's work within the social sciences to be regarded as presenting a 'postmodern' (McNay, 1994: 159; Wolin, 1988: 179–180; Hoy, 1988; Hillyard & Watson, 1996), 'relativistic' (Ramazanoglu, 1993: 8) account that is 'normatively confused' (Fraser, 1989: 32–33) in its 'nominalistic' (Porter, 1996) and 'nihilist' (Major-Poetzl, 1983: 60; Rose, 1994) denunciation of the social scientific enterprise (see, also, Osborne, 1994). From such a perspective Foucault really would have very little to offer an essentially realist, morally grounded enquiry into the scale of the miscarriage of justice phenomenon and likely forms of harm to victims of miscarriages. A thorough exploration of such charges is beyond the scope of this introduction, and is not the object of this book. However, I would like to attend to this possible (mis)interpretation at the outset by stating the reverse. It can, plausibly, be argued that rather than being an out-and-out relativist who denied the possibility of objective truth, Foucault was a *perspectivist* concerned to examine the operation of the 'truths' peculiar to 'the societies within which we find ourselves', the 'truths' of 'what we are', the 'truths' we live by (Gordon, 1986: 76). Foucault, in fact, described himself as a critic of 'present-ness' of 'Today' (Foucault, 1986: 90). This entails an entirely serious and critical commitment, if not an 'absolutist' one, to the production of credible accounts which problematise accepted and presentist thinking.

Furthermore, Foucault was not a nihilist, but a thinker whose conception of power presupposed the possibility of resistance, of a certain form of freedom (see, for example, Rose 1993, 1999), and of radical social and political change (see, for example, Patton, 1994). Indeed, for Foucault (1979b: 95), resistance to power is not simply a reaction to a pre-existing power, for this would be to misunderstand the strictly relational character of power relations. Resistance, from a Foucauldian perspective is, in fact, part of the definition of power; resistance is never in a position of exteriority in relation to power. Rather, it is more likely the reverse: states of power are continually engendered or incited by virtue of the potential counter-powers which co-exist with them – 'where there is power there is resistance' (Foucault, 1979b: 95). From such a frame of reference, it is entirely legitimate to draw from Foucault in a qualified form of realist investigation (see, for example, Cain, 1993: 74). Further, as Osborne (1998: xii) noted, Foucault was a nominalist of sorts, yet this 'oddly enough, leads to a kind of *realism*, because our only option becomes not to theorize about [the way things are] but attempt to picture it at work' (my emphasis). Moreover, as Ward (1999: 3) observed, for the purposes of analyses of 'social construction' it may make good methodological sense to 'bracket' the question of whether a criminal defendant 'really was' guilty, or whether some natural phenomenon 'really' exists. However, it certainly does not follow that one can set such questions aside once and for all when the aim of enquiry is, for instance, to correct a miscarriage of justice or quantify the harm that miscarriages of justice cause. If not obviously consonant with one another, therefore, it does not follow that constructionism/perspectivism and realism are engaged in some fatal metaphysical conflict. On the contrary, 'the results of sociological enquiries into "case construction" can help us to understand why miscarriages of justice occur' (Ward, 1999: 3). Accordingly, bringing together social constructionist analyses, whilst to an extent operating outside of the conventional disciplinary parameters of empirically grounded social research, *and* realist-style theorising, can add a significant dimension in terms of accounting for the formation of existing hierarchies of knowledge in a given field (cf. Ward, 1999: 4–5). In any case, there is, undoubtedly, some hazard in trying to colonise Foucault for any one specific line of critical enquiry (see Gane, 1986: 111; Osborne, 1994: 493–499). As Sheridan (1980: 225) has argued:

> There is no 'Foucault system'. One cannot be a 'Foucauldian' in the same way that one can be a Marxist or a Freudian: Marx and Freud left coherent bodies of doctrine (or 'knowledge') and organizations which, whether one likes it or not (for some that is the attraction), enjoy uninterrupted apostolic succession from their founders. If Foucault is to have any 'influence' it will no doubt be as a slayer of dragons, a breaker of systems.

Foucault can, thus, be taken to 'offer a set of possible tools for the identification of the conditions of possibility which operate through the obviousness and enigmas of our present, tools perhaps also for the eventual modification of those conditions' (Gordon, 1980: 258). It is in this sense that this book extends Foucauldian insights into the operations and exercise of prevailing forms of knowledge-power in the field of miscarriages of justice. The attempt is to 'break' the existing 'systems' of thought on this grave social problem and contribute to news ways of thinking about, and acting upon, miscarriages of justice that may lead to more fruitful changes to reduce the number of miscarriages and the harm that they cause.

The structure of the book

The book is presented in two parts: Part I deals with the matters of the definition and calculation of the scale of the miscarriages of justice phenomenon; Part II with the limits of the changes to the criminal justice system in response to perceived miscarriages of justice for their remedy and/or reduction.

In more specific terms, Chapter 1 distinguishes between public and political aspirations of what the criminal justice system should deliver and what it actually delivers. It sets out in greater detail the theoretical underpinnings of the book with an analysis of the shift from sovereign forms of power to existing regimes that strive towards governmental modes. It emphasises the need for vigilance from the representatives of the governed and the inclusion of all breaches of due process in the miscarriage of justice lexicon to effect remedial changes that might enhance public wellbeing.

Chapter 2 builds on Chapter 1, looking critically at the official statistics on successful appeals against criminal conviction, official breaches of due process. It constructs a typology of miscarriages of justice and proposes three categories that can be inferred from the official statistics – the *exceptional*, the *routine* and the *mundane*. This shifts the calculation of the number of miscarriages of justice that occur each year from 18 cases to over 4,700 cases each year over the last 20 years. To make sense of the official data on successful appeals, a range of complimentary analyses on the role of statistics in exercises of power are synthesised to produce what is termed a 'critical pragmatist' approach. This acknowledges that official data on successful appeals against criminal conviction is a product of socio-legal construction and, therefore, not an objective measure of miscarriages of justice. Nevertheless, official statistics determine the truths we live by and so must be engaged with *pragmatically* for the very real impacts that they have in shaping social realities on the miscarriage of justice problem.

Chapter 3 considers the question of *causality* of miscarriages of justice. It locates the official statistics on successful appeals against criminal conviction (official miscarriages of justice) within a critical analysis of the structures and procedures of the criminal justice process which cause miscarriages of justice but which may never be overturned or act as barriers to overturning miscarriages of justice. In this light, official miscarriages of justice as evidenced by the official statistics on successful appeals are seen, themselves, as only a partial indicator of all miscarriages of justice that occur and a very limited indication of the full extent of the damage caused to the victims of miscarriages of justice.

Turning to the analysis of the voices that participate in the negotiation of exceptional miscarriages of justice and the modifications of the criminal justice system, Chapter 4 considers the voice of government on miscarriages of justice. It presents an historical overview of key legislative responses to miscarriages of justice in England and Wales to develop an apparent pattern to the governmentality of the criminal justice system in response to miscarriages of justice. This is important because it sets the question of the possibilities of effected changes to the criminal justice system within a broader historical perspective that can take better account of the trends in criminal justice system modification. It is through an historical analysis of the legislative responses to miscarriages of justice, that a better understanding of the nature of miscarriages in the present is provided. Drawing from Foucault's thesis on governmentality, it is argued that the focus on exceptional successful appeals that exemplify new causes or consequences of miscarriages of justice is, actually, insufficient. Alternatively, legitimate government would more vigilantly respond to the scale of miscarriages of justice that can be inferred from the official statistics on successful appeals. Such statistics signal not only an excessive scale of judicial 'error' but, also, an excessive scale of harm to victims of miscarriages of justice whose wellbeing the government is (supposed to be) mandated to enhance.

Chapter 5 considers the part that victim support groups and campaigning organisations play within the governmentality of the criminal justice system to prevent miscarriages of justice. It presents an analysis which inverts and extends Foucault's notion of a 'disciplinary society' and the panopticon, pitching campaigning organisations as 'watchdogs of government' in the processes of governmentality, prompting governmental intervention to the criminal justice system in response to particular exceptional successful appeals which show new causes or harmful consequences of miscarriages of justice. However, campaigning voices have not made the connection between the crucial part that they play in effecting progressive amendments to the criminal justice system that are achieved by exceptional cases of successful appeal and the extent to which the procedural framework of the criminal justice system is, therefore, constituted in large part by their efforts. Hence, the forcefulness of campaigning counter-discursive utterances against miscarriages of justice has not been as strong as they could be.

Chapter 6 conducts an analysis of the forms of academic counter-discourse that were produced and deployed in reply to the RCCJ. It discerns two forms of academic counter-discourse in response to apparent miscarriages of justice, focusing on the more critical expressions of the academic voice which demanded fundamental reform. Drawing, again, from Foucault, it is argued that the collective tendency of the critical academic counter-discourses viewed the RCCJ as a 'failed' 'damage limitation exercise' was profoundly problematic. On the contrary, the RCCJ is shown to be an outgrowth of a process that produced a counter-discourse that exemplified a specific problematic in the legislative framework of the criminal justice system that was able to induce a public crisis of confidence, thus prompting governmental intervention and the introduction of changes. From such a frame of reference, it is concluded that public 'crises' that are induced by successful appeals that reveal previously unacknowledged 'errors' in the criminal justice system, and attain an exceptional miscarriage of justice status, need not be conceived in entirely 'negative' terms. On the contrary, they should be capitalised upon in the general interests of improving the criminal justice system for the governed. Indeed, the more successful appeals that demonstrate 'failings' with the existing criminal justice system, then, potentially, the more 'crises' of public confidence in the criminal justice system will be induced, and the more problematic aspects of the criminal justice system will have to be subjected to governmental intervention and corrective change.

Chapter 7 considers existing articulations of the 'human rights voice' since the introduction of the Human Rights Act (1998) (HRA). It argues that whilst this voice *does* contribute to existing depictions of the harmful consequences of miscarriages of justice in important ways, it does so in an incomplete way. In particular, an inherent limitation of the human rights approach is the conception of harm to individual subjects solely in terms of the contravention of legal rights and freedoms. This omits other associated forms of harm that also accompany miscarriages of justice more widely conceived, such as the impacts upon the families and friends, and the economic costs of justice in 'error' that impact upon other areas of public spending. This chapter consequently tries to reorientate the human rights voice into more provocative territory to capitalise on the full promise contained within the HRA.

Chapter 8 engages with the zemiological standpoint. This emerging perspective offers the promise of moving beyond the boundaries of existing counter-discourses against miscarriages of justice, consolidating the call to *rethink* definitions of miscarriages of justice to include mundane and/or routine successful appeals. It brings into focus a more comprehensive perspective on the harmful consequences of miscarriages of justice along social, psychological, physical and financial lines, not only to victims in high profile cases of wrongful imprisonment but, also, those victims of miscarriages of justice of crimes thought to be trivial by comparison in magistrates courts. Zemiology, however, is not the entire solution to the problem of miscarriages of justice. In recognition, some of the key limits with the zemiological approach as it relates to the construction of a zemiological voice on miscarriages of justice and governmentality are discussed.

Finally, the conclusion reiterates that what is required is a move away from exceptionalist understandings through the construction of a 'voice for the governed' that can combine the various strengths of the existing voices, but which can also take account of their various limitations. It is not that the previous changes to the criminal justice system in attempts to prevent miscarriages of justice are wrong on their own terms. Rather, the narrow concentration on certain exceptional cases of successful appeal requires turning a blind eye to the extent of the scale of harm that exists and that requires recognition and redress. It forgoes the implementation of more far-reaching changes as part of the on-going governmentality project and the improvement of the criminal justice system for all.

1

What is a Miscarriage of Justice?

Introduction

Public and political discourses on miscarriages of justice are highly polarised. On the one hand, those committed to due process express concerns about the possible wrongful conviction of the factually innocent. On the other hand, those committed to crime control express concerns about the need to ensure that all guilty offenders receive their 'just deserts'. Intuitively, it would seem correct that the criminal justice system should be *both* about the conviction of the factually guilty and acquittal of the factually innocent and that both due process *and* crime control should be accommodated in the delivery of justice. However, as illustrated in the following quotation taken from a successful appeal judgement, the criminal justice system does not neatly correspond with the expectations of either due process or crime control advocates as expressed in public/political discourses and can neither guarantee that the factually innocent will be acquitted in criminal trials, nor that the factually guilty will be convicted.

> In our view the case against all three appellants was formidable... However we are bound to follow the approach set out earlier in this judgment, namely assuming the irregularities which we have identified had not occurred would a reasonable jury have been bound to return verdicts of guilty? In all conscience we cannot say that it would...Accordingly we cannot say that any of these convictions is safe. They must be quashed and the appeals allowed...For the better understanding of those who have listened to this judgment and of those who may report it hereafter this is not a finding of innocence, far from it (R v Davis, Johnson and Rowe, *The Times* July 25, 2000; (2001) 1 Cr App R 115).

Rather, then, the criminal justice process operates on an altogether different plane to the ideological struggle between due process versus crime control combatants. In the absence of a crystal ball or concrete certainties about the perpetrators of alleged crimes, it relies on an elaborate system of rules and procedures which attempt to ensure that suspects of crime and defendants in criminal courts receive a 'fair hearing'. From such a perspective, the criminal justice system's definition of a miscarriage of justice is not so much related to whether a person convicted of a criminal offence is innocent of the crime but, rather, whether the person received a 'fair trial'. This may seem unsatisfactory and out of step with public understandings about what the criminal justice system should deliver and what political promises say it will deliver. Nonetheless, as will be shown, if the criminal justice process functioned in any other way it would be at odds with the underlying governmental rationality that renders it legitimate.

This chapter begins with a closer analysis of the difference between popular aspirations (public and political discourses) on what the criminal justice system *should* deliver and what it *actually* delivers to illustrate the overriding concern for the criminal justice system is ensuring that all accused of criminal offences receive fair and just treatment, in accordance with the rules and procedures of due process. Then, an historical analysis is undertaken of the emergence of a new form of governmental rationality (which Foucault termed governmentality) as society shifted from sovereign exercises of power to existing forms grounded in the rule of law. In particular, this emphasises the extent to which the legitimacy of existing exercises of power in the realm of criminal justice is determined by reference to principles of due process, transparency and fairness and how this differs from previous exercises of power in response to acts deemed criminal. Finally, the need to challenge all abuses of due process, both in the interests of enhancing governmentality in the on-going shift from sovereignty and for the potential damage to governmental legitimacy that they represent, is outlined, again making use of a Foucauldian inspired perspective.

Popular discourses and what the criminal justice system actually delivers

The proposition that the criminal justice process should convict the guilty and acquit the innocent highlights a crucial incompatibility between discourses which embody public/political aspirations of what the criminal justice system should deliver and what it actually delivers.

Miscarriages of justice as they relate to the criminal justice system do not and cannot relate to the wrongful acquittal of the guilty in any practical or strict legal sense, as this undermines fundamental principles that underpin the legitimacy of the entire criminal justice process: the presumption that defendants are innocent in criminal trials until a case has been proven beyond a reasonable doubt by the prosecution against them (discussed further below). As Helena Kennedy (2004: 11) put it:

> In the adversarial criminal justice system we do not start off from a position of neutrality. We start off with a preferred truth – that the accused is innocent – and we ask the jury to err on the side of that preferred truth, even if they think she (sic) probably did do it. I explain to juries that if they find themselves in the jury room saying I think she probably committed the offence or she may well have done it, they have to stop themselves short, because probabilities are not good enough. The criminal justice system is based on the fundamental value that it is far worse to convict an innocent person than to let a guilty one walk free.

The main difficulty, then, with the idea that guilty offenders who are acquitted by the courts represent miscarriages of justice is that it works from the untenable premise that defendants in criminal trials who are acquitted are, in fact, guilty. This is not to defend the acquittal of the factually guilty in criminal trials. It is, simply, to clarify the logic of the criminal justice system as it is currently constituted and practised, as compared with popular discourse. From this perspective, this analysis is not focused on expressions of popular notions about guilty acquittals and miscarriages of justice. Rather, it concentrates on the other side of the popular miscarriage of justice conundrum as it relates to popular concerns about the possible miscarriages of justice to the innocent.

However, as conventional perceptions on miscarriages of justice relate to the possible wrongful conviction of the innocent, here, too, are significant misconceptions about what the criminal justice system is able to provide. As will be shown below, miscarriages of justice do not relate to the wrongful conviction of the innocent in any reliable sense either. This is not to infer that innocent people are not convicted by the criminal justice system, nor is it to suggest that the public should not be concerned about the conviction of the innocent. On the contrary, as already indicated and developed further below, the *belief* and widespread concern that innocent people were convicted of crimes that they did not commit has been the vital motor force behind the introduction of progressive modifications of the criminal justice system and is a crucial aspect of the governmentality project.[6] Rather, my specific aim here is to highlight the distinction between what the public want from the criminal justice system, what politicians promise the criminal justice system will deliver and what the criminal justice system can actually deliver. It is an attempt to clarify what, precisely, constitutes a miscarriage of justice according to the legal system in the interests of a more meaningful understanding about how they are managed by the criminal justice system and how they might be more effectively challenged.

What, precisely, is a miscarriage of justice?

A key characteristic of miscarriages of justice is that whatever allegations there may be, a miscarriage of justice cannot be said to have occurred unless and until an applicant has been successful in an appeal against a criminal conviction, and until such time s/he remains an *alleged* miscarriage of justice. This is, generally, the case for public, political and criminal justice system discourses alike. For instance, the Birmingham Six had two unsuccessful appeals before they were officially acknowledged and recorded in the official statistics as victims of wrongful conviction/ imprisonment following their success in their third appeal, the Bridgewater Four (Regan, 1997b; Foot, 1986), Maguire Seven (Maguire, 1994) and the Guildford Four also all had multiple appeals before they were accepted, officially, as victims of miscarriages of justice. I have noted previously that, in this sense, definitions of miscarriages of justice can be said to be entirely 'legalistic': they are defined by law, they are wholly determined by the rules and procedures of the criminal justice system, and if those rules and procedures change, then the way in which miscarriages of justice are defined will also change. Miscarriages of justice as they are understood and acted upon by the criminal justice system, however, differ from popular perceptions in an important way. They are distinct from the specific problem of the wrongful conviction of the innocent, as a successful appeal against a criminal conviction is *not* evidence of the wrongful conviction of the innocent. On the contrary, a successful appeal against criminal conviction denotes an official and systemic acknowledgement of what might be termed a breach of the 'carriage of justice', the rules and procedures that together make-up the criminal justice process, and it bears no relation to whether a successful appellant is factually guilty or factually innocent: these are not questions that our criminal justice system pursues or attempts to resolve, at least in the ordinary sense that these terms are popularly understood (Naughton, 2005c: 165–167).

The criminal justice system in England and Wales is not about the pursuit of the objective truth of a suspect's or defendant's guilt or innocence. Adversarial justice is an evidential contest, regulated by principles of due process, compliance with the rules and procedures of the legal system. In particular, the two key tenets of the criminal law in England and Wales are stated as the presumption of innocence and the standard of proof. The presumption of innocence is claimed to mean that an individual is deemed to be innocent, until proven guilty. The standard of proof states that to find a defendant guilty in criminal cases in England and Wales the evidence should establish guilt beyond reasonable doubt (Chapman & Niven, 2000: 4–5). However, criminal trials are not a consideration of factual innocence or factual guilt in any straightforward sense. They are highly technical affairs which attempt to determine if defendants are 'guilty' or 'not guilty' of criminal offences on the basis of the reliability of the evidence before the court. The following quotation, for instance, taken from the House of Lords ruling in the case of *Director of Public Prosecutions v. Shannon* [1974] 59 Cr.App.R.250 sums up the legal position fairly succinctly:

> The law in action is not concerned with absolute truth, but with proof before a fallible human tribunal to a requisite standard of probability in accordance with formal rules of evidence.

In an even more critical mode, McBarnet (1981: 12–13) noted, the criminal process is not about absolutes, but about pragmatics:

> What is involved is not a philosophical or scientific concept of proof but a much less demanding *legal* concept. The justification lies not in any idealism that 'the truth the whole truth and nothing but the truth' results, but in pragmatics. The courts are there not to indulge in the impossible absolutes of philosophy or science but to reach decisions – quickly. So the courts have drawn a line at what will do as proof. Prosecutors do not have to prove everything a jury might want to know, they only have to produce a *sufficiency* of evidence. The law defines how much evidence constitutes 'sufficient' to prove a case and it is the judge's role to decide and to persuade the jury that the required legal standard has been met (original emphasis).

Correspondingly, criminal appeals do not seek to determine the guilt or innocence of appellants or correct the wrongs of criminal trials in the sense that popular discourses may suppose: under s. 108 of the Magistrates Courts Act (1980) appeals against conviction are allowed to the Crown Court for criminal convictions given in the Magistrates' Courts, so long as the potential appellant did not plead guilty. Under s. 79 of the Supreme Court Act (1981) such appeals are by way of a full rehearing to determine if the appellant/defendant was 'guilty' or 'not guilty' in line with criminal trials. In more serious cases, appeals to the Court of Appeal (Criminal Division) (CACD) do *not* attempt to determine innocence or guilt either, but, rather, s. 2 of the Criminal Appeal Act (1995) instructs that it (a) shall allow an appeal against conviction if it thinks that the conviction is unsafe; and (b) shall dismiss such an appeal in any other case. There are also specific rules under s. 4 that regulate the CACD to 'receive any evidence which was not adduced in the proceedings from which the appeal lies', but only within certain criteria. Section 4, for instance, specifies that the CACD 'shall, in considering whether to receive any evidence, have regard in particular to (a) whether the evidence appears to the Court to be capable of belief; (b) whether it appears to the Court that the evidence may afford any ground for allowing the appeal; (c) whether the evidence would have been admissible at the trial on an issue which is the subject of the appeal; and, (d) whether there is a reasonable explanation for the failure to adduce the evidence at the trial'. In these highly technical processes, subject to common law and Parliamentary change, miscarriages of justice, as evidenced by successful appeals against criminal conviction, are routine, even mundane, occurrences, which, as will be shown in the next chapter, number over 4,500 cases per annum (see also Naughton, 2003). Importantly, however, these successful appeals are not evidence of factual innocence and may include both the guilty and the innocent who satisfy the required criteria of the appeal courts (see also Naughton, 2005c, 2006).

Public and political discourses

As indicated, and contrary to the foregoing outline of the process of criminal trials and appeals, public discourses on the criminal justice system are quite straightforward: the criminal justice system should attempt to convict the guilty and acquit the innocent. Indeed, from such a perspective, public discourses about miscarriages of justice, deriving from the media (for example, Gillan, 2001; Goodman, 1999; Foot, 2002; Woffinden, 1998, 1998a; Dodd, 2000; Rose, 2002), routinely (mis)conceive successful appeals against criminal conviction as *prima facie* evidence that supports their belief that an innocent person has been the victim of a wrongful conviction. Moreover, public discourse works from the equally mistaken premise that the appeals system exists (or should exist) precisely because the criminal justice system is a fallible, human system that can and does make mistakes and that innocent people can, therefore, be wrongly convicted in criminal trials. The function of the appeals system from this perspective, then, is to correct the 'errors' of criminal trials by overturning the convictions of the innocent. On the contrary, however, the criminal appeals system exists and functions to ensure that appellants received a fair trial, as defined by the rules of the system, and that their convictions are, therefore, 'safe' on these terms. Under such a regime, proof of innocence does not guarantee that a criminal conviction will be quashed, unless, of course, it undermines the safety of the conviction too (discussed further below in reference to the case of John Roden who was recently reported to have been refused a referral to the CACD by the CCRC after its ten year review).

Public discourse is reinforced by political discourse that also states that the intention of criminal trials is the conviction of the guilty and the acquittal of the innocent. This was recently expressed, for example, by the Prime Minister (Tony Blair) in rolling out the removal of certain long-standing procedures regarded as safeguards against the wrongful conviction of the innocent under the Criminal Justice Act (2003) (CJA). The stated intention of the CJA (2003) is to 'rebalance' the criminal justice system so that more guilty offenders are convicted (Home Office, 2002: 15). To this end, the criminal justice system is undergoing its most radical overhaul for centuries (for a critical discussion see Kennedy, 2004). For instance, the CJA (2003) put an end to the 'double jeopardy' rule, which for almost 800 years has prevented people being tried for the same crime twice (for a discussion see James et al, 2000b; Broadbridge, 2002). The CJA (2003) also introduced 'hearsay' evidence into criminal trials, allowing as admissible oral evidence in criminal proceedings which is adduced as evidence of any fact or opinion asserted even though it is not given by the alleged witness live in court (for a discussion see, for example, Arkinstall, 2003). Despite evidence from other jurisdictions and claims that such moves erode civil liberties, undermine key procedural safeguards and, thus, result in miscarriages of justice, understood as meaning the wrongful conviction of the innocent (see, for example, Lilley, 2002; Tempest, 2002; Letwin, 2002), the Prime Minister utilised a popular discourse on miscarriages of justice pertaining to guilty acquittals to push the changes through stating that: 'It is perhaps the biggest miscarriage of justice in today's system when the guilty walk away unpunished' (Blair, 2002). At the same time, however, the Prime Minister stressed that those concerned with the possible wrongful conviction of the innocent need not worry as at the heart of the changes 'there is an absolute determination to ensure that the innocent are acquitted in criminal trials' (Tony Blair cited Home Office, 2002: 11).

There are a number of immediate problems with the most senior politician's analysis of the criminal justice system and the possibility that guilty offenders acquitted by the courts would constitute a miscarriage of justice at all, let alone the greatest miscarriage of justice today. Leaving aside the fact that the Prime Minister is, himself, legally qualified, his assertions represent a complete misunderstanding of the nature of the criminal justice system. It is completely at odds with the reality of criminal justice in England and Wales. The prosecution already achieves the conviction of over 95 per cent of defendants at magistrates' courts (Griffiths, 2002) where in excess of 98 per cent of criminal trials are currently conducted (Bright & Nicklin, 2002). Moreover, over 87 per cent of defendants in the Crown Court where the remaining 2 per cent of cases are heard are also found guilty (Naughton, 2002). More significantly, perhaps, and as already discussed, any idea that criminal trials attempt to ensure the acquittal of the innocent or the conviction of the guilty is not reflective of the reality of the operations of criminal trials and/or appeals. It is, therefore, simply a 'determination' that 'absolutely' cannot be met under the present arrangements (see also Naughton, 2005b).

Miscarriages of justice from the perspective of the criminal justice system

A distinction between miscarriages of justice and the wrongful conviction of the innocent emerges, then, whereupon a miscarriage of justice is entirely *internal* to the workings of the criminal justice system, wholly dependent upon how 'justice' is defined: miscarriages of justice, as evidenced by successful appeals against criminal conviction, derive from technical decisions made from the existing rules and procedures of the appeal courts. They can appropriately be termed 'miscarriages of due process'. Alternatively, concerns about the wrongful conviction of the innocent are wholly *external* to the criminal justice system, which is *incompatible* with public/political discourses (Naughton, 2006). This is emphasised in the following quotation from Clive Walker (1993: 4

my italics) about the inherent legal nature of miscarriages of justice, which, at the same time, further emphasises the distinction between miscarriages of justice and public/political concerns about the wrongful conviction of the innocent:

> Some observers attempt to distinguish between those who are really 'innocent' and those who are acquitted 'on a technicality'. However, a conviction arising from deceit or illegalities is corrosive of the State's claims to legitimacy on the basis of due process and respect for rights...Accordingly, *even a person who has in fact and with intent committed a crime could be said to have suffered a miscarriage [of justice] if convicted on evidence which is legally inadmissible* or which is not proven beyond reasonable doubt.

From a legal perspective, then, miscarriages of justice are neither about ensuring that the factually guilty are convicted, nor that the factually innocent are acquitted. This is not merely a theoretical or abstract academic argument. It is supported by the leading legal authorities on successful appeals against criminal conviction, which demonstrate, further, that the appeal courts do not consider the question of an appellant's innocence or guilt. Instead, for convictions to be quashed they have to be adjudged to question the integrity of the trial in which they were given and, thus, be rendered 'unsafe' by appeal court judges. This is evident, for example, in the following extract from the appeal judgement that quashed the Bridgewater case:

> This Court is not concerned with the guilt or innocence of the appellants, but only with the safety of their convictions. This may, at first sight, appear an unsatisfactory state of affairs, until it is remembered that the integrity of the criminal process is the most important consideration for courts which have to hear appeals against conviction. Both the innocent and the guilty are entitled to fair trials. If the trial process is not fair, if it is distorted by deceit or by material breaches of the rules of evidence or procedure, then the liberties of all are threatened (Hickey & Ors, R v [1997] EWCA Crim 2028).

The problem with such judgements from the perspective of public/political discourses on what the criminal justice *should* deliver is that they can fuel whispering campaigns that lump together victims of miscarriage of justice who are guilty with those who are innocent. They conceive both as 'getting off on technicalities', as, indeed, they generally do, as criminal appeals are highly technical affairs governed by strict rules and procedures. This, in turn, can act to allow the issue of accountability for miscarriages of justice and/or the wrongful conviction of the innocent to be sidestepped. It, in effect, acts to subjugate the problem of the wrongful convictions of the innocent from the public/political gaze until such time that the real perpetrators of the crimes for which they were convicted are apprehended and convicted. It suggests that until such an unlikely scenario occurs, their innocence should remain in doubt.

A case that starts to unearth the wrongful conviction of the innocent and separates it from the general problem of technical miscarriages of justice, however, is the Cardiff Three. But, the Cardiff Three, convicted for the murder of Lynette White in 1988, did not overturn their convictions in 1992 because they were innocent. On the contrary, in line with all successful appeals they had to get the CACD to agree that a lack of integrity in the way that their convictions were obtained rendered them unsafe. This was achieved when Lord Taylor quashed the convictions asserting that whether Steven Miller's admission to the murder of Lynette White were true or not was 'irrelevant', as the oppressive nature of his questioning (he was asked the same question 300 times) required the interview to be rejected as evidence. It was a breach of due process, more specifically the rules of evidence under the Police and Criminal Evidence Act (1984) (PACE) (R v Paris, Abdullahi & Miller (1993) 97 Cr App R99). In keeping with the general uncertainty that results from successful appeals, doubts prevailed for the next decade about whether or not the Cardiff Three were involved in the murder until the case made British legal history and the real killer of Lynnette White, Jeffrey Gafoor, who had been traced by the National DNA Database, was convicted for her murder in July 2003 (BBC News, 2003).

The case of the Cardiff Three, then, not only provides a milestone in British policing, it, also, confirms the wrongful conviction of the innocent, distinguishing it from the general problem of technical miscarriages of justice. At the same time, the case of the Cardiff Three highlights the difficulties that the innocent face in overturning criminal convictions and, then, in their attempts to prove their innocence: given the limits of the appeals system, not all innocent victims of wrongful conviction will be able to overturn their convictions and attain a miscarriage of justice; nor will all victims of miscarriages of justice be fortunate enough to have the real perpetrators of the crimes for which they were convicted brought to justice and their innocence proven (see Naughton, 2006).

Despite the factual innocence of the Cardiff Three, however, the current structures of criminal trials and criminal appeals remain, meaning that a possible strategy exists whereby guilty offenders could maintain innocence to keep alive the possibility of overturning their convictions on appeal by showing an abuse of process. Abuse of process has been defined as 'something so unfair and wrong that the court should not allow a prosecutor to proceed with what is in all other respect a regular proceeding' (Hui Chi-Ming v R [1992] 1 A.C. 34). Although there is an inbuilt incentive to plead guilty to criminal offences to receive a sentence discount (s. 144 Criminal Justice Act, 2003), the disincentive of pleading guilty to criminal offences is that it guarantees conviction. Moreover, it virtually closes off the possibility of overturning the conviction on appeal.[7] So, some guilty offenders will plead not guilty at trial, some of these will be convicted and sent to prison, and some of these will then maintain innocence in the hope of achieving their release through a successful appeal.[8]

A notable abuse of process case that was successful on appeal and which further clarifies the official position of the criminal justice system in England and Wales is the case of Nicholas Mullen. In his judgment on the merits of Mullen's appeal, Lord Justice Schiemann spelt out the position of the criminal justice system and miscarriages of justice as follows:

> The phrase 'miscarriage of justice' does not simply mean that a guilty man has escaped, or that an innocent man has been convicted. It is equally applicable to cases where the acquittal or the conviction has resulted from some form of trial in which the essential rights of the people or the defendant were disregarded or denied (R (Mullen) v Secretary of State for the Home Department [2002] EWCA Civ 1882).

Leaving aside the fact that Lord Justice Schiemann, himself, apparently misconceives the criminal appeal process by feeding from and into public and political discourses with the suggestion that the wrongful acquittal of the guilty and wrongful conviction of the innocent *would* constitute a miscarriage of justice, although entirely satisfied that the appellant was factually guilty, the CACD quashed Mullen's conviction because it had involved 'a blatant and extremely serious failure to adhere to the rule of law.' Mullen's conviction had been deemed unsafe after it was found ten years into his 30 year sentence that all involved in his deportation from Zimbabwe – the police, MI6, the Security Service and officials from the Foreign Office and the Home Office as well as the relevant authorities in Zimbabwe – had colluded to secure his extradition in breach of domestic law in Zimbabwe and internationally recognised human rights. The quashing of the conviction is seen as the CACD's way of denoting its condemnation of the behaviour of the prosecuting authorities in ever bringing the case of Mullen to trial (see Roberts, 2003: 441).

In quashing Mullen's conviction, Lord Justice Rose was clear about the legal system's (lack of) position on innocence or guilt and the possible advantage to offenders likely to be guilty who plead not guilty and maintain their innocence whilst preparing their appeals: '...for a conviction to be safe, it must be lawful; and if it results from a trial which should never have taken place, it can hardly be regarded as safe' (R v Mullen [1999] EWCA Crim 278).[9]

This analysis is further evidenced by the official legal definition of miscarriages of justice, found in s. 133(1) of the Criminal Justice Act 1988, enacted to give effect to the UK's obligations under Article 14(6) of the International Covenant on Civil and Political Rights (ICCPR), which states:

> ...when a person has been convicted of a criminal offence and when subsequently his (sic) conviction has been reversed or he (sic) has been pardoned on the ground that a new or newly discovered fact shows beyond reasonable doubt that there has been a miscarriage of justice, the Secretary of State shall pay compensation for the miscarriage of justice...unless the non-disclosure of the unknown fact was wholly or partly attributable to the person convicted.

To qualify for compensation, then, successful appellants need not prove their innocence and may even be guilty. Rather, they must be able to demonstrate that their convictions were rendered 'unsafe' by a newly discovered fact, providing the non-disclosure of the new fact was not wholly or partly attributable to the claimant. In this sense, s. 133 of the CJA (1988) does not define what is meant by a miscarriage of justice but, rather, states that compensation is only payable when a convicted person has been pardoned or a conviction quashed on an appeal out of time, or on a reference to the CACD by the CCRC. As Stephanie Roberts (2003: 441–442) noted:

> The rationale for this is that it has to be a decision which is no longer open to challenge under the normal judicial process so if a conviction has been quashed within the usual time limits the appellant will not be eligible for compensation. This gives effect to the Article's intentions that compensation should be paid where a new fact has emerged and where the normal working of the judicial system has not revealed the wrongful conviction.

An obvious critique of the existing official definition of a miscarriage of justice from the perspective put forward by this analysis is that it works to disqualify the thousands of victims who will be shown in the next chapter to annually achieve a successful appeal against a criminal conviction. This abdicates governmental responsibility for the harm caused by 'errors' of the criminal justice system. As will be shown in the next section, it, simultaneously, indicates a wide scale governmental failure to ensure the wellbeing of the population it is mandated responsibility for.[10]

Governmentality and the birth of due process

Historically, criminal justice was not subject to the elaborate system of rules and procedures that govern acts deemed criminal today. Ideas such as the 'presumption of innocence' and the 'burden of proof' on the prosecution to prove its case 'beyond all reasonable doubt' simply did not exist. On the contrary, under previous regimes of truth and power, 'justice' was an eminently subjective and arbitrary affair. This was a time when the pronouncements of the sovereign went unchallenged, whether they were correct or otherwise. There were no formal opportunities for appeal and, hence, no official acknowledgement that a miscarriage of justice had occurred.

Apart from being unsatisfactory against current criminal justice ideas and practices, the arbitrary exercise of power presented a considerable constraint to social change. Norbert Elias's (1978) analysis of what he termed 'the civilizing process' traced the delicate changes in manners within European societies as they processed from feudal systems to modern nation states governed by the rule of law, showing how seemingly mild changes in etiquette reflected deep transformations of the power relations in society. In particular, Elias's sociology identified a dynamic relationship between the structures of society and the psychology of the population that together comprise society: changes in the structures of society effect changes in how people think about what is and is not possible and, accordingly, how they act in social reality. As this relates specifically to this discussion of the birth of due process and fair trials as a governing principle in criminal justice matters, for modern capitalist societies to flourish they required populations that were not hindered by a perpetual anxiety about the arbitrary exercise of power. On the contrary, modern capitalist societies (are supposed to) provide structural conditions that allow people to go about their daily lives and commercial activities freely and openly without undue fear or impediment of arbitrary discrimination or persecution. Hence, the introduction of due processes in exercises of power in what might be termed rule of law societies to render governmental interventions into public life legitimate. This is not intended as an advocacy of capitalist societies *per se*. It is a descriptive sociological analysis of the transition of power relations in society. It is an attempt to highlight the very different problematic that links government and governed in a complex relationship of power in existing rule of law societies in which government has a key role to play in the management of the structures of society to enable us to live open and fear-free lives.

Foucault's (1979a, 1991) analysis of the emergence of the modern nation state dovetails with Elias's (1978) analysis in showing the links between new forms of governance and the consequent freeing-up of the citizenry to think and act in different ways. Indeed, from a Foucauldian inspired reading, it is not possible to study the technologies of power without an analysis of the political rationality underpinning them (Lemke, 2000). However, for Foucault (1979a), the modern state is not to be regarded in the conventional way, as a kind of power which ignores individuals in the interests of the totality, nor in the Marxist sense, as being concerned only with the interests of a particular class group in society. Rather, state power is both an 'individualizing and a totalizing form of power' (Foucault, 1979a, 1991; Rabinow, 1984: 14; Gordon, 1991: 3) it includes and involves all. Foucault's history of government highlighted that from the middle of the 16th century a series of treatises began to appear which not only concerned the traditional questions of the nature of the state, nor even with the problems of how the prince could best guard his (sic) power. Their scope was much wider concerning the 'art of government', in almost every area of social life such as the 'governing of a household, souls, children, a province, a convent, a religious order, or a family' (Rabinow, 1984: 15). Political reflection was, thus, broadened to include 'almost all forms of human activity, from the smallest stirrings of the soul to the largest military manoeuvres of the army' (Rabinow, 1984: 15).

Foucault's history of government also emphasised the centrality of statistical forms of analysis in the modes of government that distinguish the modern world and the ways in which they are (or should be) used to enhance the wellbeing of the population:

> ...the population is the object that government must take into account in all its observations and 'savoir', in order to be able to govern in a rational and conscious manner. The formation of a 'savoir' of government is absolutely bound up with the knowledge of all the processes related to the population (Foucault, 1979a: 18).

In particular, Foucault's (1979a: 14–16, 1991) analysis showed that from about the 18th century on, the 'arts of government', which replaced Sovereign authority, emerged as a consequence to the problem of population and 'consist(ed) essentially of the knowledge of the state, in all the different elements, dimensions and factors of its power, termed precisely "statistics", meaning the "science of the state"'. Statistics, argued Foucault, gradually revealed that the population had its own lawlike regularities such as its own rate of death, of suicide, of disease, its own cycles of scarcity, etc. He asserted that under the 'art', 'population' management became the ultimate interest of government, embracing the *welfare* of the population to improve its conditions, increase its wealth, longevity, health etc. Hence, individual interest and that of the population as a whole becomes both the target and the instrument of government (1979a: 18, 1991). For Foucault, (1979a: 17, 1991) 'statistics...make it possible to quantify the phenomena specific to population', such that 'the art of government and empirical knowledge of the state's resources and condition – its statistics – together formed the major components of a new political rationality' (Rabinow, 1984: 16).

From such a perspective, governmental rationalities in modern societies are intrinsically linked to developments in statistical forms of knowledge and to the powers of governmental expertise which attempt to improve the overall welfare of society and its members – the improvement of its conditions, the increase of its wealth, health, and so on (Foucault, 1991: 100). Existing modes of power are, thus, not so much a matter of 'imposing' constraints or limitations upon citizens, but become rather a matter of 'making up' citizens capable of bearing 'a kind of regulated freedom' (Rose & Miller, 1992: 174). Personal autonomy from this perspective 'is not the antithesis of political power, but a key term in its exercise, the more so because most individuals are not merely the subjects of power but play a part in its operations' (Rose & Miller, 1992: 174). To be sure, to regard the state as some kind of 'monstre froid' 'confronting and dominating' is to 'over-value the problem of the State' (Rose & Miller, 1992: 174). Of primary importance, from this model of societal power relations 'is not so much the State-domination of society, but the "governmentalization" of the State' (Rose & Miller, 1992: 175). This highlights a certain paradox of governmentality: whilst modern liberalism is usually defined as a political philosophy which limits the legitimate exercise of power by political authorities over society, it, at the same time, also *obliges* the government with regard to the organisation and wellbeing of society (Rose & Miller, 1992: 179).

Much akin to models of power in the sphere of corporate governance, then, government can be seen as an *ideal type* that can be conceived as the 'board', whilst population/governed can be seen as analogous with the 'shareholders' or 'stakeholders' in whose beneficial interests the board exists to exercise its decision making responsibilities with fairness, transparency and accountability. This is not to suggest that all governmental decisions and/or activities of the 'board' are benign. Nor is it to imply that all members of the population/governed are equal 'shareholders'. However, (as will be explained further below) unlike under sovereign exercises of power which were not open to challenge by the populous, the governmentality project is premised on the need for members from sections of the population/governed to struggle against apparent instances that they (we) believe detract from their (our) wellbeing; under governmentality, it is incumbent on the governed (us) to inform government of changes needed to address social problems to enhance their (our) interests. As this relates specifically to the issue of miscarriages of justice, then, alleged victims of miscarriages of justice are obliged to challenge the aspect of the existing criminal justice system that is said to be the cause of the miscarriage of justice. And, in line with the governmentality process, only if such claims achieve support in the form of a successful appeal against criminal conviction can government even consider making an intervention to change the offending aspect of the criminal justice system (outlined in detail in Chapter 4). In this sense, the main point to be made here is that the shift from sovereignty ushered rationalities of due process into the general realm of the governmentality of society and the specific realm of the governmentality of the criminal justice system, deviations from which call into question the legitimacy of governmental exercises of power. In short, governments cannot make changes to the criminal justice system in response to miscarriages of justice without the authorisation that a member of the population/governed/public has suffered a miscarriage of justice as evidenced by a successful appeal against criminal conviction (outlined in detail in Chapter 5).

An oft cited defining moment in the appearance of due process as the guiding principle in the governmentality of the criminal justice system is the Magna Carta. A lot has been written about the motivations of King John when he signed the Magna Carta, the consensus view seeing it as an attempt to protect his own position (for a discussion see, for example, Holt, 1992: 188–236). Nevertheless, of most significance for this discussion is what the Magna Carta has come to mean and stand for since it was signed:

> ...despite the fact that the words 'due process' do not appear in any of the documents that have come to be known as the Magna Carta...King John's attaching his seal to those documents in 1215 was nonetheless an explicit commitment to the principle that no one, not even the king, was above the law, that the governed shall not be subjected to capricious rule (Forst, 2004: 11).

From the perspective put forward here, the Magna Carta, then, can be conceived as indicative of a shift in the power relations in society and a new relationship between government and governed. It represents a very early acknowledgement of a shift to a rule of law system and due process in criminal justice matters. As Holt (1992: 2) noted, it 'lays down that no free man (sic) is to be imprisoned, dispossessed, outlawed, exiled or damaged without lawful judgement of his (sic) peers or by the law of the land'. It established the foundations for our ideas about what justice ought to be about – judgement by our peers, the presumption of innocence until proven guilty and the burden of proof on the prosecution to prove guilt beyond a reasonable doubt.

Government in rule of law societies, then, need not be conceived as an intrinsically conspiratorial, negative or coercive form of control or domination over a population or domain of government. On the contrary, *legitimate* government is obliged to take as its object the enhancement of the population or domain to which it is mandated to be responsible. As Foucault (cited Rose, 1996: 44) noted, 'legitimate government will not be arbitrary government, but will be based upon intelligence concerning those whose wellbeing it is mandated to enhance' (also Foucault, 1991: 100). In this process, statistics on all aspects of the domain to be governed or managed are drawn from that inform government about the needs of the population to be managed. 'Pastoral' government attains the 'intelligence' to enhance the well-being of those individuals and domains for which it has responsibility through new forms of rationality that also emerged alongside the replacement of 'sovereignty' by 'governmentality' that are intrinsically connected to the production and deployment of statistical forms of knowledge, calculation, categorisation and expertise (see, for example, Foucault, 1991: 96; Hunt & Wickham, 1994: 27). Statistics on success-ful appeals against criminal conviction, for instance, (should) inform government about the scale of the miscarriage of justice problem, indicating the likely number of people that are harmed by 'justice in error'.

These developments – the emergence of governmental rationality and what might be termed statistical forms of reason – ushered in a new regime of power, namely 'bio-power'. The notion of bio-power as a political rationality is essential to Foucault's thoughts on governmen-tality and was crucial to his analysis of power within modern societies. For Foucault, a society's 'threshold of modernity' has been crossed when power, a particular kind of power – 'bio-power' – is primarily a matter of the 'administration of life' and 'life-processes' (Foucault, 1979b: 143). He asserted:

> ...'bio-power' brought life and its mechanisms into the realm of explicit calculations and made knowledge-power an agent of the transformation of human life...Modern man (sic) is an animal whose politics places his existence as a living being in question (Foucault cited in Rabinow, 1984: 17).

It is bio-power that makes the management or governmentality of post-sovereign rule of law societies possible: in order to manage or govern a population/the governed, administrative knowledge of 'life' and of 'life-processes' is a necessary prerequisite. In order to manage a population well, governmental rationality requires detailed knowledge about the population or the domain to which it is directed. Bio-power made possible the fostering of life and the growth and care of popula-tions by bringing 'life and its mechanisms into the realm of explicit statistical calculations and made knowledge-power an agent for the transformation of human life' (Foucault cited Rabinow, 1984: 17). Moreover, for Foucault, bio-power/population management is achieved, not through the exercise or threat of physical or economic power, but rather, through 'disciplinary techniques'. *Discipline* referred to the *instruments* and *techniques* utilised in the operations of 'disciplinary power' that can be taken over and used by *any* social institution: prisons, certainly, but also schools, hospitals, the military, factories, and so on. Discipline requires surveillance knowledge, by which those to be 'known' and acted upon are made 'visible' and knowable (Foucault, 1977). This is provided through a whole array of governmental devices and techniques such as school, factory, health and/or prison inspectorates, royal commissions, departmental committees of inquiry, social surveys, journalistic reportage and so on (Osborne, 1996: 114) that are utilised to visualise and statistically represent populations and societal domains. The purpose of such knowledge, often seen in entirely negative terms, is, also, to inform government as to the norms proper to the particular domain, rather than to provide the direct rationale for government itself (Osborne, 1996: 101). To repeat, this is not to infer that all exercises of governmental power are equally benign for all members of society. Nor is it to suggest that governmental exercises of power are not open to abuse. Rather, it is to present a new relationship between government and governed, situating legitimate exercises of governmental power in a relational role with the population/governed whose welfare it is mandated to enhance. Moreover, as we shall see, discipline is a two-way-street in a society in which power is relational between government and governed. However, the governed must participate in the governmentality process by bringing to light and contesting occurrences such as miscarriages of justice to activate government to address aspects of the existing arrangements that they can prove are detracting from the general wellbeing of all.

Governing government

At root, then, governmentality can be conceived as a *process* by which rule of law societies are managed, operating with the professed interests or rationale of enhancing the wellbeing of the population. This introduces questions pertaining to existing exercises of power that were not possible under previous systems, bringing into focus the 'other' side of power relations, the part played by the population, the governed, which determines, ultimately, whether governmental exercises of power are legitimate or otherwise. This suggests, further, that not only are the governed not passive under governmentality, they are, actually, in the driving seat of power relations, in response to whose needs government must, under certain conditions, respond with suitable improvements to the way things are.

As already indicated, unlike sovereign exercises of power, legitimate governmental exercises of power are not arbitrary. Governmental modes of power cannot simply impose changes to societal systems. On the contrary, they must themselves follow a certain form of governmental 'due process'-governmentality – within which any proposed changes must not only be acceptable to the governed, they have to come from the governed itself. In societies where exercises of power are relational between government and governed, it is incumbent upon the governed to play their (our) active part in informing government of aspects of social life detrimental to public wellbeing. Through such engagement, which may be termed 'governing government', government knows (has forms of discourse) about societal problems in need of intervention. Only through such engagement is government legitimately *allowed* to intervene. Sticking with the example of the establishment of the CCRC in response to perceived miscarriages of justice, governmental changes to the way in which post-appeal allegations of miscarriages of justice were referred back to the CACD could not be introduced without the efforts of victim support groups and campaigning organisations that kept faith with the Guildford Four and the Birmingham Six despite them exhausting the existing legal remedies. These real cases provided the tangible *evidence* that members of the population were actually being harmed by the existing post-appeal arrangements and that governmental intervention was legitimately required. This puts a certain onus on the governed to participate in the production of counter-discourses on aspects of social life that are detrimental to our wellbeing, backed up by concrete evidence, in attempts to prompt governmental intervention and corrective change. It suggests that governmentality follows its own due processes and evidential standards (in the shape of real cases) for achieving changes to the criminal justice system in response to apparent miscarriages of justice.

This analysis is supported by Foucault's (1980: 80–81) theoretical observation of what he termed an 'insurrection' of 'subjugated knowledges' or forms of 'anti-discourse' in recent times that have interrupted established regimes of thought; forms of particular, localised and/or discontinuous criticism that have been so efficacious that they have undermined, for example, psychoanalysis, the asylum, the legal system or the prison and resulted in governmental intervention. There are two ways in which such forms of knowledge can be understood. On the one hand, they are 'those blocs of historical knowledge which were present but disguised [or buried] within the body of...systemising theory and which [meticulous erudite, exact historical knowledge]...has been able to reveal' (Foucault, 1980: 82). On the other hand, however, Foucault (1980: 82) argued that by 'subjugated knowledges one should understand something else, something which in a sense is altogether different, namely, a whole set of [local, specific and popular] knowledges that have been disqualified as inadequate to their task or insufficiently elaborated: naïve knowledges, located low down on the hierarchy, beneath the required level of cognition or scientificity'. For Foucault (1980: 83), what tied these two types of subjugated knowledge together – those buried discourses of academic erudition and those popular disqualified discourses of popular experience – is that both are essentially concerned with a '*historical knowledge of struggles*' (original emphasis). As he (1980: 83) said: 'In the specialised areas of erudition as in the disqualified, popular knowledge there lay the memory of hostile encounters which...have been confined to the margins of knowledge.' What emerged out of this 'union' between erudite academic knowledge and local experiential knowledge are 'genealogical, or rather a multiplicity of genealogical researches, a painstaking rediscovery of struggles together with the memory of their conflicts' (Foucault, 1980: 83). As Foucault (1980b: 82–87) pointed out, the utility of genealogical research that produces subjugated forms of knowledge is that it can be tactically deployed in struggles that oppose the harmful effects of the forms of power that predominate in societies like ours.

Evidence abounds in contemporary society of apparent 'failures' by government to curtail what are often termed the 'crimes of the powerful' at the expense of punitive measures in response to the crimes of the 'powerless' (for a recent critique in the context of state and corporate crime see, for instance, Tombs & Whyte, 2003). To be sure, we are surrounded with evidence of forms of bias, discrimination and inequality in the delivery of 'justice', for instance, which may lead some to the (mistaken) conclusion that exercises of power remain fundamentally sovereign in form. However, the crucial sociological point from Marx is that social systems do not emerge fully formed out of the ashes of the social system that they come to replace. On the contrary, from the perspective developed here, it is perhaps more fruitful to conceive the governmentality project as still under construction; as an on-going process that works to shake off sovereign mores and hangovers in response to forms of critique that unearth currently subjugated discourses with the forcefulness to disturb and dislodge the existing ways of managing forms of apparent social injustice. As this relates specifically to the governmentality of the criminal justice system, guiding principles such as the 'presumption of innocence' and 'burden of proof' on the prosecution (as representative of Government) to prove its case 'beyond a reasonable doubt' can, therefore, be viewed as ideals to be strived for. They provide the foundational concepts from which critiques of the way things are can be made. To be sure, without foundational ideals of fairness and due process, counter-discourses about injustice would not be possible, there would be nothing to ground such critiques in. It is only because the criminal justice system is supposed to be (and purports to be) fair and just that proven instances of unfairness, injustice and/or non-compliance with the rules and procedures of due process, such as successful appeals as evidence of miscarriages of justice, have counter-discursive strength against the way things are, the truths we live by.

In this sense, the governmentality project can, itself, be viewed as a (due) process of reform from sovereign forms of rule, which cannot itself be reformed until it has been entirely rid of all remnants of sovereignty. On this journey, however, it is vital that the representatives of the governed in the jigsaw of the miscarriage of justice problem – high profile individual victims, campaigning groups and organisations, critical academics, human rights activists, practitioners, and so on – seek out cases in support of apparent shortcomings in the existing criminal justice system arrangements to give force (power) to their voices for change. From this perspective, governmentality is as much as about how effective the surveillance techniques and tactics of the governed are at prompting governmental intervention to problematic areas of social life in need of correction, as they are about forms of government surveillance that attempt to visualise the needs of the governed.

Conclusion

This chapter has sought to provide the theoretical foundation from which the analyses in the remainder of the book will be grounded. Despite a popular desire that the criminal justice system should convict the guilty and acquit the innocent, the system relies on prevailing standards of due process to determine the guilt or not guilt of criminal defendants. At root this involves an attempt to ensure that suspects and defendants of crime receive trials deemed to be fair on the system's terms. Quashed convictions are achieved by showing that trials were unfair and, thus, unsafe and illegitimate. This stems from the complex relationship between government and governed in post-sovereign rule of law societies striving towards governmental rationalities, which determine how legitimate exercises of power must be implemented. At the same time, the onus on the governed as part of governing government is to seek out instances which show 'failures' to comply with the underlying structural requirement that legitimate expressions of power follow the principles of fairness and the enhancement of public wellbeing. Indeed, Foucault's (1980b) genealogical approach has an important relevance to this analysis of governmental interventions into the criminal justice system in response to the specific problem of perceived miscarriages of justice. In the same way that counter-discourse or 'anti-discourse' was necessary in undermining prevalent perceptions of the realities of the asylum and/or the prison, there is a corresponding necessity for the elevation of disqualified discourses that accompany routine and/or mundane miscarriages of justice. This can serve to undermine the predominant perception that miscarriages of justice are an exceptional occurrence and small in number, and provide a more comprehensive depiction of the scale and harmful consequences of the problem.

As the next chapter will show, successful appeals are not only an exceptional occurrence in England and Wales, they are also routine and mundane features of the criminal justice process that occur every day of every week of every year. Accordingly, analyses that attempt to depict the extent of miscarriages of justice that consider only those cases and forms of knowledge that derived from post-appeal procedures will, inevitably, be partial and, hence, inadequate. Alternatively, a more comprehensive depiction of the miscarriage of justice phenomenon needs also to include all successful appeals to provide access to a whole variety of currently disqualified and marginalised forms of discourse about the forms of miscarriages of justice and their consequences, both to the individual victims, their families and to society as a whole.

2
The Official Miscarriage of Justice Iceberg

Introduction

Discourses on miscarriages of justice in all relevant spheres tend to revolve around the same few notorious cases. For instance, the case of the Guildford Four has remained at the forefront of public consciousness on miscarriages of justice and political debate about the limits of the criminal justice process since it was overturned in 1989.[11] Likewise, the case of the Birmingham Six has been an ever-present touchstone in debates about miscarriages of justice since it was overturned in 1991. These cases are routinely claimed to be illustrative of the 'tip' of a much greater 'iceberg' of miscarriages of justice that are occurring. Indeed, anyone with even a vague knowledge about miscarriages of justice will be able to list other well known cases that have captured the public's attention and dominated debates about miscarriages of justice over the last 15 to 20 years. These, no doubt, will include the cases of Stefan Kiszko (Rose et al, 1997), the Bridgewater Four (Regan, 1997b), the Maguire Seven (Maguire, 1994), which, along with the Guildford Four and the Birmingham Six, were also at the heart of the debate about miscarriages of justice which led to the RCCJ (1993). More recently, the cases of Stephen Downing (see Hale, 2002), the Cardiff Newsagent Three (see Carroll, 1998; Lewis, 1999), Robert Brown (see Hopkins, 2002b; Hill, 2002a), Paul Blackburn (see Naylor, 2004) and Sally Clark (see Batt, 2005) have been the focus of miscarriage of justice discourses. Significantly, the foregoing cases share the method by which they achieved a successful appeal: they were all overturned by post-appeal mechanisms, having previously been unsuccessful in their routine appeals. At the expense of such analyses on individual cases, there has been no previous attempt to calculate precisely just how big the miscarriage of justice iceberg might be and just how many people are affected as either primary or secondary victims.

However, as the legal evidence of a miscarriage of justice is a successful appeal against criminal conviction, what about the successful appeals that are routinely overturned by the CACD? Moreover, what about successful appeals in the Crown Court against convictions given in magistrates' courts? Are these successful appeals against criminal conviction not miscarriages of justice too? If these successful appeals *are* included in the calculation of miscarriages of justice, a miscarriage of justice iceberg in England and Wales is demonstrated that far exceeds all previous estimations. It follows that the customary focus on post-appeal successful appeals at the exclusion of a more inclusive approach that takes account of all successful appeals presents only a partial indicator of the full scale of miscarriages of justice that occur.

With that in mind, this chapter draws from the official statistics of successful appeals against criminal conviction deriving from the CCRC, the CACD and the Crown Court to discern three categories of official miscarriage of justice – the *exceptional*, the *routine* and the *mundane*. It, then, points up some inherent methodological difficulties that are involved in quantifying miscarriages of justice in terms of the official statistics on successful appeals. Finally, it more generally considers the issue of official statistics usage within a theoretical account of the production and exercise of existing forms of power in the field of criminal justice. Despite their inherent limitations, official statistics on successful appeals are a vital element in depictions of miscarriages of justice and a core component in the exercise of existing forms of criminal justice system power. In other words, a more pragmatic approach towards official statistics on successful appeals needs to be adopted for critical purposes.

Towards a typology of miscarriages of justice

The criminal justice system in England and Wales provides five main routes to appeal against alleged miscarriages of justice:

- the Crown Court deals mainly with appeals by persons convicted in magistrates' courts against their conviction or sentence or both whereupon the case is reheard (for full details of the referral criteria see Magistrates' Courts Act, 1980; Criminal Appeal Act, 1995; Criminal Justice Act, 2003);

- the Court of Appeal (Criminal Division) (CACD) hears appeals in criminal matters from the Crown Court (for full details of referral criteria see Criminal Appeal Act, 1968; Criminal Appeal Rules, 1968 and the Criminal Appeal Act, 1995; Criminal Justice Act, 2003);
- the High Court, Queens Bench Division receives appeals by way of 'cases stated' from magistrates' courts and the Crown Court on the ground that proceedings are wrong in law or in excess of jurisdiction for the opinion of the High Court;[12]
- the House of Lords, the final court of appeal in the UK, hears appeals on arguable points of law of general public importance (for full details of referral criteria see Department of Constitutional Affairs, 2006: 11–12);
- the Criminal Cases Review Commission (CCRC) can reinvestigate and refer cases that have already been through the appeals system and have not succeeded for any reason back to the appropriate appeal court if they feel that there is a 'real possibility' that the conviction will be overturned (for full details of referral criteria see Criminal Appeal Act, 1995; Criminal Justice Act, 2003; Criminal Cases Review Commission, 2006).

The Department for Constitutional Affairs (DCA) (formerly the Lord Chancellors' Department (LCD)) collects, and publishes annually, statistics from each of these appeal courts/processes. The statistics for appeals allowed are represented in Table 2.1 (below).

Taken together, the official statistics on successful appeals against criminal conviction in whichever court the conviction, was given and through whichever appeal mechanism the successful appeal was allowed, provide an indicator of the extent to which erroneous criminal convictions can be conceived to officially occur each year in England and Wales – official miscarriages of justice.

Exceptional miscarriages of justice

Despite this, as indicated, public perceptions and all forms of discourse on miscarriages of justice have been almost entirely focused upon what might be termed *exceptional* cases of successful appeal that were referred back to the CACD by the CCRC or, before the CCRC was established, C3 Division of the Home Office, having previously failed through routine appeal procedures.[13] The problem with this is not that these cases were not miscarriages of justice but, rather, that they represent only one *type* of successful appeal and a tiny aspect of all miscarriages of justice, as evidenced by successful appeals. For instance,

Table 2.1   Appeals allowed in England and Wales over the last 20 years

	Crown Court: Appeals Allowed 1986–2005 (inclusive)****	High Court – Queens Bench Division: Appeals Allowed from Magistrates' Courts 1986–2005 (inclusive and includes cases allowed by Single Judge and Divisional Court)	High Court – Queens Bench Division: Appeals Allowed from the Crown Court 1986–2005 (inclusive and includes cases allowed by Single Judge and Divisional Court)	Court of Appeal (Criminal Division): Appeals Allowed Against Conviction 1986–2005 (inclusive)****	House of Lords: Appeals Allowed or Reversed in Criminal Matters in England and Wales 1986–2005 (inclusive)*	Criminal Cases Review Commission: Convictions Overturned following a referral back to CACD since it started handling casework
1986	3,718	80	18	N/A*****	4	N/A
1987	3,544	57	11	192	1	N/A
1988	3,371	68	8	223	1	N/A
1989	4,274	37	5	211	0	N/A
1990	4,693	35	3	256	0	N/A
1991	5,464	61	11	269	3	N/A
1992	6,303	64	12	299	2	N/A
1993	7,998	72	13	402	0	N/A
1994	8,139	93	30	351	3	N/A
1995	8,064	99	12	253	0	N/A
1996	5,237	70	21	250	3	N/A
1997**	3,771	67	7	236	2	1
1998	3,980	73	10	290	2	8
1999	3,573	57	6	171	0	15
2000	3,090	74	9	150	1	17
2001	2,978	44	9	135	5	15
2002	2,959	43	10	166	1	22
2003	2,089	43	11	178	2	29
2004	3,019	44	4	240	3	26
2005***	3,651	23	6	228	8	28
Total	89,915	1,204	216	4,500	41	161
Yearly Average	4,495.75	60.20	10.8	236.84	2.05	17.89

Daily Average in Crown Court, CACD (including referrals from the CCRC) and House of Lords	18.21

Sources: Lord Chancellor's Department 1986, 1987, 1988, 1989, 1990, 1991, 1992, 1993, 1994, 1995, 1996, 1997, 1998, 1999, 2000, 2001, 2002; Department for Constitutional Affairs, 2003, 2004, 2005, 2006.

   * Until 1994 the determination of appeals to the House of Lords as to whether appeals had succeeded was described in terms of the order appealed against being 'Affirmed' or 'Reversed'. Thank you to Christine Salmon, Deputy Head of the Judicial Office, for confirming in a letter dated 18 October 2006 that if an order of the lower court order is 'Affirmed' this amounts to the appeal being 'Dismissed'; similarly, where the lower court order is 'Reversed', the appeal is 'Allowed'.

  ** Figures for cases overturned following a referral by the CCRC the year 1997–1998 are from 31 March when the CCRC started handling casework.

 *** Figures for cases overturned following a referral by the CCRC for the year 2006 are up to 31 August.

 **** Figures for appeals in the Crown Court and CACD will include cases overturned following a referral by the CCRC.

***** Statistical information for allowed appeals in the CACD is not available for 1986.

Table 2.1 shows that an annual average of 18 cases have been success-ful in appeal following a referral by the CCRC in its first nine years. This compares with a total of over 1.2 million criminal convictions (excluding summary motoring offences) in the Crown Court and mag-istrates' courts in year 2001 alone, for example (Home Office, 2002b: 16). As this relates to the iceberg analogy and attempts to effect changes to the criminal justice system to prevent or reduce mis-carriages of justice, analyses that are limited to a definition of mis-carriages of justice as successful appeals that are overturned following a post-appeal referral by the CCRC (or previously C3 Division) will depict what might be termed only the tiniest of icicles, suggesting that the criminal justice system is near perfect with an error rate of 0.000015 per cent. Such analyses do little, if anything, to raise con-cerns about miscarriages of justice and/or prompt governmental intervention to reduce their occurrence. On the contrary, govern-mental intervention requires a significant statistical problem to be evident.

Routine miscarriages of justice

A major limitation of concentrating on exceptional cases of successful appeal that are brought to light via the post-appeal procedures of the CCRC, is that all manner of *routine* successful appeals in the CACD against conviction given in the Crown Court have been neglected. Indeed, if definitions of miscarriages of justice are rethought to include all those successful appeals that are routinely quashed upon appeal by the CACD, then miscarriages of justice can, perhaps, be said to be far more prevalent than is usually thought. Table 2.1 also shows that in the period 1987–2005 (inclusive), for example, the CACD abated 4,500 criminal convictions. This equates to a yearly average of 237 cases, or a 13-fold increase in the miscarriage of justice iceberg that can be cal-culated utilising a definition grounded in successful appeals following a referral by the CCRC.[14]

Mundane miscarriages of justice

In addition to successful appeals in the CACD from the CCRC and the Crown Court, criminal convictions given in magistrates' courts can be appealed in the Crown Court whereupon the case is reheard. When the criminal convictions from magistrates' courts that are quashed upon appeal to the Crown Court are also taken into account the extent of England and Wales' miscarriage of justice iceberg that can be inferred from the official statistics on successful appeals is even further extended. To be sure, conventional definitions of miscarriages of justice based on successful appeals that follow a referral back to the CACD by the CCRC overtly exclude all criminal cases in magistrates' courts, where currently 98 per cent of criminal cases are dealt with (Bright & Nicklin, 2002), excluding from the critical gaze far more than is taken into consideration.

Table 2.1 shows an annual average of 4,496 quashed convictions at the Crown Court for criminal convictions that were given by magistrates' courts between 1986–2005 (inclusive). If this average is added to the CACD annual average then an official picture of miscarriages of justice in England and Wales, the official miscarriage of justice iceberg, is increased to an annual average of 4,733 cases. As this relates to the number of miscarriages of justice that can be calculated from conventional definitions which are premised on post-appeal successful appeals from a CCRC referral, assuming that the Crown Court sits in its appellate function five days a week for 52 weeks, it shifts the depiction of the scale of the miscarriage of justice problem from around 18 cases per annum to 18 cases per day.

On top of the successful appeals against criminal convictions in the Crown Court and the CACD, the official index of miscarriages of justice also includes successful appeals in criminal matters from the House of Lords. Table 2.1 lists successful appeals in the House of Lords over the last two decades, matching the period of the statistics from the Crown Court and the CACD. These cases need, also, to be incorporated into critical qualitative analyses of the harmful consequences of miscarriages of justice for the additional victims that they show are affected.

In advocating the rethinking of definitions of miscarriages of justice in England and Wales to include all successful appeals against criminal conviction, however, a range of methodological issues pertaining to the validity, reliability and/or representativeness of the official statistics arise: how reliable, valid or representative are official statistics on successful appeals against criminal conviction as a way of quantifying miscarriages of justice in England and Wales?

Methodological issues

In a *pragmatic*, but yet still critical mode, there is a strong case for defining miscarriages of justice as embracing *all* the official statistics on successful appeals against criminal conviction. The very nature of the enterprise means that legal definitions and categorisations cannot be transcended. Thus, it seems inappropriate to consider only part of the picture – exceptional post-appeal cases of successful appeal – at the expense of broader statistical appraisals of mundane and/or routine successful appeals that derive from the same existing criminal appeals system, albeit at a different stage. Whether successful appeals are mundane, routine or exceptional in character, they each represent an official acknowledgement that a criminal conviction is considered, officially, to be flawed.

Inextricably related to the problem of definitional reliability is the matter of the potential political dimension of the official statistics on successful appeals. Official statistics on successful appeals are inherently political in the sense that they are *representative* of legal judgements grounded in politically derived legislative changes. If the law on appeals changes, so too do the criteria for defining successful appeals as well as official measurements of successful appeals (cf. Hindess, 1973: 12).

A further potential political dimension with official statistics of successful appeals against criminal conviction according to Woffinden (1987) is the possible problem of political obstruction. Drawing support from Koestler (1956), Woffinden (1987: 341) asserted that it is 'impossible to tell' how many miscarriages of justice occur, but 'it is not unreasonable to assume that the number of undetected errors may be greater than we believe' (Woffinden, 1987: 341):

> The major problem…(with) miscarriage of justice (cases) is that to acknowledge the case as such would inevitably involve admitting to a catalogue of serious errors in the detection of crime and the administration of justice. The authorities are loath to countenance this…with the result that…even allowing murderers to go free and commit further crimes becomes a small price to pay for the maintenance of the façade of judicial infallibility (Woffinden, 1987: 342).

Woffinden is correct that a finite calculation of miscarriages of justice is, probably, impossible. He is also correct to raise the issue of the political dimension of the problem of miscarriage of justice research, as well as the associated harmful consequences of such governmental inaction (discussed further in Chapter 8). However, the impossibility of a finite calculation of miscarriages is not merely due to the reasons that he proposes. As this discussion is attempting to show, it is not only about political interference, but also about the reliability and/or validity of the available statistical information and the accompanying problem of an appropriate definition of miscarriages of justice to work from. Moreover, as the above statistics on successful appeals show, even in a strictly legalistic sense, the appellate courts indicate miscarriages of justice are not only widespread, they are commonplace. In this sense, it is not the case that the agencies that together comprise the criminal justice system in England and Wales are 'loath' to acknowledge the quashing of criminal convictions. Successful appeal statistics are collected and produced from all manner of appellate court and indicate that quite the reverse is true. Rather, the 'political problem' seems to reside more with those critics who have premised their critiques on very narrow definitions of miscarriages of justice as rare and exceptional occurrences of judicial 'error' and the products of post-appeal methods for overturning potential miscarriages of justice. Alternatively, if miscarriages of justice are taken as systemic mistakes, then they can be viewed as a mundane feature of criminal justice in England and Wales. This needs wider transmission in the interests of a more realistic and sustained critical debate about the realities of criminal injustice. Official statistics of successful appeals against criminal conviction need to be taken seriously to provide a more adequate depiction of the miscarriage of justice problem. Although they may not be an objectively accurate index of all miscarriages of justice and/or wrongful convictions in England and Wales, they can be viewed as an index of the institutional or organisational processes and forms of behaviour that produce official miscarriages of justice, about which very little is currently known (cf. Kituse & Cicourel, 1963: 137).

Another interrelated challenge to such empirically grounded research into miscarriages of justice in England and Wales is the *validity* of the available statistical information and what it purports to cover. Since the 1960s there has been an on-going debate within the Social Sciences on the reliability of statistical 'data' and its usefulness (or uselessness) as a tool of sociological analysis – the very idea of statistical sociology being anathema to some. This debate has, to a large extent, been centred upon Durkheim's *Suicide* (1952) to the effect that it is commonplace for 'A' level and undergraduate Sociology students to cut their critical and methodological teeth on that text.

As this relates to research on miscarriages of justice, the problem is just as profound. If Durkheim's *Suicide* (1952) can (correctly) be criticised on the grounds that 'suicide' as an official category of social reality is the product of the interpretations of official coroners (see Douglas, 1967), then the idea of research on miscarriages of justice is open to the same criticism. Official statistics of successful appeals against criminal conviction are not an exhaustive indicator of miscarriages of justice in England and Wales. On the contrary, they are entirely legalistic and retrospective socio-legal *constructions* (cf. Box, 1971: 208–210). They are the product of the official pronouncements and categorisation of the different appellate courts of the criminal justice system. As Miles & Irvine (1979: 115) noted: 'Official statistics are not objective reflections of social reality, neutral pictures emerging from purely technical decisions. Their production involves a host of decisions about the objects, techniques and methods involved'. The official figure of successful appeals that appears in the DCA's publications relates only to the records of the various appellate courts in England and Wales as prescribed by the legislation that governs criminal appeals. These records are also subject to an acute technical problem in their compilation, as the decisions of judges are very much subject to their own *interpretations* of the law. As it is possible for different judges, in different places, at different times to interpret the same law differentially, official statistics can be conceived as inherently incorporating an inevitable degree of inconsistency in their construction which can never be overcome (cf. Reiner, 1996: 191–192).

Furthermore, if the official statistics on successful appeals are to be included in a revised definition of miscarriages of justice, it needs also to be acknowledged that they take no account of those appeals against criminal conviction that are *in the process of being quashed*. Nor do they take account of allegations and suspicions of miscarriages of justice that might never be officially adjudicated as such. As the following chapter will show, there are a whole host of procedural barriers, obstacles and/or disincentives that will also have a profound impact upon the reliability and/or validity of the official statistics on successful appeals to comprehensively represent all wrongful convictions in England and Wales, however conceived. Thus, even if all of the officially collected statistics on successful appeals were considered as miscarriages of justice they would not represent the total number of wrongful convictions in England and Wales. Rather, the official statistics are themselves only a partial indicator, an official index, of the total extent of miscarriages of justice in England and Wales. The inclusion of all successful appeals in critical analyses together with the knowledge of their partiality, however, represents a scale of miscarriages of justice has the potential to inform critical praxis in a direction that has, hitherto, received no theoretical or substantive appraisal. This raises the crucial matter of the nature and operation of power in the sphere of the criminal justice system, which informs my rationale that official statistics of successful appeals must be embraced for the counter-discursive force that they can provide. To these matters the discussion now turns and what is termed a 'critical pragmatist' approach to the official statistics on successful appeals is constructed and advocated.

A critical pragmatist approach to the inclusion of all successful appeals

In general, critical social scientific conceptions of official statistics are derived in response to 'positivist' and/or 'empiricist' approaches. The positivist simply *observes* phenomena, establishes the links between them, and *uncovers* the fundamental *laws* of human behaviour (see, for example, Aron, 1965: 62–66). Similarly, the empiricist tends to see the open-minded *collection of data*, and the unbiased *discovery of findings*, as the key to knowledge of the social world (Miles and Irvine, 1979: 115 original emphasis). Against such conceptions, critical social theorists generally tend to regard official statistics as politically biased forms of information that are systematically manipulated both by, and in the interests of, power structures in society (see for example, Nichols, 1996; Doyal, 1979; Hird & Irvine, 1979; Hyman & Price, 1979; Kincaid, 1979; Oakley & Oakley, 1979). From such a standpoint, official statistics have historically been regarded with great suspicion by critical social scientists and are generally engaged with only in the interests of theoretical and/or methodological criticism in an attempt to weaken or undermine their governmental authority; critical social scientists are generally unwilling to work 'within' the discursive agendas that have been predetermined by their adversaries; and the application of official statistics is either generally avoided, or undertaken with extreme caution, which inevitably results in the production of diffident, if not extremely weak counter-discourse.[15]

As this situation relates to the specific area of critical discourse against miscarriages of justice, the situation is even more profound. Miscarriage of justice researchers have seemingly rejected official statistics of successful appeals against criminal conviction altogether in favour of critical analyses of particular exceptional post-appeal cases of successful appeal. It is almost as if the struggle for the 'victory' of a publicly acknowledged quashed criminal conviction of an alleged innocent victim of wrongful conviction somehow makes those cases that attain a high profile status in the process somehow more noble and/or worthy than those successful appeals that result from the mundane and/or routine pronouncements of the CACD. It is as if the media attention that accompanies high profile cases of wrongful conviction in some way embarrasses the government and, consequently, weakens its power.

The problem with this is that analyses that focus only upon exceptional cases of successful appeal that are produced through post-appeal procedures, result only in small-scale critiques, which in the context of all successful appeals represent only the minutest of 'error'. Accordingly, such critical analyses cause little disruption to the everyday affairs of the criminal justice system. Moreover, against such analyses, the routine defence of the criminal justice system when exceptional miscarriages of justice are revealed, i.e. that no human system is perfect, that a certain number of miscarriages of justice is, therefore, inevitable, and that is why such appellate safeguards as the CACD exist and extra-judicial appellate safeguards were introduced, appears extremely convincing (see, for example, Royal Commission on Criminal Justice, 1993: 6–7).

Against this, a more inclusive perspective on successful appeals, for the officially acknowledged 'errors of justice' that they indicate and cannot be side-stepped, shows that miscarriage of justice is not only a small-scale problem. On the contrary, miscarriages of justice in England and Wales are a mundane feature of criminal justice. And, there is a world of difference between an annual average of 18 exceptional, post-appeal, high profile cases being quashed by the CACD and the annual average of 237 criminal convictions that are routinely quashed by the CACD, and the 4,496 cases that are mundanely quashed by the Crown Court.

The apparent wholesale disregard of the official statistics on miscarriages of justice by the social science community can be conceived to have its roots in a general critical social scientific tradition: critical social science is, generally speaking, wedded to the pursuit of truth (see, for example, Feyerabend, 1981). It is little wonder, then, that critical discourses have rejected even the consideration of official statistics of successful appeals. The general critiques produced by social science are enough for any self-respecting critic of miscarriages of justice to leave them well alone. As already mentioned, the official statistics on successful appeals are entirely legalistically determined and retrospectively directed. They contain inherent and acute theoretical and methodological problems that can never be resolved, no matter how 'technical' their encoding. This may explain why there has been no critical criminological or socio-legal assessment at all of the official statistics on successful appeals.

Official statistics, however, whether manipulated or not, truthful or not, are probably the most forceful constituent element in the interplay of competing discourses and the exercise of modern forms of power. They determine the truths we live by. As Levitas (1996: 45–63), for example, observed, official statistics on the unemployment figures generally determine the *meanings* that are attributed to 'unemployment', both in terms of public perceptions and the governmental departments that deal with unemployment. As Miller & Rose (1990) noted, official statistics are inseparable from the forms of calculation and expertise of the objects of government. Indeed, official statistics are intrinsically and intimately connected to the exercise of governmental power within the various domains that comprise society. They shape public perceptions on the various governmental problematics within society on such issues as social class, gender, ethnicity and so on. Furthermore, they determine the policies that are designed and implemented in response to those problematics (see, for example, Government Statistician's Collective, 1979). As such, the apparent unwillingness of those engaged in the production of critical counter-discourse against miscarriages of justice to engage with official statistics of successful appeals can be conceived as ensuring the discursive dominance of its adversaries. They, effectively, fail the members of the governed who experience miscarriages of justice on a routine and mundane basis, disqualifying their counter-discursive voices altogether.

Moreover, the general critique of official statistics from the critical social scientific community tends to presuppose that if statistics were not 'manipulated' or 'abused' they would be truthful. It serves to reinforce the scientific notion that statistics *are*, on the whole, or, at least, *would be* through the proper technical correction, about truth, and that only those statistics that are interfered with are false and, therefore, illegitimate. But, as we have seen, official statistics generally, as well as official statistics on successful appeals specifically, are intrinsically *socio-politico-legal technicalities*. To be sure, official statistics are not about truth in any objective or absolute sense. But, they do *produce* the discursive 'truths' that shape, guide, channel, and control modern western societies, in a Foucauldian sense, the 'truths' we live by (see Foucault, 1986). As Rose & Miller (1992: 174) noted, existing forms of power are not so much a matter of 'imposing' constraints or limitations upon citizens, upon a population, but more a matter of statistically 'making-up' citizens capable of bearing 'a kind of regulated freedom'. Thus, official statistics are not simply ways of collecting information about a State, but are in fact about 'normalisation'; about normalising the population. They are central to relations of power between government and governed in the governmentality project. In defining those outside the 'norm' such as the unemployed, the poor, criminals, the mentally ill, and so on, official statistics determine the norm. And, because 'few of us fancy being pathological "most of us" try to make ourselves normal, which in turn affects what is normal', indeed we desire to be normal (Hacking, 1990: 2). This is not to portray a bleak system of social control and domination. On the contrary, it is to make an eminently sociological observation pertaining to the processes of socialisation under the system of governmentality.

To be sure, from such a perspective: 'Even our personalities, sub-jectivities, and "relationships" are not private matters...On the con-trary, they are intensively governed...Thoughts, feelings and actions may appear as the very fabric and constitution of the intimate self, but they are socially organised and managed in minute particulars' (Rose, 1990: 1). This is because 'in modern societies "freedom" is "imposed", not through force but through the "shaping", "channelling" and "enhancement" of "subjectivity" in all of the operations of modern government; and the "government of subjectivity" which characterises modern political power is "explicitly connected" with social scientific statistical knowledge, a *technique* of the management of a popu-lation...modern government is to "know", to "proscribe", and to "monitor" the lives of those for whom one is responsible' (Rose, 1990: 221–223).

Alternatively, then, perhaps a more fruitful way of conceiving official statistics should be as intrinsically related to the construction of exist-ing structures of power and relations between governed and govern-ment. As such, they can be utilised by both governed and government as tools to aid understanding and discursive weapons in the on-going governmentality struggle to change society. As Latour (1987) has shown, because statistics are highly rhetorical they are used strateg-ically to convince people. From such a frame of analysis, official statis-tics on successful appeals do not simply passively depict social reality, they are part of the discourse of *governing*. They discursively create forms of reality. They enable centralisation by fabricating a 'clearing' within which thought and action can occur. They set up a homo-geneous domain inhabited only by other numbers. They establish a single 'plane of reality', with a single concern reducible to numbers. They, thus, enable a machinery of government to operate from centres that calculate (see Latour, 1987, also 1986). Moreover, as Rose (1991: 674) has shown, official statistics are a very persuasive form of power because they promise a 'de-politicization' of politics, 'redrawing the boundaries between politics and objectivity by purporting to act as automatic technical mechanisms for making judgements, prioritising problems and allocating scarce resources'.

It is in this kind of framework that a *critical pragmatist* application of the official statistics on successful appeals as miscarriages of justice is advocated. A pragmatic approach, not as an apology for power, but as a way of resisting dominant expressions of power, even utilising official statistics in the exercise of power for the betterment of society for the governed. It is a critical pragmatic approach that recognises that critical notions of 'truth' must not be disconnected from the practices of belief, assertion and inquiry (cf. Misak, 1999: 2); that, critical discourse needs also to concern itself with the truth of the consequences of the official statistics on successful appeals, with 'the 'truths' we live by. As James contended:

> The pragmatic method is primarily a method for settling metaphysical disputes that might otherwise be interminable...A pragmatist turns his (sic) back resolutely and once for all...from abstraction and insufficiency, from verbal solutions, from bad *a priori* reasons, from fixed principles, closed systems, and pretended absolutes and origins. He (sic) turns towards...action and power (James, 1992: 39–41 original italics; Festenstein, 1997; Murphy, 1990).

From such a perspective, despite the inherent limits and technical difficulties of official statistics in terms of reliability and validity from a conventional sociological approach to official data, they are probably the most powerful *force* in discursive struggles and disputes. The centrality of official statistics in governmental policy design and implementation suggests that existing societies can almost entirely be conceived as societies of *discursive statistical argumentation*. In the processes of governmentality and the negotiated modification of the criminal justice system, statistical forms of knowledge are vital. They both inform and enhance the force of counter-discursive productions, wherein the most convincing statistical discourse will succeed: the more miscarriages of justice that can be legitimately demonstrated, the stronger counter-discursive voices will be.

Conclusion

This chapter has attempted to further substantiate an urgent need to rethink prevalent definitions of miscarriages of justice to include all successful appeals against criminal conviction. This will provide a more adequate depiction of the scale of the miscarriage of justice problem for further critical analyses that should, simultaneously, carry greater counter-discursive weight to attempts to address the harmful consequences that miscarriages of justice cause. In so doing, a critical pragmatist approach towards official statistics on successful appeals was constructed and proposed to further strengthen the call to revise conventional definitions of miscarriages of justice to include all successful appeals in their analyses. This is not to suggest that the official statistics are somehow a reliable or even valid representation of the total extent of miscarriages of justice in England and Wales. This they are not. But, the official statistics on successful appeals do expose a scale of officially generated statistics of miscarriages of justice that might more effectively engage with official discourse and dominant exercises of power in the struggle over criminal justice.

It must be noted, however, that this chapter has only considered the likely scale of miscarriages of justice in England and Wales in the entirely legalistic and retrospective confines of the official statistics of successful appeals in the Crown Court and the CACD, including cases overturned following a referral by the CCRC, and the House of Lords. That is, a miscarriage of justice has only been considered to occur when an appeal against criminal conviction has been successfully achieved in one of these three appellate courts. This does not include the appeals represented in Table 2.1 that are allowed each year in the High Court, Queens Bench Division relating to criminal matters. To be sure, s. 111 of the Magistrates' Courts Act 1980 provides that any person who was a party to any proceeding before a magistrate's court, or is aggrieved by a conviction, order, determination or other proceedings may question that proceeding on the ground that it is wrong in law or in excess of jurisdiction by applying to the magistrates' court to state a case for the opinion of the High Court. Furthermore, s. 28(1) of the Supreme Court Act 1981 provides that, subject to an exception for criminal cases, any order, judgement or other decision of the Crown Court may be questioned by any party to the proceedings on the ground that it is wrong in law or in excess of jurisdiction, by applying to the Crown Court to have a case stated for the opinion of the High Court. The exception is that there is no power to state a case in respect of a judgment or other decision of the Crown Court relating to trial on indictment (appeal against such decision lies to the CACD). It must also be noted that in criminal cases the Crown Court may only state a case in respect of final decisions and not in respect of interlocutory rulings made in the course of the hearing.

A limitation with the inclusion of all appeals allowed in the High Court, Queens Bench Division in analyses of official miscarriages of justice is that we do not know how many cases stated which are allowed by the High Court result in an overturned conviction and how many cases stated are allowed on points of law which have no material impact on the conviction. As such, the statistics for allowed cases stated to the High Court in criminal matters need to be treated with caution. This said, it is likely that further exploration may well turn up additional cases that *are* overturned following an allowed appeal in the High Court for criminal matters. These, too, need to be incorporated into critical qualitative analyses of miscarriages of justice and the harmful consequences to victims, for the additional number of people that they show are affected. Moreover, their inclusion here provides statistical consistency and gives a further indication of the mundane nature of allowed appeals in the various appeal courts in England and Wales and the issue of 'justice in error'.

3
Causation: Beyond the Official Miscarriage of Justice Iceberg

Introduction

There are two distinct approaches to unearthing the causes of miscarriages of justice in England and Wales. On the one hand, academic and practising lawyers have conducted collaborative researchers drawn from official data on the causes of miscarriages of justice as evidenced, primarily, by exceptional successful appeals, and listed the causes in strict accordance with the reasons given by the appeal courts, i.e. false confession, malicious allegation, police or prosecutorial 'error' or 'misconduct', and so on. On the other hand, researchers from a more critical sociological/criminological perspective have operated on a more theoretical plane of analysis and sought to attribute the causes of miscarriages of justice to forms of inequality and discrimination that lie at the heart of the structures of society. The former modes of analysis, premised on the judgements of the appeal courts, tend to attribute the causes of miscarriages of justice to errant individuals who are either criminal justice system personnel or members of the public who, for whatever reason, subvert the criminal justice process, which otherwise would not have caused a miscarriage of justice. Conversely, analyses that locate the causes of miscarriages of justice in the very structures of society attribute them to the normal exercise of criminal justice system power which targets certain sections of the population, along lines of social class, gender, ethnicity, age, and so on, failing, therefore, in the fundamental governmental requirement that all should be treated as equal before the law.

The different approaches sometimes produce competing accounts for why miscarriages of justice occur. The case of the M25 Three (see Bird, 2000), for instance, in which Raphael Rowe, Michael Davis and

Randolph Johnson were convicted of a series of robberies and violent attacks just off the M25 motorway in December 1988, achieved a successful appeal on the official ground of a 'material irregularity' in the (non) disclosure of crucial evidence that undermined the prosecution case (Editorial, 2000a). Alternatively, it is also widely speculated that the M25 miscarriage of justice was due to structural racism in the criminal justice process. It transpired that among the evidence that was not disclosed by the prosecution was eyewitness testimony that two of the perpetrators of the crimes were white when all three of the appellants in the case were black (see Hardy, 1999). Rather than see this as necessarily problematic, this chapter constructs a critical perspective on the causes of miscarriages of justice that brings together critical sociological/criminological accounts and legally orientated approaches; the errant individual approach and theoretical structural accounts, for the distinctive contributions to depictions of the problem that they each provide. It emphasises the strengths and limits of each in terms of their discursive force to bring about meaningful changes that may, truly, reduce or prevent miscarriages of justice.

In addition, the perspective crafted here also identifies certain *procedures* of the criminal justice system that can cause innocent people to be wrongly convicted and then act as barriers, obstacles or disincentives to overturning their convictions through a successful appeal. This introduces a critique of the limits of the legal notion of miscarriages of justice from the perspective of popular discourse on miscarriages of justice as they relate to concerns about the wrongful conviction of the innocent. It builds on the last chapter, for if it can be shown that not all wrongful convictions that occur are successfully overturned, then, the official statistics on successful appeals can be conceived to be partial and not a comprehensive representation of all wrongful convictions, and that the official statistics on successful appeals are representative, only, of official miscarriages of justice that occur in England and Wales from the perspective of the legal system. It means that the scale of wrongful convictions is even greater than the miscarriages of justice that can be inferred from the official statistics of successful appeals. In turn, this denotes that even when all of the voices of victims of miscarriages of justice who overturn their convictions through mundane and/or routine appeals are taken into account there remain subjugated voices of wrongful conviction that need to be unearthed to provide a more complete picture.

Theoretical perspectives

In an attempt to make sense of the existing theoretical terrain, Andrew Green (1995: 46–73) discerned five ideal-type formulations that can be discerned in existing explanations of the causes of miscarriages of justice:

- a theory that generally posits the criminal justice system as unproblematic and the causes of miscarriages of justice in terms of individual procedural 'error' or transgression;
- a theory based on an inherent imbalance of rights;
- a model based on systemic prejudice against ethnic minorities;
- a social structural theory of class bias and economic disadvantage; and,
- a model that conceptualises the police as inherently corrupt.

Putting Green's analysis to work, the first, and most common explanation of the causes of miscarriages of justice is what might be termed the *error* formulation which attempts to attribute miscarriages of justice to individual 'errors' or 'defects' in the procedural framework of the criminal justice system. As indicated, in this category are problem-bearing individuals, either a criminal witness or suspect who misleads the agents of the criminal justice system or an overzealous agent of the system who break the rules (for examples of this formulation see Fisher, 1977; May 1994). In this formulation, the criminal justice system is conceived to be entirely concerned with dealing with problematic individuals and the procedural framework of the criminal justice system is in a continual state of on-going change as errors 'emerge' and show the existing procedures to be inadequate in stopping individual transgression.

Secondly, Green discerned a rights-based *system imbalance* formulation. Rights and procedural safeguards are provided to suspects because they are powerless and the system is powerful, they, thus, provide a balance between the opposing parties. This second possible formulation discerned by Green seems to contradict the first formulation because it contends that the process of criminal justice routinely denies criminal suspects their rights because the system is unbalanced. There are two versions of this unbalance theory. According to one side of the argument, the view generally put forward by agents of the criminal justice system itself is that there are too many procedural safeguards that hamper police investigations and the successful prosecution of the factually guilty (for a classic example of this formulation, see Mark, 1977, 1978; for a more recent example see Blair cited Travis & Hopkins, 2002). Against this, it is argued that the procedures of the criminal justice process are weighted against criminal suspects (for the classic socio-legal analysis of this position see McBarnet, 1981).

The third formulation discerned by Green flowed from the second and argued that criminal suspects who are denied rights or safeguards and wrongly convicted are more likely to be from minorities, especially ethnic minorities. This is because the system contains deeply rooted structural prejudices and values which are built into the system's procedures (see, for example, Scraton & Gordon, 1984; Hillyard, 1993). In particular, this formulation argues that the criminal justice system is unable to exclude external prejudices or effectively prevent them from affecting the work of its agents which is expressed through the practices of 'stereotyping' and 'targeting' (see, for example, Box, 1983; Hillyard, 1996: 13–15, 1998: 36–46).

A fourth theoretical explanation discerned by Green was a *social-structural* explanation that asserts that the criminal justice system cannot be balanced, because rights and safeguards cannot compensate for social structural inequality. In this formulation, victims of miscarriages of justice are most likely to be 'poor' and, therefore, 'powerless' (McConville et al, 1991: 206; Box, 1983). This formulation argues that the criminal justice system comprises people whose social background and class affiliations make them unsympathetic or even hostile to the working class, on whom most of the police's attention is focused (for example, see Hall et al, 1977; Hall, 1980; Woffinden, 2001; Reiman, 1995: 4–5, 114–117; Pantazis, 1998).

Finally, Green discerned a fifth theoretical formulation of the causes of miscarriages that is opposed to the previous four formulations, and this he termed the *corruption* explanation. According to this formulation, rights and/or safeguards count for nothing if criminal suspects are 'fitted up' by the agents of the criminal justice system by 'planting' evidence against them, fabricating witness statements, and not disclosing evidence that might support a defence case. These things can occur for reasons of ambition or other personal gain. This is perhaps the most straightforward theoretical perspective on the cause of miscarriages of justice, and the one that appears most in media coverage: 'Corrupt groups of police officers are not rotten apples, but are cancerous growth in an otherwise healthy criminal justice body, whose other organs are unaffected; the system is composed of discrete elements police and courts, and the first can mislead the second' (Green, 1995:

49; examples of this formulation include, Hillyard, 1994: 75–78; McConville, 1989: 5–6; Morton, 1994).

From the foregoing, a distinction can be made between the first formulation and the other four formulations. The 'error' theory operates *within* the remit of the criminal justice system and conceives the structures and/or procedures of the criminal justice system as generally unproblematical, with the causes of miscarriages set in terms of problematic individuals who transgress the procedures of the system either by intent or 'error'. Against this, the remaining theories work *outside* of the criminal justice system, all conceiving miscarriages of justice as caused by some form of structural discrimination, disadvantage or institutional source, within which the individuals who cause miscarriages of justice, either by 'error' or intended misconduct, are of lesser importance. In terms of discursive force, the 'error' formulation apportions the blame firmly upon individual miscreants and attempts to contribute more directly with the procedural remedies of the criminal justice system to deter problematic individuals from causing miscarriages of justice. As the following chapter will show, it is in response to these forms of analysis that the most significant changes to the criminal justice system have been introduced in attempts to ward off miscarriages of justice. For example, the introduction of formal guidelines under PACE (1984) to govern police investigations followed the revelation that the police officers who investigated the murder of Maxwell Confait had 'fitted-up' three young suspects, two of whom had learning disabilities (Fisher, 1977). Likewise, as already noted, the establishment of the CCRC came about because successive Home Secretaries (miscreant individuals) failed in their duty to send potentially meritorious cases (which turned out to be meritorious) back to the CACD for political as opposed legal reasons (RCCJ, 1993). The limitation of this approach is that such changes to the legal system do not question the underlying structures of the criminal justice process which cause miscarriages of justice. Rather, by contributing to grafting changes to the existing criminal justice system in response to exceptional miscarriage of justice cases they reinforce the notion that the criminal justice system, at root, functions with the aim of acquitting the innocent, which does little to disturb the dominant paradigm.

Alternatively, the discursive strength of critical theoretical perspectives on the structures which govern the operation of criminal justice is that they serve to shed further light upon the possible ways in which miscarriages of justice may be caused, feeding into public/media discourses and raising public concern. Although they apportion the blame elsewhere and are, therefore, less directly engaged with the attempt to effect changes to the criminal justice system, they demand radical *reform* of the existing arrangements of the criminal justice system that may truly prevent and/or reduce miscarriages of justice. They extend perceptions of the miscarriage of justice iceberg by emphasising the increased likelihood of miscarriages of justice to criminal suspects from, for example, ethnic minorities or the economically disadvantaged. The composition of the prison population alone tends to substantiate the claim that the criminal justice system in England and Wales tends to discriminate against the poor (for example, Hall, 1980) and ethnic minorities (for example, Hillyard, 1996, 1998), and that this translates into the routine imbalance of suspects' rights (McBarnet, 1981). Moreover, as will be illustrated below in the examples of the continuing problem of police misconduct, there is ample evidence of continuing forms of police corruption, despite the introduction of PACE (1984).

Overall, then, whilst critical theories of the causes of miscarriages of justice that cite class bias or ethnic minority prejudice, for instance, are not wrong as such, they tend to operate on a plane of critical analysis that is *external* to the procedures of the criminal justice system through which successful appeals are produced. In consequence, they can be conceived to practice an anti-pragmatist approach to law that renders their critiques largely ineffectual in terms of their specific ability to effect successful appeals which underpin the introduction of changes to the criminal justice system as part of the governmentality process. As the next section will show, successful appeals in England and Wales are not achieved through general arguments that the structures of the criminal justice system are inherently problematic or prejudicial against certain individuals and/or groups, no matter how accurate they might be. On the contrary, they are achieved through working within the 'error' paradigm and showing in concrete cases that due process – the rules and procedures of the criminal justice system – were in some way *not* correctly adhered to, either by 'error' or some form of errant intent and that individuals *were* victims of miscarriages of justice. Accordingly, from the perspective advanced in the last chapter on the need to engage pragmatically with the criminal justice system for the truths that it represents, the forms of counter-discourse that are generated by critical theories that work outside of the procedural agenda of the criminal justice system provide images of the routine abuse of the ideals of due process from a sociological perspective but they do not carry much discursive force to overturn miscarriages of justice and/or effect radical reforms of the system that they are so rightly critical of.

The focus on individual causes

There have been three previous notable attempts to catalogue miscarriages of justice in England and Wales caused by individuals who make inadvertent 'errors' or intentionally do not comply with the procedures of due process. The first account was presented by Brandon and Davies (1973: 21) who conducted an analysis of Home Office pardons and referrals between 1950 and 1970, as well as material on individual cases of wrongful imprisonment provided by JUSTICE, the all-party law reform organisation, and identified a seven-fold categorisation: unsatisfactory identification; confessions made by the feeble-minded and the inadequate; evidence favourable to the defence withheld by the prosecution; certain joint trials; perjury, especially in cases involving sexual or quasi-sexual offences; badly conducted defence; criminals as witnesses. Then, JUSTICE (1989: 76–94), updated Brandon and Davies' earlier research, drawing from their own case files, and produced a more sophisticated analysis of the four stages of the criminal justice process – pre-trial, trial, appeal and post-appeal – and discerned five common threads that cause miscarriages of justice: wrongful identification; false confessions; perjury by a co-accused and/or other witnesses; police misconduct; and, bad trial tactics by the defence. More recently, Clive Walker's (2002) analysis continued the exercise to attribute the causes of miscarriages of justice to wayward individuals who fail to comply with the rules and procedures of due process. Drawing from Dixon's approach to the relationships between law and policy, however, Walker (2002) produced a more sophisticated analysis which took account of what he termed the legalistic-bureaucratic in which law determines policy, the ways in which internal working cultures determine policy and the way in which policy is structured by law and culture. For Walker (2002), miscarriages of justice are overwhelmingly an 'inside job', by and large caused by actors within the criminal justice process rather than induced by external agency. Following the tradition to cite already achieved exceptional successful appeals to support analyses of the ways individuals cause miscarriages of justice, Walker's (2002) study cited the CCRC's analysis of the first 80 cases it referred to the CACD, extending the existing literature on the ways in which individuals cause miscarriages of justice by adding the additional categories of forensic science expert witness evidence and defective summing up by the trial judge.[16] From these analyses, the following typology of the ways in which wayward individuals have caused miscarriages of justice emerges:

- wrongful identification;
- false confessions;
- perjury by a co-accused and/or other witnesses;
- police and/or prosecution misconduct, especially non-disclosure of vital evidence to the defence;
- bad trial tactics by the defence;
- forensic science expert witness evidence; and,
- defective summing up by the trial judge.

Putting these categories of causes to work, this section applies them to the literature on successful appeals.[17] Because of space constraints this section will not provide an extended discussion of each of the causes that can be discerned from the literature on successful appeals against criminal conviction. Rather, each of the causes listed will be briefly considered in turn to illustrate the pragmatic need to apportion blame to concrete transgressions of the due process procedures of the criminal justice system as a way of overturning alleged miscarriages of justice, as opposed to general critiques of the structures that underpin the criminal justice system.

Wrongful identification as a cause of miscarriage of justice in the current literature of successful appeals has generally been blamed on the errant behaviour of the agents of the criminal justice system to obtain miscarriages of justice by offering some form of inducements in return for wrongful identification evidence. For example, one of the main problems has been identified as *'prison grasses'* who provide false evidence (that causes a miscarriage of justice) in exchange for some kind of sentence discount or other bargain as in the recent cases of Reg Dudley and Robert Maynard who each served over 20 years of wrongful imprisonment as a consequence of a 'bargain' between the police and an informant who received a reduced sentence for his part in a robbery in exchange for the necessary evidence for conviction (for details, see Dudley, 2002; Dodd, 2002; Campbell, 2002; Campbell & Hartley-Brewer, 2000). Another cause of miscarriages of justice that stems from the intentions of the agents of the criminal justice system is when they offer a *financial payment* for wrongful identification evidence. An example of this in the literature on successful appeals is the case of Mahmood Mattan, who was executed at Cardiff prison in September 1952 for the murder of Lily Volpert. As the CACD quashed Mattan's conviction in February 1998, it was revealed that at his trial the prosecution case relied almost entirely on the evidence of Harold Cover, who claimed that he had seen Mattan in the area where Volpert had been murdered on the night that she was murdered. But, what the jury were not told was that Cover, who was himself jailed for life in 1969 for the attempted murder of his own daughter, had been paid by the prosecution to give his evidence (for details see Wilson, 2001; Lee, 1998). Wrongful identification evidence can also derive from *false accusations that are induced by the hope of obtaining criminal compensation*. An example is the case of David Jones, the former manager of Southampton Football Club, who was cleared of care home child abuse when his trial collapsed when an alleged victim refused to give evidence against him (for details see Chrisafis, 2000). The blame for this cause of miscarriage of justice is generally attributed to the criminal intentions of individuals outside of the criminal justice system (for a discussion of the phenomenon see Webster, 2005; Falsely Accused Carers and Teachers, 2006; Woffinden, 2001a). The ways in which forensic science expert witness evidence can cause miscarriages of justice will be discussed in a separate category below, it needs to be noted here, however, that wrongful identification can also derive from forms of evidence that rely on forensic science expert witnesses. *Fingerprint evidence* as a reliable means of identification, for instance, was significantly undermined in the case of Danny McNamee, convicted in 1987 for his alleged part in the Hyde Park Bombings by the Irish Republican Army and given a 25-year prison sentence. Eleven years later, however, McNamee's conviction was overturned by the CACD when it transpired that the jury at his trial were told that the standard required for fingerprint evidence to be regarded as reliable had been reached when it had not. The standard for fingerprint evidence states that there must be at least 16 matching characteristics. At his appeal, however, not one of 14 leading fingerprint experts found more than 11 matching characteristics (see Woffinden, 1999b, 1999c).[18] In another case concerning the limits of forensic science techniques and identification evidence, Mark Dallagher spent seven years of a life sentence in prison for the murder of 94-year-old Dorothy Wood on the basis of *earprints* found on the glass of the window through which an intruder had entered her house. When Dallagher was convicted at Leeds Crown Court in 1998 the case made British legal history as the first in which earprints led to a successful prosecution and was even hailed by Norman Sarsfield, of the Wakefield CPS, as 'a great step forward for forensic science'. Dallagher, however, who had always protested his innocence, claiming that he was handicapped by an ankle injury at the time of the murder, overturned his conviction in January 2004 when a DNA profile obtained from the earprint proved that it was not his (see, Woffinden, 2004; R v Dallagher [2002] EWCA Crim 1903).

JUSTICE (1989: 15–16) discerned three categories of *false confessions*: (1) the 'voluntary group' who confess to notorious crimes because they want publicity or have fantasies about committing crime; (2) the 'guilt group' who want to be punished for a crime because they have general feelings of guilt about some aspect of their lives; and, (3) a range of 'coerced groups' who are essentially suggestible in personality or in a situation which they find intolerable.[19] In the literature on successful appeals, all of JUSTICE's categories can be discerned, and are blamed upon the actions of individual police officers who transgress the rules of interrogation. For example, the case of Andrew Evans, who confessed to the police in October 1972 that he had murdered Judith Roberts resonates with JUSTICE's first category of the 'guilt group'. In December 1997, however, after he had served 25 years in prison, Evan's conviction was quashed by the CACD when new psychiatric evidence showed him to be susceptible to 'false memory' because of his extreme anxiety and hysterical state (see Duce, 1997; Randall, 1997; Vasagar, 2000a). An example of JUSTICE's third category of suspects who are 'coerced' is the case of Stephen Downing. In one of the longest cases of wrongful imprisonment in England and Wales, Downing's conviction for the murder of Wendy Sewell in February 1974 was quashed by the CACD in January 2002, after he had spent 27 years in prison maintaining his innocence, on the grounds that, 'police officers who questioned him before he confessed had committed "substantial and significant" breaches of the rules on the interrogating suspects' (Rozenberg, 2002). Downing was 17 years old with the mental age of an 11-year-old when he was arrested after he had found Sewell unconscious in the Derbyshire cemetery where he worked (see Ward, 2002). At the police station, Downing was interrogated for seven hours without being informed that he was under arrest or that he had a right to consult a solicitor before he finally made oral and written confessions to Sewell's assault (see Rozenberg, 2001). Moreover during Downing's interrogation, he had, at times, to be shaken awake and the officers took bets on whether he would confess (Vasagar & Ward, 2001). Sewell died two days later without recovering consciousness and, hence, without revealing the identity of her murderer (see, also, Vasagar, 2000, 2002; Weaver, 2000; James, 2002). A possible critique of the Downing case could be that it predated the introduction of PACE (1984). It has been argued that such miscarriages of justice can no longer occur (Steele, 1997).[20] However, a post-PACE (1984) example of JUSTICE's second category of the 'voluntary group' has resonance with a phenomenon in the literature that revolves around the vulnerability of the young and the predisposition of certain criminal suspects to make false confessions/statements. An example is the case of Ashley King and Billy Waugh who were jointly convicted in 1986 of the murder of Margaret Greenwood. In December 1999, however, the CACD quashed King's conviction, after he had spent 13 years in prison, on the ground of 'new psychological evidence of King's vulnerability during police questioning' (Dyer, 1999a). Waugh, who was one of the youngest people ever to be convicted of murder in England and Wales, was released from custody in 1987, after the CACD ruled that his conviction was 'unsafe and unsatisfactory'.[21]

There are numerous examples in the literature on successful appeals of *perjury by a co-accused and/or other witnesses* or what might be termed malicious accusations in England and Wales, all of which are attributable to errant individuals who are external to the criminal justice system. Whilst the discussion above on the potential of financial inducement as a cause of miscarriages of justice focused upon teachers and care workers, it must also be noted that teachers and care workers are also subjected to many false accusations for entirely malicious reasons (see, for example, Webster, 2005; Carvel, 1999, 2000). Miscarriages of justice can also occur following malicious accusations of rape and sexual assault such as in the case of Roy Burnett who spent 15 years of wrongful imprisonment for a rape that the Court of Appeal said 'almost certainly never happened' (Editorial, 2000c), or Roger Beardmore who spent three years in prison (of a nine year sentence) for the paedophile rape of a young girl who later admitted that she had lied to get her mother's attention (Peek, 2001). There have also been a number of successful appeal cases following convictions for 'date rape' as evidenced by the cases of Austen Donnellan (see Berlins, 2000) and Nicholas Buoy (see Merritt, 2000). More recently, Warren Blackwell overturned his conviction for indecent assault in September 2006 after he had spent more than three years in prison. The case was referred back to the CACD by the CCRC who reported that the woman who made the allegation against Blackwell has made at least five other fake allegations of sexual and physical assault to police in three separate forces; was married twice and made false allegations against both husbands – one of whom was a policeman; once accused her own father of sexual assault, but police concluded she had made it up; and, accused a boy of rape when she was a teenager, only for a doctor to discover she was still a virgin. The CCRC concluded that in the case of Mr Blackwell, the woman who made the allegations had 'lied about the assault and was not attacked at all, her injuries being self-inflicted' (see Greenhill, 2006).

From the literature on successful appeals, a range of subcategories of *police misconduct and prosecution non-disclosure* are evident which often overlap to cause miscarriages of justice, and which are all attributed to the errant actions of individual police officers and/or prosecution staff. In June 2003, for instance, Anthony Poole and Gary Mills had their convictions quashed by the CACD on the grounds that the prosecution withheld evidence that might have undermined the testimony of a key witness and a detective's 'misleading' 'hearsay' summary of an account given by another witness, Ian Juke, who did not attend the trial 'revealed a level of impropriety that tainted the whole police investigation' (see Bowcott, 2003). In addition, the literature on miscarriages of justice displays other forms of police misconduct including *police collaborations with major criminals* and 'losing' key evidence, both in the interests of obtaining convictions of the innocent and in the interests of securing the acquittal of the guilty (Sweeney et al, 2000); the *misuse of informants* (Hopkins & Dodd, 1999); *planting evidence* (Hopkins, 2000; Woffinden, 2000); and, *fabricating evidence* and *sabotaging cases* (Thompson, 2000; Pallister, 1999). Additionally, a main factor in 'prosecution misbehaviour' remains an alleged 'culture of non-disclosure' (see Gillard & Flynn, 2000). In May 2000, for example, the CACD quashed John Kamara's conviction for the murder of Liverpool bookmaker John Suffield in 1981 during a robbery on the ground that the prosecution failed to disclose over 200 witness statements taken by Merseyside police to the defence lawyers at the original trial. Kamara had spent 20 years in prison (see Carter & Bowers, 2000; BBC News, 2000; Liverpool Echo, 2000).[22]

There is evidence in the material on successful appeals that demonstrates the continuing relevance of *bad trial tactics by the defence* as a cause of miscarriages of justice in England and Wales. For example, *inadequate representation* was blamed in the separate successful appeals of John Taylor (see Criminal Cases Review Commission, 2006c) and Mark Day who was convicted for murder with two others despite the fact that he did not know his co-defendants, a fact that his defence failed to bring to the court's attention (Woffinden, 2001b). Significantly, the associated problems of poor defence will have a profound impact upon the official statistics on successful appeals to fully represent all miscarriages of justice as an inadequate defence is almost certainly *not* grounds for appeal, whether the failure lies with lawyers or with expert witnesses (Brandon & Davies, 1973: 101–102; JUSTICE, 1989: 51–55).

The problem of *forensic science expert witness evidence* as a cause of miscarriages of justice was mentioned above in terms of how failures of fingerprint and earprint evidence can contribute to the problem of wrongful identification. In addition, the limits of forensic science experts witness evidence is radically challenged in a clutch of recent successful appeal cases, questioning its very foundation. For example, Sally Clark overturned a mandatory life sentence for the murder of two of her children when conflicting forensic evidence suggested that the chances were they died of natural causes (Batt, 2005); Angela Cannings was given a double life sentence for the murder of her two children who were, probably, the tragic victims of 'cot death' (Cannings & Davies, 2006); Sheila Bowler was cleared of the murder of her aunt, Florence Jackson, after she had served four years of a life sentence, when new forensic evidence showed that she most probably died of accidental drowning (Devlin & Devlin, 2000; Jessel, 1994: Chapter 11); Patrick Nichols spent 23 years in prison for the murder of Gladys Heath, a family friend, until competing forensic science compelling argued that she had probably suffered a heart attack and accidentally fallen down a flight of stairs (Tendler, 1998); and, Kevin Callan served three years for the murder of his four-year-old step-daughter, Amanda Allman, until he, himself, became an expert in neurology and was able to counter the convicting evidence and offer the more plausible explanation that she died as a result of a fall from a playground slide (Bunyan, 1995). These are just a small sample of such cases that have been overturned following new forensic evidence. Critically, if the forensic evidence that overturned the foregoing convictions is correct, not only is the widespread belief in forensic science expert witness evidence undermined, it suggests a new category of miscarriages of justice when defendants are convicted, and even given life sentences, for 'crimes' that may never have occurred (Naughton, 2005).

As far as miscarriages of justice relate to defective summing up by the trial judge, in July 1998, Derek Bentley, executed in January 1953 for the murder of P.C. Sidney Miles, and a long-standing alleged miscarriage of justice, received a posthumous pardon. This followed his successful appeal in the CACD, which severely criticised Lord Goddard, the trial judge, ruling that the conviction had been unsafe because of the judge's 'intemperate summing-up' (see Campbell, 1998). (Re)emphasising that miscarriages of justice result from breaches of fairness in criminal trials, as opposed to proof of innocence, Lord Bingham of Cornhill, Lord Chief Justice stated:

> ...since the trial judge in his summing-up failed to direct the jury on the standard and burden of proof, to give sufficient direction on the law of joint enterprise, or adequately to summarise the defence case, made prejudicial comments about the defendants and their defences, and indicated that the police officers' evidence, because of their bravery on the night in question, was more worthy of belief than that of the defendants, Bentley was denied the fair trial to which he was entitled and his conviction was in consequence unsafe (Times Law Report, 1998).

The foregoing analysis contributes to the existing terrain, then, by updating analyses of the individual causes of miscarriages of justice in England and Wales and by showing that all of the causes of miscarriages of justice previously discerned by JUSTICE over a decade ago, and by Brandon and Davies over 30 years ago, are still evident in contemporary successful appeals. This emphasises, clearly, the limits of previous changes to the criminal justice system that have attempted to eliminate miscarriages of justice. As Walker (2002) noted, the criminal justice system is a human system and there will always be individuals who transgress whatever rules and/or procedures are put in place to give supposed safeguards to criminal suspects and/or defendants in criminal trials and profess to avoid miscarriages of justice.

Moreover, as the foregoing analysis was grounded in already achieved successful appeals, it illustrates the point that successful appeals are not achieved through general arguments to the effect that the structures of the criminal justice system are inherently problematic or prejudicial against certain individuals and/or groups. On the contrary, successful appeals are pragmatically achieved by working within the appellate procedural framework and by showing that the procedures of the criminal justice system were in some way not correctly adhered to, either by 'error' or some form of errant intent, and that specific individual victims of miscarriages of justice *were* wrongly convicted. From such a standpoint, however, existing accounts that focus on how individuals can cause miscarriages of justice do not tend to problematise the *procedures* through which successful appeals are produced. Nor do they consider the possible ways in which certain procedures may cause wrongful convictions and/or act as deterrents to their remedy (Greer, 1994), which are distinct from legal notions of miscarriages of justice and related to popular discourses and the concern about the wrongful conviction of the innocent. Rather, victims of alleged miscarriages of justice and their supporters attempt to determine some form of procedural irregularity (breach of due process as defined by the existing criminal justice system) to account for their miscarriage of justice and achieve a successful appeal. Essentially, this is achieved by working from the premise that the existing procedures of the criminal justice system are problem-free and apportioning blame to an agent of the criminal justice system, either through procedural 'error' or transgressive misconduct from a procedure. In so doing, such forms of activity, inevitably, serve to create, sustain and reproduce the dominant discourse that the existing criminal justice system is fundamentally fair and just, apart from the apparent exceptional miscarriage of justice at issue. They assume that such miscarriages of justice can be corrected for with relatively minor procedural add-ons to the existing system, which serves, only, to strengthen the need to work within the existing system in attempts to overturn alleged miscarriages of justice. They act against the fundamental *re-forms* of the criminal justice system that are indicated as necessary by structural critiques that might radically reduce and/or prevent the perennial causes of miscarriages of justice evident in the foregoing analysis. They are unable to conceptualise the wrongful convictions to the innocent that popular discourses are so fundamentally against (cf. Gordon, 1980).

Another major limitation with such accounts is that they are grounded in prevalent definitions of miscarriages of justice that concentrate on successful appeals that are produced through the post-appeal procedures. As such, although such accounts catalogue a wide range of causes of, predominantly exceptional miscarriages of justice, they tend not to map the likely causes of routine and mundane successful appeals. Nor do they map the likely procedural causes of miscarriages of justice and/or the possible deterrents to a successful appeal that legitimate procedures might, even inadvertently, present. Therefore, such accounts are not very persuasive (counter-discursively strong) as they only consider a tiny aspect of all successful appeals – post-appeal exceptional cases – which, as shown in the previous chapter, amount to around 18 cases per year. The irony is that by working entirely within the agenda of the criminal justice system in a pragmatic attempt to overturn a miscarriage of justice through post-appeal methods, the forms of counter-discourse against miscarriages of justice that can be levelled against the criminal justice system are inevitably statistically small scale and, therefore, discursively weak.

Methodological approaches

Two broad methodological approaches, then, have informed the existing approaches to the causes of miscarriages of justice: the *interactionist* and the *structuralist*. On the one hand, the interactionist approach is a micro-sociological attempt to explain the effectiveness, or otherwise, of the law and measure the 'gap' between the 'black letter' of the law and the law in practice. This is the favoured methodology for researches which attempt to explain the ways in which individual criminal justice system administrators such as police officers, prosecutors, judges, and so on, have been unintentionally erroneous or have intentionally subverted the law in their attempts to obtain miscarriages of justice (for a discussion see Black, 1972; Feeley, 1976; McBarnet, 1981). The structuralist account, on the other hand, is a less common macro-sociological approach that focuses on the socio-economic structures and legal-bureaucratic rules of law. In so doing, it asserts the political function and permissive character of legal rules to legitimate forms of behaviour by the agents of the system that cause miscarriages (for examples of this approach see McBarnet, 1981; Jefferson & Grimshaw, 1987). This is the favoured approach of critical theorists who attempt to locate the causes of miscarriages of justice within the context of broader structures and forms of discrimination that exist within society. In addition, and in between these two opposing approaches, McConville et al (1991: 11) followed Henry (1983: 62) and applied an *integrated* approach that attempted to unite the interactionist and structuralist approaches to explore 'the interpenetration of the micro-structures with the macro and vice versa'. Following, the kind of methodological approach adopted by McConville et al (1991), the remainder of this chapter also considers a number of *procedures* and *practices* of England and Wales' criminal justice system that might contribute as causes of wrongful convictions that are not included in the official miscarriage of justice iceberg; procedures that cause wrongful convictions and/or present barriers, obstacles or disincentives to an eventual successful appeal to innocent victims:

- procedural barriers that cannot be overcome by innocent victims of wrongful convictions;

- procedural obstacles that can be overcome by some innocent victims of wrongful conviction, but the difficulties mean that there will inevitably be some victims that will not achieve a successful appeal; and/or,
- procedural disincentives that serve to deter innocent victims of wrongful conviction from even making an appeal.

This marries the accounts of how rogue individuals can cause miscarriages of justice that presently fail to problematise the procedures of the criminal justice system that might cause wrongful convictions and/or act as deterrents to a successful appeal with more critical theoretical perspectives that do problematise the underlying structures that govern the procedures of the criminal justice system but do not presently engage with statistical analyses of the likely extent of miscarriages of justice and/or wrongful convictions. Such a union shifts existing expressions of the interactionist account onto a new theoretical and methodological footing that can serve to strengthen the forcefulness of forms of counter-discourse against miscarriages of justice and wrongful convictions. It demonstrates, more practically, that there are likely to be many wrongful convictions that are caused by the procedures of the criminal justice system that may never achieve a successful appeal and, hence, the official statistics do not present a comprehensive depiction of all wrongful convictions. Rather, they are entirely orientated to legal definitions of miscarriages of justice. This consideration, however, will not be exhaustive in the sense that every procedure and/or practice will be covered. Rather, some of the more significant procedural candidates that cause wrongful convictions and/or act against a successful appeal are pointed up to show that there are, indeed, possible causes of wrongful convictions that might never feature in the official indices of successful appeals against criminal conviction.

Procedural causes

Plea-bargaining is, perhaps, the most obvious and widespread cause of wrongful conviction and *procedural barrier* to a successful appeal that has a profound impact upon the official statistics to adequately depict the full extent of wrongful convictions in England and Wales. Plea-bargaining can be defined as a judicial practice whereby judges and barristers strike a secret deal in return for a guilty plea (Gibb, 2000). Accordingly, plea-bargaining can be conceived as interactionist in the sense that it is determined though the negotiations of individual social actors. Plea-bargaining, however, is also a routine procedural practice of the criminal justice system and, hence, it is also appropriate to conceive and analyse it within an integrated methodology. In their discussion of plea-bargaining in the US, Huff et al (1996) started with the observation that perhaps the most puzzling of all wrongful conviction cases, as well as the least publicised, are those in which innocent people plead guilty. After all, asked Huff et al (1996), why would a perfectly innocent person plead guilty? In response, Huff et al (1996) drew from a social psychological experiment conducted by Gregory et al (1978) and discerned ample reasons why some innocent people might plead guilty. For example, criminal defendants might be more likely to accept plea bargains when they are faced with a number of charges or when the probable severity of punishment, as they perceived and feared it, was deemed to be great (Huff et al, 1996: 73). Moreover, innocent criminal defendants in the US who face execution might be induced to make deals (Sheck et al, 2001). Even though they might face long prison sentences, such defendants can live in the hope that eventually the truth of their innocence will be discovered and they will be freed (Huff et al, 1996: 73). As for the lack of publicity in plea bargain cases in the US, Huff et al (1996: 73) noted that one of the reasons is probably that most plea bargains result in immediate freedom, suspended sentence, or perhaps probation and, hence, in such cases there is no aftermath, no continued investigation, no exoneration. In the US, the revocation of a guilty plea is legally permitted only under limited conditions, for example, when a judge refuses to abide by a plea-bargain that has been made between the defendant, through defence counsel, and the prosecution. Ordinarily, a plea-bargain closes the case (Huff et al, 1996: 73).

Although the practice of plea-bargaining is widely acknowledged in the US (see also, for example, Guidorizzi, 1998; Mather, 1979; Heumann, 1978), there is much controversy, indeed secrecy, about the use of such a practice in the judicial pronouncements of England and Wales' judiciary. In line with a court ruling of 30 years ago which stated that plea-bargaining should not occur (Gibb, 2000), officially plea-bargaining does *not* take place in English courts (Dyer, 2000b). Despite this, the practice of plea-bargaining was exposed to be widespread in two criminal cases that were widely publicised in the year 2000 (see Gibb, 2000).

One of those cases was that of Robin Peverett, the former headmaster of Dulwich College Preparatory School in Kent, who walked free from Maidstone Crown Court in July 2000 with an 18-month suspended prison sentence after pleading guilty to nine offences of sexual molestation between 1969 and 1977 (see, for example, Ahmed, 2000), an offence which could have carried a maximum custodial sentence of ten years (see Weale, 2000). Peverett's lenient sentence, it transpired, was the result of a bargain that had been struck between the defence and prosecution lawyers with the co-operation of the trial judge in return for his guilty plea (see, for example, Dyer, 2000a; Weale, 2000).

In response to the public fury that accompanied the sentence in the Peverett case, the Attorney-General, promptly restated the earlier court ruling that plea-bargaining is a breach of a barrister's professional conduct and is banned (Gibb, 2000). In addition, the Attorney General also referred the case to the CACD on the grounds that the sentence was too lenient. The CACD ruled, however, that the sentence stand as the prosecution's involvement in the 'lamentable' plea bargain, in effect, barred the crown from going back on the deal (Times Law Report, 2000). More specifically, on the general practice of plea-bargaining, the CACD judgement issued by Lord Justice Rose stated that:

> There were, of course, wholly exceptional cases [of which the Peverett case was not one] where that [plea-bargaining] might properly be done, for example if a defendant were dying...Apart from such wholly exceptional cases, no good usually came of this kind of activity...[which] affronts the public (cited Times Law Report, 2000).

This indicated that, contrary to the Attorney General's earlier statement, plea-bargaining is not an altogether breach of a barrister's professional conduct, nor is it entirely banned in England and Wales. On the contrary, then, it is truer to say that plea-bargaining is a legitimate procedure of England and Wales' criminal justice system which should only come into play under rigid 'exceptional' circumstances. This served to fuel the debate on plea-bargaining and the possible 'exceptional' circumstances of its applicability. For instance, retired Recorder, Geoffrey Davey, distinguished between plea-bargaining where the effect is to 'pervert the course of justice', and the kind of plea-bargaining, which was commonplace during his judicial career, that might elucidate an early guilty plea, thus achieving the ends of justice and saving court time and expense (Davey, 2000). More recently, Lord Justice Auld's Report into the criminal courts recommended that there should be a graduated scheme of sentencing discounts should be introduced so that the earlier the plea of guilty the higher the discount for it. This should be coupled with a system of advance indication of sentence for a defendant considering pleading guilty (Auld, 2001: paras 91–114, recs 186–193; see also, Travis, 2001; Dyer, 2001).

Strictly speaking, whilst the events of, and the debate surrounding the Peverett case served to shed some light upon the socio-legal realities of plea bargain practice, the Peverett case was not a miscarriage of justice. To be sure, Blackstone's principle: 'better that ten guilty persons escape than one innocent suffer' is still a foundational stated aim of criminal justice in England and Wales. Accordingly, the system is weighted to the extent that the non-conviction of the factually guilty is not normally conceptualised as a miscarriage of the criminal justice system. But, having established the existence and widespread practice of plea-bargaining, it must be noted that it can work both ways. As Huff et al (1996) observed, it can also be about the inducement of innocent people to plead guilty to criminal offences that they did not commit, which *would* constitute a wrongful conviction and, even, miscarriage of justice if it breached the procedures which govern the criminal justice process.

Such was the finding of Baldwin and McConville's (1977) classic research of the extent to which plea-bargaining occurred in the Birmingham Crown Court. In particular, Baldwin and McConville (1977) showed that plea-bargaining was not unusual in the Birmingham Crown Court, that the bargains that are negotiated are not always in the defendant's interests, and that the processes that are involved in the bargain being struck sometimes went beyond the publicly acknowledged guidelines on plea-bargaining as they existed within the law of England and Wales at the time. Perhaps, more disturbingly Baldwin and McConville's (1977) research also showed that from the defendant's perspective the process of plea-bargaining may be perceived as involving pressure or forms of coercion to plead guilty to charges of which they regard themselves as innocent of (see Campbell & Wiles, 1977: ix). In their analysis, Baldwin and McConville (1977) found that a fundamental source of judicial defect is the customary 'sentence discount' that is awarded to defendants who indicate their apparent repentance by pleading guilty. The present rules on sentence discount are that judges and magistrates are required, when sentencing an offender who has pleaded guilty, to take into account the stage at which the guilty plea was entered, and the circumstances in which the plea was made. If a discounted sentence is passed, this must be stated in court. The CACD has stated that a discount of one-third should normally be given for a timely guilty plea (Chapman & Niven, 2000: 37). As in Davey's (2000) recent assertions on plea-bargaining cited above, Baldwin and McConville (1977) saw the argument in favour of the sentence discount being centred around an attempt to discourage defendants from wasting the valuable time of the court by needlessly contesting lost causes. As Williams (1976) put it:

> ...offenders who have no defence must be persuaded not to waste the time of the court and public money; pleas of guilty often save the distress of witnesses in having to give evidence, as well as inconvenience and loss of time; and in present conditions such pleas are essential to prevent serious congestion in the courts (cited Baldwin & McConville, 1977: 106).

Against this, Baldwin & McConville (1977) turned the concept of sentence discount on its head by asserting that it is customary within the law of England and Wales to boast of a person's fundamental right to require the prosecution to prove their case beyond reasonable doubt, yet people are in effect penalised when the prosecution are able to do so (Baldwin & McConville, 1977: 108). Moreover, as Baldwin and McConville (1977) drawing from Trasler (1976) pointed out:

> Counsel and judges...may...complain of the waste of their time. Yet their time (unlike that of the accused, should he (sic) be convicted) is sufficiently repaid...the cost falls not upon them, but upon the people at large, who may be content to pay a price for the assurance that others will not be convicted upon inadequate evidence...To impose so severe a penalty [an extra third to the sentence] for wasting the time of a group of notably well-paid men (sic) seems excessive (cited Baldwin & McConville, 1977: 109).

As this relates to the official statistics on successful appeals, plea-bargaining has an undoubted effect on their accuracy to account for all wrongful convictions that occur. An effect that makes a precise calculation impossible, but which, nonetheless, illustrates that the official statistics on successful appeals do not fully represent wrongful convictions in England and Wales.

The *parole deal* is another major *procedural barrier* to a successful appeal that has an impact upon the accuracy of the official statistics. In his analysis, Hill (2001) defined the parole deal as very much akin to a plea bargain for it attempts to make innocent prisoners acknowledge guilt for crimes that they did not, in fact, commit. Significantly, for Hill (2001), both offer the same essential deal in an attempt to obtain judicial finality in cases: 'We say you are guilty. Admit it and you get something in return'. The rationale behind the parole deal is connected to a range of 'cognitive skills', 'thinking skills', 'reasoning and rehabilitation' and various other 'offending behaviour' programmes and courses that have come to dominate regimes within prisons in England and Wales over the last decade. These courses are almost universally based on the work of psychologists in the correctional service of Canada and work from the premise that as offenders 'think' differently to law abiding citizens, once their 'cognitive distortions' are corrected then they could be released with a reduced risk of recidivism (Wilson, 2001a). The effect is that whilst the prison service acknowledges that it is unlawful to refuse to recommend release solely on the ground that a prisoner continues to deny guilt, it tends to work under the simultaneous assumption that denial of offending is a good indicator of a prisoner's continuing risk (Naughton, 2004b, 2005e). Accordingly, prisons proceed on the basis that convictions are safe, which, in principle, seems an entirely reasonable and practical policy. In practice, however, this serves to exacerbate the harmful consequences of the injustice already done to the wrongly convicted prisoner (Woffinden, 2000b, 2001c; Hill, 2002, 2002a; Berlins, 2002). In consequence, prisoners who protest their innocence experience a range of discriminatory practices and inevitably serve longer sentences, as the basis for release under the parole system is that prisoners attend offending behaviour courses and acknowledge their offence that they have not in fact committed (Naughton, 2006b). For example, *Stephen Downing* whose conviction was quashed in January 2002 spent 27 years incarcerated for an offence which he might normally have served 12 years had he not been classified 'IDOM' – in denial of murder. His continued denial of a murder that he did not commit meant that he was also deprived of better jobs, training opportunities and parole consideration (see Editorial, 2002a). To emphasise the point, Hill (2002b) reported that: 'All the prison officers knew Stephen [Downing] was innocent. They were begging him to say he had done it [murdered Wendy Sewell] so they could release him.' Other similar appeal cases followed such as Robert Brown (see Hopkins, 2002b; Hill, 2002, 2002a) and Paul Blackburn (see Naylor, 2004), each of whom spent 25 years in prison maintaining their innocence. They, too, were eligible for release almost a decade before they overturned their convictions on appeal and discriminated in a range of ways from their counter-parts who acknow-ledged their guilt for the crimes for which they had been convicted. It is claimed that some prisoners have been maintaining innocence for the last 35 to 40 years and may never be released. Despite having exemplary prison records, they will not admit to crimes that they say that they did not commit.[23]

Wilson (2001a) conceptualised the situation as one which political philosophers would describe as a *throffer* – the combination of an offer or promise of a reward if a course of action is pursued, with a threat or penalty if this course of action is refused. This plays out with the pri-soner being offered an enormous range of incentives including more out-of-cell time, more visits and a speedy progress through the system, to follow the course of action desired by the prison regime – to go on an offending behaviour course to ensure that the prisons performance target is met. This is made to appear as an entirely rational and sub-jective choice, especially as it will be the basis for ensuring early release through parole. At the same time, if the prisoner does not go on a course, the threat of continued imprisonment remains, as the prisoner will be deemed too much of a 'risk' for release at all (Naughton, 2006b). Accordingly, the practice to treat prisoners more harshly who maintain their innocence, whilst at the same time rewarding prisoners to accept their 'guilt' can be conceived as an additional cause of wrong-ful convictions that may never come to light. A likely consequence will be for many innocent prisoners to 'acknowledge' their 'guilt' in the interests of a more tolerable prison experience or existence and early release through parole. Once embarked upon this course of action, however, not only will it be virtually impossible for the wrongly imprisoned innocent to overturn their wrongful conviction, there will also be a profound impact upon the number of successful appeals that it is possible to quantify.

The *Criminal Procedure and Investigations Act (1996)* (CPIA) serves as a further *procedural barrier* that facilitates wrongful convictions that will be almost impossible to overturn and, hence, impact upon the ability of the official statistics of successful appeals to depict all wrongful convictions. Under the CPIA (1996) a disclosure process between pros-ecution and defence was introduced that is at odds with the opera-tional practices of police officers, the CPS and defence solicitors (for a discussion see, for example, Davies, Croall & Tyrer, 1998: 12). The CPIA (1996) introduced a new and in many ways more restrictive scheme for how material is handled. Whereas previously the defence could go and inspect all the material, now in most cases a police officer will decide the materials that undermine the prosecution's case and only then, in theory, pass it on to the accused. As Bennathon (2000) noted, the CPIA (1996) 'is an awful and dangerous piece of legislation, but just how bad it is tends to get hidden by its technical nature.' As a consequence, 'errors', whether inadvertent or otherwise, may not be recognised and the result is a system that presents real risks of future miscarriages of justice (see Taylor (2001). The CPIA (1996) also questions the possible limits of the notion contained in the official account of the criminal justice process and the idea of the prosecution and defence parties' ability to *freely* present their respective 'opposing' or 'adversarial' cases in court 'as they see fit', as the case must be now substantially set out before it gets to court (see Green, 2000a; Emmerson, 1999; Woffinden, 1999). In concrete terms, questionnaires by the Law Society and the British Academy of Forensic Sciences (BAFS) have produced a list of over 200 examples of wrongful conviction caused through non-disclosure (see Langdon-Down, 1999). Thus, although the CPIA (1996) was a legislative consequence of the cases of the Guildford Four and Judith Ward (see Ward, 1993) in which key evidence pointing to the defendant's innocence was not disclosed to the defence by the prosecution, the CPIA (1996) is, probably, causing more wrongful convictions, and possibly miscarriages of justice if it can be shown that there was a failure to disclose evidence that either supports the defence case or undermines the case for the prosecution (Dyer, 1999b, 2000c; Rowe, 2000). In this context, perhaps the most obvious consequence of the CPIA (1996) is that no one knows how many wrongful convictions and/or miscarriages of justice are being caused simply because no one knows how much material is being withheld (Woffinden, 1999). Accordingly, although the CPIA (1996) can be conceived to cause wrongful convictions and act as a barrier to a successful appeal it is impossible to know how many successful appeals are not achieved.

A *procedural obstacle* to overturning wrongful convictions, that some victims may be able to overcome, and others may not, lies at the heart of the criteria for alleged miscarriage of justice cases to be referred to the CACD, for example. As discussed in the previous chapter, s. 4 of the Criminal Appeal Act (1995) regulates the CACD to 'receive any evidence which was not adduced in the proceedings from which the appeal lies', but only within certain criteria: if the evidence appears to the Court to be capable of belief; if it appears to the Court that the evidence may afford any ground for allowing the appeal; if the evidence would have been admissible at the trial on an issue which is the subject of the appeal; and, if there is a reasonable explanation for the failure to adduce the evidence at the trial' As such, innocent victims of wrongful conviction who are unable to satisfy these requirements may be unable to overturn their convictions. The recent decision by the CCRC not to refer the case of John Roden, despite claims that the Case Review Manager who investigated his application believed that he had a 'compelling' case, emphasises the limits of both the CCRC and the CACD, as the CCRC is subordinate to the criteria of the CACD under the 'real possibility test'. To be sure, under the provisions in the Criminal Appeal Act 1995, the CCRC merely *reviews* cases of alleged or suspected miscarriage of justice with a view to referring them back to the CACD if it is believed there is 'a real possibility' that the case will be overturned. In this sense, the CCRC can be said to act as a filter for the CACD and sanction the successful appeals of guilty offenders if their convictions were procedurally incorrect, whilst, at the same time, remaining helpless to refer the cases of innocent victims of wrongful convictions if they are unable to fulfil the 'real possibility test'. The 'real possibility test' as applied by the CCRC is, essentially, then, an attempt by the Commission to 'second-guess' the appeal courts (James, 2002a). The CCRC, then, can be conceived as entirely concerned about miscarriages of justice as defined by criminal law, as opposed to the possible wrongful conviction of the innocent as expressed in public/political discourses. It operates entirely within the parameters of the criminal justice process to uphold the integrity of due process, but does not question the possibility that due process procedures can cause miscarriages of justice and/or the wrongful conviction of the innocent (Naughton, 2005b). It cannot refer cases back to the appeal courts in the interests of justice as understood and expressed by public and political discourse (James et al, 2000: 140–153). If, for example, the CCRC turns up evidence that indicates an applicant's innocence that was available at the original trial it may not constitute grounds for a referral (Nobles & Schiff, 2001: 280–299). It is claimed that the CCRC are unable to refer Roden's case precisely because the evidence that indicates his innocence was available at his original trial and, thus, does not satisfy the CACD requirement (see Lewis, 2004).

Finally, an example of a *procedural disincentive* to a successful appeal is the *time loss rule*. In essence, the time loss rule refers to the information provided to applicants who intend to make appeals against their criminal convictions that if their appeal is ultimately unsuccessful it could result in substantial increases to their sentence. Very little research exists about the time loss rule. Research conducted by JUSTICE (1994: 7), however, found that 'the effect is to transform a minor check on wholly groundless applications into a major barrier in some meritorious cases'. The time loss rule, then, discourages appeals against possible wrongful convictions, and further illustrates the inability of the official statistics to adequately depict all wrongful convictions that occur.

Conclusion

This chapter synthesised an analysis of the individual causes of miscarriages of justice with critical theoretical analyses of the ways in which the underlying structures of the criminal justice system serve to cause miscarriages of justice and wrongful convictions. In addition, existing depictions of the miscarriage of justice iceberg were extended to include a range of significant procedures of the criminal justice system that can cause wrongful convictions and/or act as deterrents to overturning miscarriages of justice through a successful appeal. What this chapter has not determined, however, is the precise number of wrongful convictions that are engendered by the routine operations of the procedures of the criminal justice system that were discussed. On the contrary, it has demonstrated that a precise figure of wrongful convictions is impossible to arrive at. But, a precise depiction of all wrongful convictions was not the object of this chapter. Rather, the primary purpose was to emphasise that there are indeed structures and procedures that cause wrongful convictions and miscarriages of justice and/or act as deterrents to their remedy through a successful appeal. This analysis can, then, be used as a tool of analysis against which the official indices of successful appeals can be assessed to show that they can be conceived to be only a partial indicator of all wrongful convictions and miscarriages of justice in England and Wales. Hence, the official statistics on successful appeals against criminal conviction are not an exhaustive or comprehensive indicator of England and Wales' miscarriage of justice iceberg.

4
Government

Introduction

Governmental intervention on the perceived problem of miscarriages of justice has been prompted by exceptional cases of successful appeal which fail to be overturned through existing appeal procedures. Thus, the RCCJ was not established in response to a crisis caused by concerns of an excessive number of successful appeals as evident in the official statistics but, rather, in response to the specific cases of the Guildford Four, the Birmingham Six, and so on, which exemplified a procedural problem with returning potentially meritorious cases back to the CACD when appeal rights had been exhausted (Royal Commission on Criminal Justice, 1993: 1–6).

This chapter is premised on the findings of the last chapter which noted that England and Wales' criminal justice system is a case-law system within which change to the criminal justice system is not effected through speculative critique. On the contrary, the due process of governmentality requires the demonstration of procedural 'error' or irregularity in concrete cases, i.e. by showing that particular individuals are being detrimentally harmed by the existing arrangements. From this starting point, an historical analysis of governmental responses to perceived miscarriages of justice is conducted to emphasise a kind of 'governmental voice' which responds to certain forms of counter-discourse in a particular official way. Interestingly, however, the governmental voice shares with counter-voices the assumption that miscarriages of justice are exceptional cases of successful appeal that have failed to be overturned through existing appellate procedures. Given the arguments in Part One, this constitutes a crucial limitation if the terrain of miscarriages of justice is to be properly understood.

There are three parts in the development of this analysis. First, an historical analysis of governmental legislative responses to specific successful appeal cases at the centre of key changes to the criminal justice system is conducted. In so doing, a broader analysis of the operations of the governmental voice is provided. Following this, Foucault's thesis on power, knowledge and resistance is outlined to show that procedural changes to the existing criminal justice system can be seen as intrinsically bound up with forms of counter-discourse – counter-voices – that are grounded in successful appeals that provide the necessary concrete evidence of new causes or harmful consequences of miscarriages of justice. Finally, the limits of the focus upon exceptional cases as a governmental driver for changes to the criminal justice system, as opposed to a wider analysis of the scale of miscarriages of justice indicted by governmental statistics, is discussed.

The governmentality of the criminal justice system

A historical analysis of the criminal justice system shows that whichever era one chooses for analysis, governmental responses to the perceived problem of miscarriages of justice has never addressed the general issue of miscarriages of justice. On the contrary, it has always been addressed to specific high profile cases that revealed new 'errors'. To illustrate this point, four of the most important legislative events that have defined the historical phasing of the criminal justice system are:

- the establishment of a Court of Criminal Appeal under the Criminal Appeal Act (1907) (CAA (1907));
- the first step towards the permanent abolition of capital punishment under its temporary abolition in the Murder (Abolition of Death Penalty) Act (1965) (MADPA (1965));
- the introduction of formalised police codes of practice and conduct under the Police and Criminal Evidence Act (1984) (PACE) (Police and Criminal Evidence Act, 1985); and,
- the establishment of the Criminal Cases Review Commission (CCRC), an 'independent' body responsible for investigating suspected miscarriages of criminal justice in England, Wales and Northern Ireland (Annual Report, 1998–2000) under the Criminal Appeal Act (1995) (CAA (1995)) (Criminal Appeal Act, 1995).

Crucially, each of these legislative events was also connected with an extra-judicial inquiry previously set up by government to address the problem of miscarriages of justice as perceived at the time. The CAA (1907) was connected with a Committee of Inquiry, which reported in 1904, set up in response to the Beck case (Report of the Committee of Inquiry into the Beck Case, 1904). The MADPA (1965) was connected to the parliamentary debate about the establishment, terms of reference and recommendations of the Royal Commission on Capital Punishment (1953) (RCCP (1953)) (Block & Hostettler, 1997; Royal Commission on Capital Punishment, 1953). PACE (1984) was an outgrowth of some of the recommendations of the Royal Commission on Criminal Procedure (1981) (RCCP) (Royal Commission on Criminal Procedure, 1981). And, the CAA (1995) was a consequence of some of the recommendations advised by the RCCJ (Royal Commission on Criminal Justice, 1993).

Furthermore, as will be shown below, although each of these events and inquiries followed long legal and political campaigns it is also significant they were not initiated because of campaigning pressures alone. Nor were they a consequence of the overwhelming weight of the statistics on successful appeals against criminal conviction. On the contrary, they were triggered by specific cases of successful appeals against criminal conviction that exemplified the most problematic aspect of the procedural framework of the criminal justice system as perceived at that particular time (Naughton, 2001).

The establishment of the Court of Criminal Appeal

Throughout the 19th century there was a longstanding Parliamentary campaign for the establishment of a court capable of hearing criminal appeals (see Colvin, 1994). This was fuelled by the recurrence of miscarriage of justice cases that were evidenced by Home Office pardons (see Pattenden, 1996: 5–33). Despite this, the eventual establishment of the Court of Criminal Appeal in 1907 was attributable to the combined counter-discursive public pressures exerted by the cases of Maybrick (Ryan, 1977), Edalji (see Lahiri, 2000) and Beck (see Coates, 2001). These cases exemplified the urgent need for a court of criminal appeal as they showed, categorically, that people such as Edalji and Beck were being wrongly imprisoned and others, as exemplified by the Maybrick case, were given the death penalty for crimes that they, probably, did not commit, and, more importantly in terms of the process of change to the criminal justice system, which the public believed that they did not commit. Taken together the Maybrick, Edalji and Beck cases served to diminish public confidence in the criminal justice system to the extent that a committee of inquiry was established to investigate the Beck Affair. Subsequently, a court of criminal appeal had to be established to dispose of the public crisis and restore confidence in the criminal justice system (see Woffinden, 1987). Indeed, in announcing the establishment of the Criminal Court of Appeal under the CAA (1907) the then Home Secretary, Herbert Gladstone, told the House of Commons that 'the only way to reverse the public belief that miscarriages of justice were an every-day occurrence...was the establishment of a court capable of hearing appeals of fact, law and sentence' (cited Pattenden, 1996: 31).

The abolition of capital punishment

Following the establishment of the Court of Criminal Appeal in 1907, the concern that people were being, or could be, convicted of criminal offences, and in some cases executed, without an appeal soon dissipated from the public consciousness and the 'normal' assumption that the criminal justice system was operating correctly was re-established. The belief that the criminal justice system now contained the necessary legislative safeguards to correct miscarriages of justice created what in Elias's (1978) analysis could be termed a new 'figuration' of criminal justice. In a Foucauldian sense, it created a new regime of criminal justice. This period of 'normality', however, would be temporary, lasting only until the success, or otherwise, of the Court of Criminal Appeal could be determined and the knowledge entered the public domain that even with a criminal appeal system people were still being given the death penalty in questionable circumstances. This intensified the longstanding campaign for the abolition of capital punishment but did not, in and of itself, result in abolition (see Capital Punishment UK, 2006). For abolition to be, finally, achieved, it took the cases of Bentley, (Parris, 1991; Trow, 1990), Evans (see Kennedy, 1961) and Ellis (see Jones, 2001; Hancock, 1963), which together exemplified to the public the unjustness of the continuance of capital punishment (see, for example, Ryan, 1983: 10–16; Christoph, 1962). In disposing of the public crisis surrounding the cases of Bentley, Evans and Ellis the MADPA (1965) temporarily abolished capital punishment for a five-year period (see Block & Hostettler, 1997). Upon its expiry in 1969, capital punishment was permanently abolished (see Callaghan, 1997).

The introduction of the Police and Criminal Evidence Act (1984)

With the abolition of capital punishment a space was provided wherein critical thoughts could turn to other potential 'errors' or problems with the criminal justice system. Despite longstanding allegations of police corruption and calls for police accountability (see, for example, Chibnall, 1979: 138–142; Manning, 1979: 45; Miller, 1979: 21–22; Jefferson & Grimshaw, 1984: 71–72; Reiner, 1985; Punch, 1985), guidelines for the conduct of police conduct could not be formally introduced. Once again, it was a specific case that exemplified improper police conduct and provided the evidence to forms of counter-discourse that, in turn, induced a public crisis and subsequently prompted (allowed) government to intervene. The Confait Affair (see Price & Caplan, 1976; Kettle, 1979; Price, 1985) exemplified the need for police accountability, both in the interests of greater reliability of evidence and the enhancement of suspect's rights, and led to the establishment of the RCCP (Royal Commission on Criminal Procedure, 1981, para, 10.1). In particular, the Fisher (1977) inquiry into the case had been especially critical of the police practices that led to the wrongful convictions of the three youths for the murder of Maxwell Confait. The whole prosecution, argued Fisher (1977), was geared simply to providing the case against the boys. In response, the RCCP's main recommendation was translated into PACE (1984) (for a discussion see Leigh, 1985; Birch, 1985; Gibbons, 1985; Mirfield, 1985; Munro, 1985) and the public crisis of confidence in the criminal justice system was, again, temporarily disposed of.

The establishment of the Criminal Cases Review Commission

Following the introduction of police codes of conduct under PACE (1984), one of the next most significant procedural 'errors' to emerge with the criminal justice system was the need for an independent body for the investigation of suspected or alleged miscarriages of justice once routine appeal processes had been exhausted. The limits of the appeal process in terms of the criteria of fresh evidence coupled with the apparent reluctance of successive Home Secretaries to refer cases back to the CACD, for political, as opposed purely legal reasons, raised further concerns about the safety of the high profile criminal convictions of the Guildford Four and the Birmingham Six.[24] On 14 March 1991, the day the Birmingham Six had their convictions overturned by the CACD, the governmental response was to set up the RCCJ, in response to a widespread public crisis of confidence in the criminal justice system. One of the most significant outcomes of the RCCJ was the establishment of the CCRC, an independent body for the investigation of alleged or suspected miscarriages of justice that have previously failed to be overturned through routine appellate procedures. In so doing, the public crisis of confidence in the law on criminal appeals was once again, temporarily, dispelled.

A possible criticism of the foregoing analysis is that it oversimplifies and, even, de-contextualises the history of changes to the criminal justice system and avoided or neglected what might be considered to be complex or awkward issues. For instance, the connection between Bentley and the abolition of the death penalty may seem problematical as the MADPA (1965) was some 14 years after Bentley. But, the purpose of this chapter is not to explicate the precise details of Bentley, and, anyway, the influence of Bentley on the eventual abolition of capital punishment is already very well documented (see Parris, 1991; Trow, 1990; Ryan, 1983; Christoph, 1962). Further, the purpose of this, admittedly, somewhat crude sketch of the processes of governmentality in changes to the criminal justice system is not to present an exhaustive account of the machinations of each of the various cases, inquiries and/or legislative events. Rather, my aim is to demonstrate, on a sociology of ideas level, an alternative schematic of *how* the criminal justice system is amended in response to apparent challenges to its legitimacy. I am trying to develop the beginnings of a different depiction of the *processes* or stages of modification; to show, through a broader historical analysis of the criminal justice system, a discernible pattern to the governmentality of the criminal justice system that exhibits the conventions or sequential steps set out as follows: at particular times, exceptional successful appeal cases that exemplify 'errors' in the existing legislative framework of the criminal justice system attain a high profile status. In consequence, the criminal justice system and public/media spheres are thrown into chaotic collision as the counter-discursive forces inform government of a crisis of public confidence in its management of the criminal justice system. In response, extra-judicial inquiries are launched, the recommendations of which are subsequently translated into corrective changes to the criminal justice system that restores public confidence and reaffirms governmental authority in the criminal justice system, and harmony between the colliding spheres, is, temporarily, restored. This sequence of events is conceived as resulting in only a 'temporary' resumption of criminal justice system 'normality', as it will prevail only until the next occasion that counter-discourse against miscarriages of justice is deployed in response to a specific case of successful appeal that exemplifies and provides evidence of a new 'error' in the existing framework of the criminal justice system. At such time, a public crisis of confidence *could* once again be induced, and if it is, the governmentality sequence of events will, once again, be initiated.[25]

This is not to convert a historical trend into an eternal truth. Nor is it to trivialise the crucial processes in the negotiation of miscarriages of justice in the changes to the criminal justice system. Rather, it is to observe that the structural confines within which the existing criminal justice system operates tends to produce the same pattern of criminal justice system modification. As the governmentality project relates to government, unlike the sovereign system, governmental changes are prevented without a mandate from the governed. Government cannot introduce changes to the criminal justice system arbitrarily. Indeed, the due processes of governmentality require government to have a justification for any interventions to the criminal justice system. It is operationalised by forms of counter-discourse supported by solid evidence of aspects of the criminal justice process which call for governmental intervention and remedy, apparent cases of miscarriages of justice supported by successful appeals against criminal conviction.

Power, knowledge and resistance

Foucault's 'micro-physical' researchers were concerned with the strategies and practices of modern forms of power; with expertise; and the techniques by which 'power/knowledge' produces discourses (bodies of knowledge), which in turn determine the conditions within which modern 'regimes' of truth are socially and historically produced and function. From this perspective, the foregoing examples of the governmentity of the criminal justice system throw up the following three significant features:

- certain exceptional post-appeal successful appeals against criminal conviction which represent new causes of miscarriage of justice attain a high profile status;
- a widespread moral concern about the harm caused to victims of miscarriages of justice in these cases induces a public crisis of confidence in the particular aspect of the criminal justice system which appears to be the cause of the miscarriages of justice; and,
- a concern by government to correct the criminal justice system with the stated aim of remedying/eradicating the apparent cause of the miscarriage(s) of justice that is causing the public crisis of confidence in the criminal justice system and to restore public faith that the system is operating as we think it should, i.e. not causing undue harm to people believed to be innocent.

Each of these features raise critical questions pertaining to power and knowledge in the operations of criminal justice system power, the possibilities of *resistance* and the role and rationality of government in the disposal of public crisis of confidence in the criminal justice system. In analysis, the remainder of this chapter makes use of a Foucauldian inspired perspective. To be sure, perhaps the most significant contribution of Foucault's thesis on existing forms of power was his stress on the *productive* or *constitutive* nature of its exercise. His major achievement was to have turned a negative concept on its head and to attribute the production of concepts, ideas, and the structures of social institutions to the operations of power in its existing forms. As he argued:

> We must cease once and for all to describe the effects of power in negative terms: it 'excludes', it 'represses', it 'censors', it 'abstracts', it 'masks', it 'conceals'. In fact, power *produces;* it produces reality; it produces domains of objects and rituals of truth (Foucault, 1977: 194 my emphasis).

For Foucault (1980a) existing accounts of power conceive it in either of two ways. On the one hand, power is equated with law and its exercise conceptualised in juridical terms of constitution and sovereignty: sovereign rule exists as a result of a contract between two consenting parties or agents. On the whole, this kind of analysis was common among conservative theorists on the right of politics and was inspired from early forms of political theory such as Hobbes' theory of the State. Alternatively, power is analysed on the left of politics, largely inspired by Marx, in terms of the State apparatus and its ideological representations of power. Foucault (1980a: 115–116) noted that:

> The way power was exercised – concretely and in detail – with its specificity, its techniques and tactics, was something that no one attempted to ascertain; they contented themselves with denouncing it in a polemical and global fashion as it existed among the 'others' in the adversary camp.

Foucault argued, despite their surface differences, both the 'juridical' and 'discursive' analyses of power share a fundamental abstract similarity – that power acts on something already constituted; that both the 'sovereign' who wields power and the 'subject' upon whom power is exercised exist in this relationship *prior* to the exercise of power; that power is the *result* rather than the productive *cause* of this relationship. Both forms of analysis merge all forms of power relations into the framework of a general relationship of sovereign and subject. To reinforce this point Foucault characterised the two types of analyses as being the 'juridico-discursive' conception of power. He caricatured it by identifying the 'uniformity' of power's exercise within such a conception:

> Whether one attributes to it the form of the prince who formulates rights, of the father who forbids, of the censor who enforces silence, of the master who states the law, in any case one schematises power in a juridical form, and one defines its effects as obedience. Confronted by a power that is law, the subject who is constituted as subject – who is 'subjected' – is 'he' (sic) who obeys. To the formal homogeneity of power in these various instances corresponds the general form of submission in the one who is constrained by it – whether the individual in question is the subject opposite the monarch, the citizen opposite the state, the child opposite the parent, or the disciple opposite the master. A legislative power on the one side, and an obedient subject on the other (Foucault, 1979b: 85).

Foucault's conception of 'modern' 'power', then, is very different from traditional socio-political conceptions of it. Power is not 'owned' by some privileged person or group and exercised 'simply as an obligation or a prohibition on those who "do not have it"' (Foucault, 1977: 27). On the contrary, 'power', or 'force' for Foucault, is not just the ruthless domination of the weaker by the stronger, in fact, it is not to be 'had' at all:

> Power is everywhere; not because it embraces everything but because it comes from everywhere...there is no binary and all-encompassing opposition between ruler and ruled at the root of power relations, and serving as a general matrix – no such duality extending from the top down and reacting on more and more limited groups to the very depths of the social body. One must suppose, rather, that the manifold relations of force that take shape and come into play in the machinery of production, in families, limited groups and institutions, are the basis for wide-ranging effects of cleavage that run through the social body as a whole (Foucault, 1979b: 93–94).

On this basis, the changes to the criminal justice system, that were introduced in governmental response to exceptional successful appeals that exemplified forms of harm to victims believed to be innocent that could not be remedied by the existing criminal justice system, can be conceived to have *produced* or *constituted* new forms of criminal justice system reality: a criminal justice system without a Court of Criminal Appeal and the possibility of overturning wrongful convictions, for example, is a fundamentally different 'product' to a system that is constituted to contain such an appellate procedure.

Moreover, from such a perspective, Foucault conceived that forms of resistance to power are not simply a reaction to a pre-existing power. 'This', he argued, 'would be to misunderstand the strictly relational character of power relations' (Foucault, 1979b: 95). Forms of resistance, for Foucault, are, in fact, never in a position of *exteriority* in relation to power. Rather, it is more likely the reverse: states of power are continually engendered or incited by virtue of the potential counter-powers which co-exist with them: 'Where there is power there is resistance' (Foucault, 1979b: 95):

> The sense and object of governmental acts do not fall from the sky or emerge ready formed from social practice. They are things which have had to be – and which have been – invented. Foucault observed that there is a parcel of thought in even the crassest and most obtuse parts of social reality, which is why criticism can be a real power for change, depriving some practices of their self-evidence, extending the bounds of the thinkable to permit the invention of others (Burchell et al, 1991: x).

Power, then, presupposes resistance of some form. He asserted: 'Relations of power are not in a position of exteriority with respect to other types of relationships (economic processes, knowledge relationships, sexual relationships), but are immanent in the latter; they are the immediate effects of the divisions, inequalities, and disequilibriums which occur in the latter, and conversely they are internal conditions of these differentiations; relations of power are not in superstructural positions, with merely a role of prohibition or accompaniment; they have a directly productive role, wherever they come into effect' (Foucault, 1979b: 94).

The key to understanding Foucault's conception of resistance lies in his meaning of a 'force' or 'power relation'. In the context of the present discussion, 'power' within the sphere of criminal justice can be conceived as nothing more than the multiplicity of force relations extant within the socio-legal body. Power's conditions of possibility actually consist of this moving substrate of *force relations*: the struggles, confrontations, contradictions, inequalities, transformations and integrations of these force relations. Thus individuals are 'positioned' within any struggle only as a consequence of the existence of a struggle for power. Accordingly, both existing forms of power and resistance to them involve the invention of 'tactics' and the co-ordination of these various tactics into coherent strategies by government and the governed. This is, perhaps, the most important practical political consequence of Foucault's thesis on power: a *strategic* manoeuvre must be countered by an opposing manoeuvre; a set of 'tactics' must be consciously 'invented' in opposition to the setting in place of another; a different procedural 'art' of criminal justice system, for example, is what will oppose the existing one. 'One is always "inside" power, there is no "escaping" it' (Foucault, 1979b: 95). Moreover, Foucault argued, resistance is more effective when it is directed at a *technique* or specific exercises of power rather than at 'power' in general. It is *techniques* of power which *allow* for the exercise of power and the production of knowledge. Resistance consists of 'refusing' these techniques. Most importantly, Foucault argued, oppressive forces of domination do not hold the monopoly in the capacity to 'invent' 'tactics'. If resistance is to be effective, it requires the acknowledgement that tactics *are* being employed in a struggle, and the active interrogation of those tactics. Foucault suggested that in the interrogation of 'tactics', 'power' is intelligible, and susceptible to analysis down to its most minute details, in terms of the historical strategies and sets of 'tactics' designed to mobilise these *techniques* to political advantage (Foucault, 1979b: 95–96).

From such a frame of reference, what might be termed the 'ear' of government is, perhaps, even more significant than the voice of government. Legislative change to the criminal justice system is inevitable in a system where power and resistance are about the governmental management of competing discourses (also cf. Nobles and Schiff, 1995). In this process, governmental techniques, such as committees of inquiries and the royal commissions into problematic aspects of the criminal justice system, represent an arena within which an enactment in the power struggle between dominant forms of criminal justice system power and its counter-discursive resistance takes place (see, for example, Osborne, 1996: 114). And, the success of the governmental *translation* of their recommendations into corrective criminal justice system legislation that disposes of public crises represents an episode of governmentality in the on-going negotiated management of the criminal justice system.

From this it follows that exceptional successful appeals that exemplify new 'errors' need not be conceived in entirely negative terms. As Coser (1956) noted: 'Far from being only a "negative" factor which "tears apart", social conflict may fulfil a number of determinate functions in groups and other interpersonal relations' (Coser, 1956: 8). Accordingly, the more critical counter-discourse that is produced around cases that exemplify apparent 'failings' with the criminal justice system, then, potentially, the more crises of public confidence in the criminal justice system will be induced, and the more problematic aspects of the criminal justice system will have to be subjected to disposal and legislative domestication by the processes of governmentality. Moreover, as Coser (1956), in a reformulation of Simmel's (1955) proposition, also noted: 'Struggle may be an important way to avoid conditions of disequilibrium by modifying the basis for power relations' (Coser, 1956: 137).

The limits of the existing governmental voice

On the face of it, the governmentality of the criminal justice system in response to perceived miscarriages of justice would seem to indicate that the governmental voice has followed its remit and introduced a range of legislative changes to the criminal justice system that have, indeed, served to amend identifiable problems and, hence, to enhance the wellbeing of the population for which it is mandated. The highlighted changes to the criminal justice system illustrate that some of the most significant changes to the criminal justice system have been introduced in the express attempt to prevent miscarriages of justice or remedy them when they occur. As shown, the debate about the case of Timothy Evans contributed to the abolition of capital punishment and the focus upon the Confait Affair resulted in the introduction of PACE (1984) and guidelines on police investigation. To be sure, the introduction of new ways to achieve an appeal that were outlined in the governmentality of the criminal justice system, such as the introduction of the Court of Criminal Appeal, can be conceived as representing what Foucault (1979b) might term tactical victories in the discursive interplay of existing forms of criminal justice system discourse and its counter-discursive opposition. In this sense, introductions such as the CCRC, for instance, are products of resistance from voices of the governed that refused to give up their belief that the Birmingham Six, Guildford Four, and so on, were innocent and the present system needed modification to overturn such cases. Prior to the Court of Criminal Appeal there was no official mechanism for overturning miscarriages of justice. And, although miscarriages of justice are extensive, the abolition of capital punishment also appears to be a step in the right direction in the sense that prior to its abolition many of the victims in exceptional cases of successful appeals would not have been alive to overturn their wrongful convictions, for example, the Birmingham Six, the Guildford Four, and so on.

On the surface, such changes would seem to indicate that significant *reforms* of the criminal justice system arrangements have been achieved. However, if the intended aims of the forms of resistance that effected the establishment of the CCRC and the abolition of capital punishment, for example, were attempts to *prevent* miscarriages of justice they can be conceived as consummate failures: they have in no way prevented or reduced miscarriages of justice from occurring. Rather, the changes to the criminal justice process in response to apparent miscarriages of justice, such as the establishment of the Court of Criminal Appeal, the abolition of capital punishment, PACE (1984) and the CCRC tend to introduce new methods for remedying possible miscarriages of justice, reinforcing notions that the criminal justice system is, ordinarily and fundamentally capable of delivering popular aspirations, i.e. just outcomes as they relate to opportunities for innocent victims of miscarriages of justice to overturn their convictions. They suggest that such changes can correct the apparent 'failings' of the system and prevent miscarriages of justice from occurring in the future. The reality is that they do not disturb the underlying structural causes of miscarriages of justice at all: the introduction of the Court of Criminal Appeal in 1907 provided a possible means to overturn miscarriages of justice, on the system's terms, if they could show breaches of due process; the abolition of capital punishment meant that victims of miscarriages of justice and/or wrongful conviction are no longer executed in 'error', but it did nothing about the possibility of the innocent spending their whole lives in prison maintaining their innocence; PACE (1984) formalised codes of police conduct in investigations and provided alleged victims of miscarriages of justice who can show breaches from PACE the possibility of overturning their convictions; the CCRC enhanced the possibility of overturning out-of-time appeals for certain qualifying applicants. The critical point, however, is that none of these changes has any impact at all on *preventing* miscarriages of justice from occurring in the first place.[26] Moreover, as highlighted in the previous chapter, nor do they question the procedures of the criminal justice process that cause miscarriages of justice and/or act against innocent victims of wrongful conviction overturning their convictions.

In his analysis, Foucault's history of governmentality also emphasised the centrality of statistical forms of analysis in the modes of government that distinguish the modern world and the ways in which they are (should be) used to improve society and enhance the wellbeing of the governed/the population. In particular, Foucault (1979a: 14–16; 1991) argued that from about the 18th century on, the 'arts of government', which replaced Sovereign authority, emerged as a consequence to the problem of population and 'consist(ed) essentially of the knowledge of the State, in all the different elements, dimensions and factors of its power, termed precisely "statistics", meaning the science of the State'. Statistics, argued Foucault, gradually revealed that the population had its own lawlike regularities such as its own rate of death, of suicide, of disease, its own cycles of scarcity, etc. He asserted that under the 'art', 'population' management became the ultimate interest of government, embracing the welfare of the population to improve its conditions, increase its wealth, longevity, health etc. Hence individual interest and that of the population as a whole becomes both the target and the instrument of government (Foucault, 1979a: 18; 1991). For Foucault (1979a: 17; 1991), 'statistics…make it possible to quantify the phenomena specific to population', such that 'the art of government and empirical knowledge of the State's resources and condition – its statistics – together formed the major components of a new political rationality' (Rabinow, 1984: 16).

Another significant limitation with the focus of the existing articulation of the voice of government from this perspective, then, is its complicity with prevalent notions that miscarriages of justice constitute only exceptional cases of successful appeals, taking no account whatever of the thousands of mundane and routine successful appeals that occur each year. It, therefore, can be conceived to divert attention away from, even disqualify, the potential voices of the thousands of victims of mundane miscarriages of justice that occur annually in the Crown Court. It also excludes from the dialogue about miscarriages of justice the potential voices of the many hundreds of victims of miscarriages of justice each year in the CACD. Accordingly, it is not that the existing tendency of the governmental voice to focus upon exceptional cases of successful appeals that exemplify newly discovered procedural 'errors' in the operation of the criminal justice process is wrong. Rather, there has been no governmental 'eye' at all upon the scale of miscarriages of justice as evidenced by successful appeals that are not exceptional, or do not exemplify new causes of miscarriages of justice, despite the evidence of such miscarriages of justice being derived from the government's own official statistics. In this sense, the legitimacy of the governmental voice can be called into question.

To be sure, if legitimate government is about enhancing the well-being of the population to which it is mandated, then, it can be argued that the responsive 'ear' of the government should not be entirely fixed upon listening to forms of counter-discourse that emphasise exceptional successful appeals. On the contrary, there should also be a governmental eye upon its own collected statistics of successful appeals, the method by which government knows about the population that it is mandated responsibility for. As it stands, however, the governmental voice on miscarriages really says very little about the real extent and forms of injustice within the domain of criminal justice. This is contrary to its remit and indicates a governmental neglect of a severe judicial lack of wellbeing. As Rose (1991) noted, all aspects of the social economy are evaluated through their numericisation. For instance, poverty is transformed into the numbers claiming social benefits; public order statistics define the crime rate; the divorce rate becomes synonymous with the nation's morality; the spread of AIDS (or the lack of it) is regarded as a sign of the success of the government of sexual conduct. In the same way, the current scale of successful appeals indicates far too many miscarriages of justice and, therefore, can be conceived to undermine the entire judiciary. To be sure, 'if sceptical vigilance over politics has long been a feature of liberal political thought, it is today increasingly conducted in the language of numbers' (Rose, 1991: 674).

Conclusion

This chapter has considered four of the most significant legislative events in the history of the criminal justice system. It discerned a pattern to these key changes to the criminal justice system that can be interpreted within a Foucauldian power/knowledge theoretical perspective as follows: governmental interventions to the criminal justice system are prompted by forms of resistance which are intrinsically connected to forms of knowledge (counter-discourse) supported by cases that exemplify new 'errors' in the criminal justice process which cause apparent harm to victims of miscarriages of justice believed to be innocent of the crimes they were convicted of. The point to be made about this is that the previous changes to the criminal justice system in response to apparent miscarriages of justice does not stop them from occurring. Rather, apart from the example of the abolition of capital punishment, they tend to introduce new ways of overturning them. To be sure, a defining feature of governmentality as it is conceived here is that it inherently precludes reforms of the criminal justice that eradicate or prevent miscarriages of justice, which are immanent or integral to the criminal justice process.

Moreover, the governmental voice, articulated in response to counter-discursive voices of particular cases of successful appeal, has not fulfiled its mandate to ensure the wellbeing of the population as a whole from the harmful consequences of occurrences such as miscarriages of justice. It has taken no account whatsoever of its own collected official statistics of successful appeals against criminal conviction which show that thousands of direct victims each and every year continue to experience the harmful consequences of miscarriages of justice, to say nothing of the many more thousands of indirect victims. It has made superficial changes to the criminal justice system in response to exceptional miscarriages of justice, fundamentally failing to introduce more wide-ranging amendments to the structures of the criminal justice system that might truly prevent miscarriages of justice from occurring.

5
Campaigns

Introduction

There is a general absence of literature on campaigns against the criminal justice system in England and Wales, and a specific dearth of literature on campaigns against miscarriages of justice and the wrongful conviction of the innocent. In the course of this research, the closest sources that I could find were two analyses by Mick Ryan (1978, 1983) on the performance of the penal lobby in England and Wales. In those analyses, Ryan (1978: 1; see also 1983: 105–121) argued that 'governments discriminate against radical pressure groups in favour of liberal or conservative groups whose views imply no fundamental critique of the existing economic and political order'. In addition, there have been other numerous critical researches into the general unjust 'treatment of the confined' with a view to a radical restructuring or complete abolition of the existing penal regime (for example, Scraton et al, 1991: 154–160; Ruggiero et al, 1995; Fitzgerald & Sim, 1982; Mathiesen, 1974). Such researches routinely draw upon the testimony of victims of miscarriages of justice who achieve exceptional successful appeals to support or substantiate their theoretical claims, but do so only in the limited context of the general unjust treatment of prisoners as a whole or as a critique of the 'politics of incarceration'. Scraton et al (1991: 152–153), for example, presented an extensive quotation by Paul Hill, one of the Guildford Four, as evidence of their argument about the general unjust treatment of Irish prisoners, which may not be an entirely appropriate analogy with the treatment of guilty offenders as the Guildford Four were subsequently provided with a public apology from the Prime Minister who stated that they should be 'completely and publicly exonerated' (Editorial, 2005).

In an attempt to redress this neglect, this chapter presents an analysis of the part that campaigning voices[27] play in the discursive dialogue about the criminal justice system in response to miscarriages of justice in England and Wales, perceived by victim support/campaigning organisations as the wrongful conviction of the innocent. This presents an analysis divergent from Ryan's (1978, 1983) findings of a governmental conspiracy to block radical forms of counter-discourse in favour of more friendly forms of reform discourse. On the contrary, it will be shown that successful campaigns against miscarriages of justice produce the cases that provide the counter-discursive force behind some of the most significant changes to the criminal justice system, as outlined in the previous chapter. In this sense, however, campaigning organisations are not in radical opposition to government. They are an integral part of the government of the criminal justice system, articulating the voice of the governed and the need to redress problematical aspects of the existing criminal justice system. As was shown in the previous chapter, the opportunity to appeal against alleged miscarriages of justice derived from the controversy and responding governmental intervention to the high profile case of Adolf Beck which exemplified the need for such a facility following criminal trials to remedy miscarriages of justice. This was in no way a 'friendly reform'. It was a necessary amendment to reinstil public faith that the criminal justice system could be trusted to correct its mistakes as and when they occur. Moreover, I would maintain that a criminal justice system that introduces a system of criminal appeals in acknowledgement that criminal trials can produce wrongful convictions is a world apart from a system without such a facility, representing a radically different governmental rationality on criminal justice system; a new regime of criminal justice system truth. Crucially, however, such progressive and radical changes to the governmentality project need to be underpinned by evidence of a real case/cluster of cases that give forcefulness to critical analyses and calls for change.

In general terms, what follows, firstly, draws attention to organisational diversity, campaign aims and types of cases that are assisted. Despite their important differences, all campaigning organisations share the same primary and secondary aims. Second, the processes through which campaigning organisations contribute to transforming previously unsuccessful appeal cases into forms of evidence which give force to forms of counter-discourse and changes to the criminal justice system are traced. Third, the proclivity of campaigning organisations to focus upon serious cases that involve lengthy sentences of imprisonment is explored to indicate the possible factors behind such an approach. Finally, an assessment of the achievements and limitations of existing forms of campaigning discourse against miscarriages of justice/the wrongful conviction of the innocent is conducted.

Campaigning organisations: diversity and complementarity

A whole host of diverse groups and organisations exist to support alleged victims, provide information that might assist in overturning miscarriages of justice and/or actively campaign to reform the criminal justice system to eliminate miscarriages of justice. These include United Against Injustice (UAI) (United Against Injustice, 2006), a federal system of miscarriage of justice organisations which support more than a single case in their geographical location. The organisations affiliated to UAI, which generally provide support to victims and their families through regular meetings and information-sharing, include Manchester-based INNOCENT, Liverpool-based Merseyside Against Injustice (MAI), Falsely Accused Youth Leaders (FAYL), Yorkshire and Humberside Against Injustice (YHAI), Kent Against Injustice (KAI) and London Against Injustice (LAI) (United Against Injustice, 2006). Besides these are a varied host of national miscarriage of justice organisations and/or support groups including Miscarriage of Justice Organisation (MOJO), a human-rights-based organisation founded in 1999 by Paddy Hill (of the Birmingham Six case) and Mike O'Brien (of the Cardiff Newsagent Three case) to support miscarriage of justice victims and their families, and to attempt to redress the lack of welfare and aftercare provision for the wrongly imprisoned (Miscarriage of Justice Organisation, 2000), Miscarriages of Justice UK (MOJUK), which provides details of a large number of alleged miscarriage of justice cases, works closely with prisoners and produces bulletins and newsletters which circulate and co-ordinate information to and between campaign groups/organisations (see Miscarriages of Justice UK, 2006), The Portia Campaign, which specialises in cases in which mothers are accused or jailed for murder or manslaughter of their children in contested circumstances (see The Portia Campaign, 2006), and, The Five Percenters, a cause-specific organisation that was established in January 1998 to campaign on behalf of people wrongly accused and/or convicted of 'shaken baby syndrome' (causing brain injury by shaking their baby) (The Five Percenters, 2006). In addition, to the foregoing, specific miscarriage of justice groups and organisations that campaign exclusively for alleged victims and their families and friends,

there are a whole range of organisations concerned with false allega-
tions of physical and/or sexual abuse as a specific cause of miscarriage
of justice. These include False Allegations Support Organisation (FASO)
(False Allegations Support Organisation, 2006) and Falsely Accused
Carers and Teachers (FACT) (see Falsely Accused Carers and Teachers,
2006) Support Organisation for Falsely Accused People (SOFAP)
(Support Organisation for Falsely Accused People, 2006), Supporting
All Falsely Accused with Reference Information (SAFARI) (Supporting
All Falsely Accused with Reference Information, 2006).[28]

On top of the groups and organisations that specifically campaign
against miscarriages of justice, whether on a general or cause related
basis, there are a number of civil liberties, human rights, anti-racist and
feminist organisations that campaign against and/or support alleged
miscarriage of justice cases that occur in England and Wales.[29] These
include, Liberty, founded in 1934 and one of the oldest human rights
and civil liberties organisations in the UK, that campaigns on a wide
range of civil liberties and human rights issues – from privacy to free
speech and protest, anti-terror legislation and young people's rights.
Liberty lobby Parliament, attempting to expose laws that undermine
civil liberties and human rights and to correct them (Liberty, 2007);
JUSTICE, founded in 1957, is an all-party, law reform and human
rights organisation that works to improve the legal system and the
quality of justice (JUSTICE, 2007);[30] the Institute of Race Relations
(IRR), an umbrella for campaigning organisations as well as a 'think
tank', that campaigns against injustices and miscarriages of justice
stemming from 'racial oppression' (Institute of Race Relations, 2007);
Campaign Against Racism and Fascism (CARF), which also supports
miscarriage of justice campaigns where the possible cause is 'racism'
(Campaign Against Racism and Fascism, 2007); Amnesty International,
the world-wide human rights organisation, which campaigns against
miscarriages of justice that derive from human rights abuses (Amnesty
International, 2007); National Civil Rights Movement (NCRM), which
supports cases of injustice that are caused by an infringement of civil
liberties (National Civil Rights Movement, 2007); Statewatch, which
extensively reports on miscarriages of justice deriving from deviations
from civil liberties (Statewatch, 2007); Justice For Women (JFW), a feminist organisation that campaigns to reveal miscarriages of justice that
are caused through what they term 'the gendered limitations of existing legal defences to a charge of murder for women who have fought
back against or killed violent male partners'. JFW was established in
1990 in Leeds, there are now groups in London, Leeds, Norwich and

Manchester (see Justice For Women, 2007); and, Southall Black Sisters (SBS), an Asian women's organisation based in Southall, London, SBS are concerned with miscarriages of justice that might affect black and Asian women in the areas of domestic violence and racism (Southall Black Sisters, 2007; Benn, 2000; Dunne, 1997).

The range and diversity of the groups and organisations that exist to support alleged victims of miscarriages of justice renders any attempt to discern a universal underpinning identity or voice which speaks on behalf of all miscarriage of justice groups/organisations profoundly problematic. Moreover, within and between the various, and sometimes competing and conflicting, organisations that campaign against miscarriages of justice there are ostensibly different affiliations and/or motivations. As such, any attempt to construct a single campaigning identity or consensual campaigning/victim support voice would almost inevitably produce a 'straw' construction that would not be representative of any particular group or organisation and with which none of the groups or organisations would be likely to identify. Yet, the Citizen's Commission on Scandals in Justice (CCSJ) (2006: 1) defines a miscarriage of justice in a way that seems to encapsulate the operational practice of victim support and campaigning organisations in the following terms: 'A miscarriage of justice comes into being when a Single Judge and/or the Full Court of Appeal or the Criminal Cases Review Commission reject an appeal or refuse a referral in circumstances where doubts remain as to the Appellant's guilt'. A problem with such a conception is that it runs counter to the reality of miscarriages of justice as determined by the criminal appeals system. Instead, as the test of a miscarriage of justice is a successful appeal, a miscarriage of justice can be said to officially *come into being* – is recorded in the official statistics on successful appeals as such – when a Single Judge and/or a Full Court of Appeal *allows* an appeal or when the CCRC refer a case back to the appeal courts which is, subsequently, successful in appeal. Further, it takes no account whatsoever of mundane and routine successful appeals.

The existing organisations against miscarriages of justice have two further things in common. They are not at all interested in victims who may have been wrongly convicted for 'technical' reasons, i.e. convicted of murder when they think it should have been manslaughter. On the contrary, and in keeping with popular notions of miscarriages of justice, the consensual *primary* aim that is collectively expressed among and between campaign organisations is to support/campaign for those believed to be factually innocent.[31] This is evident in the following quotations, representative of the general campaigning organisation stance:

> INNOCENT exists to support people who have been wrongly convicted, because they did not commit the crimes for which they were convicted (INNOCENT, 2006).

> F.A.C.T....believe that the vast majority of complaints of child abuse that are made against carers and teachers have been exaggerated, and that significant numbers of them have been induced, fabricated, or are entirely false (Falsely Accused Carers and Teachers, 2006).

> *faso* is a refuge of the innocent, not a safe house for abusers in denial (False Allegations Support Organisation, 2006).

> The Miscarriages of Justice Organisation is...dedicated to assisting innocent people both in prison and after their release (Miscarriages of Justice Organisation, Scotland, 2006).

A major flaw, however, with the emphasis on the support of the alleged victims of miscarriages of justice who are believed to be factually innocent is that such a state is almost impossible to prove. The quashing of a previous criminal conviction by the appeal courts cannot be uncritically accepted as *prima facie* evidence of factual innocence. The judicial pronouncements of the appeal courts are framed entirely within the parameters of the rules, procedures and/or practices of the criminal justice system, within which, the judgement of the Crown Court is whether a criminal defendant is 'guilty' or 'not guilty'. As this relates to the CACD, it, too, is not an attempt to determine the guilt or innocence of the appellant, but rather to determine whether the previously obtained criminal conviction is 'safe' or 'unsafe'. This does not provide the kind of factual objective knowledge required to prove or state the factual innocence of victims of miscarriages of justice that is both, generally, assumed and claimed by organisations that campaign against exceptional miscarriages of justice. Accordingly, any attempt to determine factual or truthful innocence in a system where even the 'guilt' of a criminal suspect can be conceptualised as a legal technicality can be conceived as an almost impossible pursuit. To be sure, the discursive rules and practices that together comprise England and Wales' current criminal justice arrangements can be conceived to *technologise* the innocence of criminal defendants beyond such reach.[32]

Campaigning organisations and governmentality – observing the observers

The various organisations that campaign against miscarriages of justice also display a diverse range of *motivations*: there are organisations that are concerned with the general problem of miscarriages of justice whatever the specific cause, and provide a support network for the families and friends of victims, essentially the organisations affiliated to UAI – INNOCENT, MAI, KAI, YHAI, LAI; there are organisations that are concerned with false allegations of sexual abuse such as FASO, SOFAP; there are organisations specifically concerned with the vulnerability of teachers and/or care workers to be falsely accused and/or convicted of sexual and/or physical abuse, for example, FACT; there is an organisation that campaigns for the provision of welfare upon the release of the wrongfully imprisoned (MOJO); there is an organisation that is specifically concerned with the associated problems of infant mortality and its potential to be a mistaken cause of miscarriages of justice (The Portia Campaign); there is an organisation concerned with miscarriages of justice that accompany mistaken diagnoses of 'Shaken Baby Syndrome' (The Five Percenters); there are organisations concerned with racism as a cause of miscarriages of justice (IRR, CARF); there is an organisation against how miscarriages of justice befall women because the law represents the interests of men (JFW); there is an organisation against miscarriages of justice against black and Asian women (SBS); and, there are organisations that stand against miscarriages of justice that derive from failures to adhere to civil liberties and human rights (Amnesty International, Statewatch, National Civil Rights Movement).

Taken together, these groups and/or organisations that strive to achieve exceptional miscarriages of justice can be conceived as covering the most problematic aspects of the existing criminal justice system that *may be* (are claimed to be) in need of amendment. What I mean by this is that campaigning organisations are the discoverers of the causes of miscarriages of justice in the sense that already acknowledged causes of miscarriages are accounted for by the existing procedures through which routine and mundane successful appeals are achieved. Campaigning organisations support alleged causes of miscarriages of justice that are not yet officially acknowledged. To be sure, exceptional miscarriages of justice are precisely *not* about working within the existing legal agenda. Rather, they are about working *outside* of the general confines of the existing 'letter of the law' in attempts to ascertain the causes and/or the reasons why alleged innocent victims of miscarriages of justice were unsuccessful in their routine and/or mundane appeals. Following which, campaigning organisations can then turn their attention towards a *secondary* consensual aim of attempting to effect corrective legislative changes to the criminal justice system in the hope that such identifiable causes are not (or are at least less of) a cause in the future. Taking another quotation to provide a textual feel for a specific campaigning voice, MAI state that it 'is *dedicated to bringing about change in the current criminal justice system* by campaigning against improper practices by the judiciary and the police (Merseyside Against Injustice, 2002 my emphasis). Similarly, FACT state that it 'exists to support carers and teachers falsely accused and/or wrongly convicted of child abuse, and to lobby for change in the criminal justice system (Falsely Accused Carers and Teachers, 2006; see also The Portia Campaign, 2002).

As such, attempts to understand the motivations of the organisations that campaign against miscarriages of justice should not merely view them from the perspective of their ostensible differences. Such differences are important in terms of the production of different images of miscarriages of justice and the different audiences that they represent. However, it is also appropriate to conceive the way that campaigning organisations aggregately or collectively deal with miscarriages of justice as intrinsically related to the governmentality of the criminal justice system. Campaigning organisations can be conceived as fulfiling their governmentality mandate as they engage in a power struggle to change the criminal justice system for the better for all. They can be seen as 'watchdogs of government' on behalf of the governed in their support of claims of miscarriages of justice that fail to be overturned through the existing appeals mechanisms. This extends Foucault's notion of 'disciplinary society' by clarifying the role of the other side of power relations, the side of the governed.

In particular, for Foucault (1977), 'disciplinary society' requires surveillance knowledge, by which those to be 'known' and acted upon, worked into the form required, are made 'visible' and knowable to government. A possible limitation in Foucault's (1977) original analysis of disciplinary society, however, is that he saw the traffic of surveillance travelling only one way, towards the subject upon whom the technique is exercised. He failed to see (or if he did to develop the idea) that the subjects of surveillance have the reciprocal power to 'observe the observer', to know, to visualise, and to effect significant exercises of governmental power, too. Instead, Foucault (1977) presented a rather negative vision that may seem contrary to the argument put forward here that the observed (the governed) can, indeed, observe the observers (government). In the light of his later thoughts on governmentality and bio-power, however, Foucault addressed the limits of his earlier thoughts on disciplinary society at least acknowledging that the governed are not entirely passive in the processes of governmentality. As Colin Gordon (1991) noted, 'in his American essays and interviews, on his views about power, freedom and hope, Foucault seems to have found fault afterwards at least with his rhetoric in [his analysis of discipline and disciplinary power], where this may have seemed to give an impression of certain uses of power as having an almost absolute capability to tame and subject power' (Gordon, 1991: 5). Consequently, Foucault (cited Gordon, 1991: 5) affirmed that:

> ...power is only power (rather than mere physical force or violence) when addressed to individuals who are free to act in one way or another. Power is defined as 'actions on others' actions': that is, it presupposes rather than annuls their capacity as agents; it acts upon, and through, an open set of practical and ethical possibilities. Hence, although power is an omnipresent dimension in human relations, power in a society is never a fixed and closed regime, but rather an endless and open strategic game.

This analysis of the role of campaigning organisations as observers of the observers or governors of government extends this still further. Campaigning organisations from this perspective are inherently and intrinsically about the production of evidence that gives power to forms of knowledge of previously unaccounted for limitations with the criminal justice system at any particular historical moment which come to fruition when cases are overturned and, hence, officially acknowledged. Such knowledge being expressly produced as part of a struggle for power to effect changes to the criminal justice system in response to apparent miscarriages of justice which find life through successful appeals. As Foucault (1977: 27–28) noted, 'power-knowledge, the processes and struggles that traverse it and of which it is made up...determines the forms and possible domains of knowledge.' To be sure, power can be conceived to work both ways in a system where power is relational between government and governed. Just as government apply forms of surveillance in attempts to know the governed so, too, the governed, in this case represented by campaigning organisations against miscarriages of justice, utilise claims of miscarriages of justice as part of the surveillance of, and attempt to, improve the criminal justice system for the benefit of all.

This inverts Foucault's (1977) analogy of the panopticon, revealing the way in which the governed can be conceived to 'discipline' government, hence, working the criminal justice system into a more appropriate form for the benefit of all. For Foucault (1977), Bentham's design for the panopticon was an important effect of 'disciplinary power' and a significant contribution to the 'machinery' required for its functioning. Indeed, the panopticon was the exemplary technique through which disciplinary power is able to function. Essentially, the panopticon consisted of a central tower surrounded by a circular building of cells, each intended to house a prisoner. The panopticon allowed a political economy of criminal supervision; an efficiency of prison population control; for the continuous observation of inmates, while simultaneously requiring few supervisory resources. The guards in their central tower could see into each of the separate cells in which the prisoners were held. But they themselves could not be seen. The result was that the inmates never knew when they were being watched; this became internalised; and they came to 'watch' themselves. Furthermore, the guards too, were under surveillance, being observed through a series of mirrors: no one can escape the 'gaze' of surveillance. Power exercised in this way is not a property, but rather is *produced* through the mechanism of surveillance itself. 'Hence', for Foucault, 'the major *effect* of the panopticon' was:

> ...to induce in the inmate a state of conscious and permanent visibility that assures the automatic functioning of power; so to arrange things that the surveillance is permanent in its effects, even if it is discontinuous in its actions; that the perfection of power should tend to render its actual exercise unnecessary; that this architectural apparatus should be a machine for creating and sustaining a power relation independent of the person who exercises it; in short, that the inmates should be caught up in a power situation of which they are themselves the bearers (Foucault, 1977: 201).

For Foucault the panopticon represents a stage in the 'normalisation' of individuals in post-sovereign societies which is necessary for the government of 'life-processes' and central to the exercise of bio-power. He argued, the investigation of the dividing line between 'normal' and 'abnormal' is crucial in a social organisation dedicated to the administration of life. It finds one such application in the study of criminals – their impulses, psycho-social make-up, and so on. This form of study harnesses general knowledges about any individual: 'The individual and the knowledge that may be gained of him (sic) belong to this production' (Foucault, 1977: 194). From the perspective developed here, campaigning organisations can, equally, be viewed as investigating the dividing line between the normal 'carriage of justice' and the abnormal 'miscarriage of justice' in their participation in the administration of the governmentality of the criminal justice system. Moreover, the various alleged problems that campaigning organisations stand against (alleged causes of miscarriages of justice that have not yet been proven by real cases of successful appeal) can be conceived as rendering the criminal justice system in a state of conscious and permanent visibility that assures the automatic functioning of the power of the governed in the governmentality of the criminal justice system. The criminal justice system and the knowledge that may be gained about it, likewise, belong to this production.

Why the focus on exceptional cases?

The governmentality of the criminal justice system highlighted the extent to which all debates on miscarriages of justice have, hitherto, been very firmly focused towards an historically specific, exceptional case or small group of exceptional cases of successful appeal. In accordance with this trend, an analysis of the focus of organisations that campaign against miscarriages in England and Wales shows that they, too, are also only overwhelmingly concerned with individual exceptional cases of alleged or suspected miscarriages of justice, as opposed to the general problem of miscarriages of justice. Such cases are generally for serious criminal offences, murder, rape, armed robbery, and so on, as opposed to apparently less serious crimes such as shop lifting, parking offences, drink driving, and so on. They have often already failed in their routine and/or mundane appeals.[33] And, they continue to present concerns that innocent people continue to suffer the injustice of wrongful imprisonment. To be sure, campaigning organisations are, generally, in line with the following criteria constructed and applied by JUSTICE (before the establishment of the CCRC and they ceased to assist alleged innocent victims of wrongful conviction/imprisonment) (1989: 1–2):

- the allegation is of actual, rather than technical, innocence;
- lengthy terms of imprisonment of four years or more were being served;

- no other legal help was available to the prisoner; and,
- an investigation might achieve something, given the present operation of the appellate courts.

This criteria works from the premise that the length of time needed to investigate cases, along with the delays in getting potentially meritorious cases back to the CACD, enforces the need to focus on serious criminal convictions with substantial prison sentences. There are a number of other interrelated reasons for this.

First and foremost, the release of individuals that are thought to be wrongly imprisoned and/or changes to the criminal justice system is not effected though theoretical generalisation. They are effected through *real individual cases* in which *real individual people* can be *shown* to have been denied their legal and/or political rights. Within such constraints, campaigning organisations have found it necessary on pragmatic grounds to focus on individual cases and strive to get the cases that they support back within the given legal agenda. Moreover, because of such parameters, it is not so much that campaigns against miscarriages of justice are not interested in routine or mundane successful appeals. Rather, campaigning organisations can be said to be less concerned with, apparently, less serious cases that can be remedied by existing appellate procedures in the pragmatic interests of directing their efforts and priorities into those cases in which alleged innocent people have exhausted their appeal rights and remain wrongly imprisoned.

Another factor in the campaigning focus on cases of wrongful imprisonment for serious criminal offences relates to the moral commitment of campaign organisations. Victims of exceptional miscarriages of justice, who have previously failed in their routine or mundane appeals and who also experience wrongful imprisonment and denial of liberty, are of the greatest priority to victim support/campaigning organisations as they are thought to have suffered the greatest wrong and/or the most harm. Accordingly, it is, perhaps, not surprising that campaigning organisations do not look at the phenomenon of miscarriages of justice as a statistical whole and include routine and mundane successful appeals into their analyses, as such cases are routinely and/or mundanely taken care of and accounted for. Moreover, it might conceivably be thought that if campaigns paid attention to already achieved successful appeals then attention would be diverted away from the cases that they assist.

There is also a temporal aspect whereby campaigns focus on serious cases of alleged miscarriages of justice that involve substantial prison sentences. In the same way that JUSTICE decided which cases it could assist, the voluntary nature of campaigning organisations, their lack of staff and resources has meant that the volume of requests to investigate alleged miscarriages of justice has also had to be limited to those cases that carry substantial prison sentences.

A further possible factor that might account for the campaign focus on exceptional cases probably relates to economic realities. Campaigning organisations are run on a voluntary basis with meagre budgets. They rely upon the contributions of supporters and upon fundraising activities. In such a context, and in the context of the other procedural, pragmatic, moral and temporal reasons for the focus on exceptional cases, exceptional cases in which the innocent are wrongly imprisoned remain the primary focus.

There are, however, profound limitations with the focus on exceptional cases, indicating that the scope of campaigning organisations in the part that they play in governing government has not gone far enough. Firstly, it is not always the case that the victims of exceptional cases of wrongful imprisonment necessarily suffer the most 'serious' harm. Even some of the most seemingly mundane cases (e.g. miscarriages of justice for shop lifting and/or drink-driving) can contain a significant and often comparable amount of harm for the individual victims concerned (attempted suicide, mental health problems, imprisonment, loss of jobs and reputation) (developed further in the chapter on the contribution of zemiology below). Secondly, the tendency for campaigning organisations to focus on individual cases, whether successful or not, will tend to be less successful in disturbing the broader context of the existing exercise and functioning of power in the criminal justice sphere that they may do if they were to include all cases in summary courts where currently over 98 per cent of all criminal cases are dealt with. Thus, campaign organisations provide no real sense of the everyday nature of miscarriages of justice; of their routine and/or mundane occurrence. Moreover, by focusing entirely upon exceptional cases, organisations against miscarriages of justice actually reinforce the perception that miscarriages of justice are an intermittent, high profile phenomenon that affects only a small number of victims which serves to conceal the harm experienced by the thousands of routine and/or mundane victims each year.

The production of the raw material for governmentality

There is a tradition among those concerned about miscarriages of justice to construct and deploy forms of scenario-based counter-discourse on the potential problems that particular criminal legislation and proposed criminal legislation may contain and/or the potential harmful consequences that it may engender. When the Human Rights Act (1998) (HRA) was announced, for example, the organisation Liberty (1998) produced a briefing detailing a range of existing judicial procedures and/or police investigative practices that *might* be conceived to contravene the HRA and the *possible* challenges that could be made under the various Articles of the Act. Despite the intellectual validity of the various critiques, Liberty's (1998) analysis, as are all such counter-discursive productions, was regarded by the legal system at that stage as entirely speculative, as fictitious. What were needed were *real* cases with *real* people who could demonstrate that they had *really* been denied their ascribed rights and/or freedoms. Governmentality does not intervene in response to speculations of potential (or even inevitable) future causes of miscarriage of justice and/or harm. Instead, it *requires* miscarriages of justice/harm to be proven in concrete cases, whereupon what was formally considered as criminal justice system fiction is *transformed* into criminal justice system 'fact'.[34] This indicates a form of 'due process' in the logic of the processes of governmentality and changes to the criminal justice system.

To stay with the same examples in the previous chapter, throughout the 240-year campaign to abolish capital punishment[35] there were many suspicions and allegations that people had been killed following judicial 'error', and posthumous pardons were a common feature of the 19th century (Pattenden, 1996: 5–33). Despite the fact that any human system can make mistakes, and that miscarriages of justice do occur and, therefore, some victims will have, inevitably, suffered capital punishment in 'error', this was not enough to justify ending the death penalty. What was required to abolish the death penalty was a case in which it was indisputable that such a judicial 'error' had occurred and that a real person had really lost his/her life. The case of Timothy Evans *transformed* the criminal justice system fiction that some people *could have been killed* in 'error' into the criminal justice system 'fact' that people really *were being killed* because of criminal justice system 'error'. This provided the necessary counter-discursive force required to induce a public crisis of confidence in the continued validity of the law of capital punishment. It effected the abolition of capital punishment. It brought a conclusion to the campaign against capital punishment.

Similarly, prior to the introduction of PACE (1984) there were many criticisms of the unjustness of police investigations. Again, however, what were required were 'hard' cases which provided the necessary evidence that real people were really being subjected to police mal or bad practice, or were victims of miscarriages of justice due to poor police investigations. Until which, such critical discourse was generally regarded as speculative, as fictitious, unable to disturb the existing regime of truth. With the Confait Affair, however, the necessary evidence that the police were, indeed, routinely in breach of the informal Judges' Rules was presented in an indisputable way with the necessary force (power) to effect the changes that so many had campaigned for and for so long.

This indicates the moral dimension of legislative changes to the criminal justice system to prevent miscarriages of justice, as the wrong/harm must be proven. It, also, emphasises a distinction between the morality of existing exercises of criminal justice system power and what popular discourses might expect. Despite the inevitability that the criminal justice system *can* sometimes get it wrong, and that as a consequence innocent people *will* inevitably be wrongly convicted and/or harmed, governmentality as a process allows such a system to continue until such time as that knowledge has been substantiated, as a precursor to the exercise of governmental power in the realm of criminal justice. The fundamental difference between the *morality* of the application of the rules of the criminal justice system and that of the morality of the governed as represented by victim support/campaigning organisations is evident in the following quotations, the first is representative of the stance of criminal justice system, the second illustrative of the stance of the governed:

> It is better to keep innocent men (sic) in prison, than to let them go free and bring the system into disrepute (Lord Denning, former Master of the Rolls cited Miscarriages of Justice UK, 2002a).

> We campaign...on...cases that we *believe* to be miscarriages of justice (South Wales Liberty, 2002 my emphasis).[36]

In assessing the above quotations it is acknowledged that the criminal justice system operates on the assumption that without the formalised *rule of law* itself there is no such thing as 'justice'. However, the above quotations emphasise that the morality of the existing application of criminal justice can be conceived as the adherence to the rules of law without question, whether or not those rules are just or fair in the everyday popular notion, and without regard to the harmful consequences that law might engender. From such a standpoint, miscarriages of justice and the harmful consequences that derive from previous mistakes or which emerge from hindsight cause little concern to those wedded to the criminal justice system. A pertinent example is the Birmingham Six's attempt to sue the West Midlands Serious Crime Squad for the beatings that they had suffered before five of them 'confessed' (see, for example, Sedley, 1999). It has since transpired that the West Midlands Serious Crime Squad were responsible for dozens of exceptional wrongful convictions (see, for example, Burrell & Bennetto, 1999). In his judgement, however, in which he refused their application, Lord Denning ('the people's judge') appeared to be more concerned with the consequences for the criminal justice system and the police than with the due process of law and the possible validity of the allegations:

> Just consider the course of events if this action is allowed to proceed to trial...If the six men win, it will mean that the police were guilty of perjury, that they were guilty of violence and threats, that the confessions were involuntary and were improperly admitted in evidence and that the convictions were erroneous. That would mean that the Home Secretary would either have to recommend they be pardoned or he would have to remit the case to the Court of Appeal. This is such an appalling vista that every sensible person in the land would say: It cannot be right that these actions should go any further (Denning cited Mullin, 1986: 216).

To give Denning the benefit of the doubt, the above, now notorious judicial assertion, may, perhaps, be read as meaning that a criminal case could not be settled in a civil court. However, there can be no such confusion with a later remark by Denning about the Birmingham Six, who by this time were looking increasingly likely to overturn their wrongful convictions: 'We shouldn't have all these campaigns to get the Birmingham Six released if they'd been hanged. They'd have been forgotten and the whole community would have been satisfied' (Denning cited Dyer, 1999d). Whether or not the 'whole community would have been satisfied', the hanging of the Birmingham Six would have been a judicial 'error' from the perspective of popular discourse.

An 'error' that, apparently, would not have 'troubled' Lord Denning as 'donning his black cap to pass a death sentence had never troubled him' (Denning cited Dyer, 1999d), for such a 'judicial error' would have been entirely legal.

Against this, the morality of campaigns against miscarriages of justice is expressed on a number of different levels and in a number of different ways. At a semantic level the names of the campaigning organisations can be said to be *moral signifiers*. For example, the word 'injustice' in 'United Against Injustice', the overarching federal system of organisations, is by definition synonymous with 'unfair' or 'wrong'. So, the explicit message is that those affiliated to UAI are 'United Against Unfairness', or, 'United Against Wrong'. Similarly, the campaign organisation 'Conviction', which helped to establish 'Innocent' and UAI, can be read as synonymous with the act of being 'convinced' or holding a firmly held 'belief'. Being 'convinced' and having a 'belief' in this context meaning, being convinced and/or believing in the innocence of the alleged victims of wrongful conviction that are the focus of the campaigns. Likewise, the campaign organisation 'INNOCENT', one of the longest standing and most influential organisations affiliated to UAI, can be read as synonymous with the absence of 'evil', 'sinless', 'blameless' and/or 'pure'. This again emphasises the moral foundations of campaigning organisations against miscarriages of justice, as well as further emphasising their approach and attitude to the people that they represent.

Along with the morality of campaigning organisations is a form of *integrity* that also differs from the form of integrity evident in criminal justice system discourse. Integrity within criminal justice system discourse can be conceived as the attainment of the operational goals of the agencies of the criminal justice system (police, CPS) in the context of the logic of an adversarial system. Often this can mean an attempt to prove the guilt and/or obtain the conviction of criminal defendants, whether or not they are actually guilty of the offences with which they have been charged or tried (JUSTICE, 1989: 23–41). This is evident in the degree to which the police or CPS can break the stated rules of the criminal justice system without a detrimental effect on the 'truth' produced by the agents of the criminal justice system and the ability of such 'truth' to secure the conviction of the innocent. For example, the rules that govern how to obtain confession evidence are routinely transgressed, but this does not generally disqualify what are essentially illegitimately obtained 'confessions'. On the contrary, Green's (1997: 8–12) researches would indicate that the working premise of those charged with the job of obtaining confession evidence is that criminal suspects are inevitably not telling the truth; that when they deny their alleged part in the criminal offences for which they are being questioned they (suspects) are, in fact, employing strategies of *resistance* to conceal the truth, i.e. their guilt. In such a context, counter-strategies are employed to overcome the suspects' resistance and reveal the concealed truth of their guilt. This often results in the transgression of the supposed safeguards that were designed to protect innocent suspects from inappropriate pressure or inducement (e.g. beaten confessions, charge, plea and sentence bargains, planting of evidence, and so on), but the evidence so obtained is often regarded by the courts as the most truthful. The reasoning is: why would someone admit to something that they didn't do, whatever their treatment or inducement?

Alternatively, campaigning integrity dictates that campaigns are not just about 'winning' a quashed criminal conviction for the alleged victims that they represent. On the contrary, integrity in campaigning discourse is about ensuring that only truly innocent people are successful as a consequence of the support provided by the campaigning organisations. This is most evident in the following quotation that can be read as a disclaimer to the continued support of those who might allege to be innocent victims of miscarriages of justice, but who might in reality be guilty, or at the least, highly suspect:

> FACT is against ALL forms of child abuse, however, *in the interests of justice and truth*, we must ensure that our legal system protects both the falsely accused and innocent, as well as punishing the guilty (Falsely Accused Carers and Teachers, 2002 my emphasis).

The integrity displayed in the above quotation is also displayed by all of the various campaigning organisations (see, for example, False Allegations Support Organisation, 2002; False Allegations Support Organisation, 2002b; Green, 2000b: 1; The Five Percenters, 2002; United Campaign Against False Allegations of Abuse, 2000). This is highly understandable, perhaps even morally pragmatic. When a campaigning organisation or a campaigning individual, especially an organisation or an individual that has previously been successful in overturning an exceptional miscarriage of justice case, agrees to support an alleged or suspected miscarriage of justice case, that case is immediately afforded a kind of moral endorsement. Following his expositions of the Evans-Christie Affair and the eventual posthumous pardon of Timothy Evans, Sir Ludovic Kennedy, for instance, established a reputation for correcting miscarriages of justice that adds weight to any cause to which he becomes involved with[37] (see, for example, Kennedy, 2002; Berlins, 2002a; Ingrams, 2001; Greenslade, 1998; Hardy, 1999). Similarly, the *Rough Justice* team (see Hill, Young & Sargant, 1985) and David Jessel's *Trial and Error* series (see Jessel, 1994) were widely regarded as emblematic of the innocence of the alleged miscarriage of justice victims in the cases that they chose to investigate[38] (see also Gibson, 1999).

As this relates to the important issue of legal representation, campaigning organisations are keen to use solicitors and barristers that have confirmed their moral stance and integrity in previously overturning exceptional miscarriages of justice. In terms of solicitors, Gareth Pierce (Judith Ward; Guildford Four; Birmingham Six; Cardiff Newsagent Three; Frank Johnson; Satpal Ram), Campbell Malone (Stefan Kiszco; Kevin Callan; John Brannan) and Jim Nichol (Bridgewater Four, Colin Wallace, Peter Fell) stand out. In terms of Barristers, Michael Mansfield QC[39] (Judith Ward, Birmingham Six; Tottenham Three; Bridgewater Four; Gurnos Three) would be right at the top of most campaigning organisations' wish list. As Mathiesen (1974) noted, 'grass roots' campaigns can be effective for direct victims of injustice when they establish what he termed 'horizontal contacts' among like-minded individuals in a variety of key positions in the power nexus.

This emphasises that the moral stakes of campaigns against miscarriages of justice can be conceived of as extremely high. If a campaigning organisation or campaigning individual with a reputation for overturning miscarriages of justice were to continue to support an alleged victim no longer *believed* to be innocent, or perhaps discovered to be actually guilty, then the integrity of the organisation would be immediately called into question. As a consequence, other cases supported by the campaigning organisation/campaigning individual would be brought into disrepute.

This also emphasises another crucial difference between criminal justice system discourse and campaigning discourse. Criminal justice system discourse is adversarial, within which miscarriages of justice, mundane, routine and exceptional, are inevitable as defenders 'succeed' in the acquittal of the factually guilty and prosecutors 'succeed' in convicting the innocent. Against this, campaigning organisations can be conceived as not adversarial at all. They are entirely about truth, about social justice, fairness and harm avoidance, including an attempt to avoid even the most apparently speculative or fictitious harm. From such a standpoint, whether or not the analysis of future harm is highly speculative, campaigning organisations regard it as yet to be proven fact, their task, then, being to set about proving it through real cases which give voice to sub-jugated discourses of miscarriages of justice. Once proved, the aim then is to campaign to effect changes of the criminal justice system as part of the on-going modification of the criminal justice system to reduce the possibility of harm to other innocent members of the public.

Achievements and limitations

On a qualitative and fairly straightforward level, successful campaigns achieve successful appeals for individuals in cases that had previously been unsuccessful in their mundane or routine appeals. In so doing, campaigning organisations contribute to the release from prison of victims of miscarriages of justice for serious criminal offences that might otherwise not be acknowledged nor remedied; they reunite families and friends; they contribute to the restoration of damaged reputations; and, they help to achieve financial compensation for exceptional victims of wrongful imprisonment. In addition, as illustrated in the last chapter, if the particular exceptional miscarriage of justice case is one that provides evidence of a previously unacknowledged 'error' with the criminal justice process, then campaigning organisations also contribute to the achievement of changes to the criminal justice system to overturn future miscarriages of justice of the same sort through mundane and routine routes.

However, when campaigns are successful in contributing to the production of exceptional miscarriages of justice that would otherwise have gone unacknowledged and/or unremedied they can be conceived from a certain perspective as contributing to the *legitimacy* of the very system that they are in programmatic opposition to (see, for example, Hillyard & Tombs, 1999: 21). It could be argued that campaigning voices actually legitimise the system that they purport to stand against as they work within the given legal agenda. Miscarriages of justice, exceptional or otherwise, are entirely legalistically defined. An alleged or suspected miscarriage is always provisional unless and/or until the appeal courts quash a criminal conviction that was previously obtained. And, when successful, campaigning organisations produce the vital cases that back-up the knowledge of the most significant systemic 'errors' and/or 'failings' in the criminal justice process in need of modification, which from a certain perspective inevitably strengthens the system (see, for example, George, 1991).

A problem with the possible conception that campaigning organisations actually or inadvertently contribute to the legitimacy of the criminal justice system is that campaigns that are successful in overturning previously unsuccessful cases through the identification of previously unrecognised faults in the system (or, more likely proving previously unacknowledged faults), in effect, contribute to *changing* the nature of the criminal justice system. In so doing, campaign organisations do not work *inside* the legal agenda, but on the *outside*, fulfilling their role as watchdogs of the criminal justice system for the governed. When campaigning organisations take up cases that have previously been unsuccessful in their mundane and/or routine appeals, the legal agenda has been exhausted. For example, prior to the introduction of the Court of Criminal Appeal off the back of the Beck case, officially acknowledged miscarriages of justice simply did not exist. Without an appeals system there were no successful appeals. With the establishment of a court capable of hearing appeals in criminal cases, then, a fundamentally different system of criminal justice was *created* that introduced miscarriages of justice into socio-legal reality as an official phenomenon. In the same way, the successful campaign to abolish capital punishment through the exemplary counter-discourse of the exceptional cases of Evans, Bentley and Ellis created a fundamentally different system of criminal justice than a system that contained capital punishment. In this sense, despite the fact that the criminal justice system seems not only to survive exceptional miscarriages of justice, but the relations of power also appear to remain unchanged by the changes to the criminal justice system, a new legislative regime of truth has been established (cf. Foucault, 1980a: 122–123).

Hence, campaigns that help to produce exceptional miscarriages of justice can also be conceived to be successful on a quantitative level. Campaigns that successfully overturn previously unsuccessful cases and then effect changes to the criminal justice system can also be conceived as providing the very procedures through which mundane and/or routine miscarriages of justice are determined in the future. Consequently, all appeals against criminal conviction that are successful, mundane, routine and exceptional, are rooted in the Beck case that provided the exemplary counter-discourse of the shortcomings of a criminal justice system without an appeal facility. Similarly, all of the mundane and/or routine successful appeals against police contraventions of codes of good conduct contained in PACE (1984) can be conceived to have their origins in the exceptional case of the Confait Affair and the interrogated false confessions of Lattimore, Leighton and Salih which effected PACE (1984). Therefore, exceptional miscarriages of justice should not be conceived as distinct or discrete from mundane and/or routine ones. Mundane, routine and exceptional successful appeals against criminal conviction are inextricably linked – today's exceptional miscarriage of justice case becomes the mundane and/or routine case of tomorrow. Thus, any measurement of the reduction of miscarriages of justice and their harmful consequences must be attributed, at least in part, to the campaigning organisations that help to achieve exceptional successful appeals and contribute to the changes to the criminal justice system.

This, however, has not been recognised by campaigning organisations who have, rather, continued in their counter-discursive struggle in the context of individual alleged cases of miscarriages of justice that have already been through the appeals process and/or exceptional cases of successful appeal that were products of the post-appeal procedures of the CCRC. Both of these strategies are inevitably weak. Alleged cases of miscarriage of justice that have failed in their existing appeal rights carry hardly any discursive force at all unless and until they achieve a successful appeal. Furthermore, exceptional successful appeals that are achieved through the post-appeal procedures of the CCRC are such a tiny aspect of all successful appeals that they, too, do not carry the discursive weight that they might if coupled with forms of counter-discourse of all successful appeals, which have their roots in the achievements of campaigns. Exceptional miscarriages are not discrete from mundane and/or routine miscarriages because they determine the routes through which they are successfully overturned. Moreover, the neglect of mundane and routine successful appeals serves to underestimate the true scale of miscarriages of justice. It renders the counter-discourse of campaigning organisations in a profoundly and unnecessarily feeble position. Alternatively, campaigning organisations could not simply focus on individual cases of alleged exceptional miscarriages of justice. They could make the connection that mundane and routine successful appeals are a consequence of exceptional successful appeals that provide the changes to the criminal justice system through which future mundane and routine miscarriages of justice are overturned. This would strengthen campaigning discourse and make clear the effect of the current scale of miscarriages of justice and the impact that this has on the legitimacy of the existing criminal justice system.

Conclusion

Contrary to conventional critical analyses, campaigning organisations against miscarriages of justice are not in radical opposition to government in their struggle to improve the criminal justice system. In their role as watchdogs for the governed, they represent a constant surveillance presence of alleged problems with the criminal justice system as part of the on-going governmentality project in this realm. They are part of the moral conscience of society in criminal justice matters, searching out apparent failings with the criminal justice system in need of change. Moreover, when campaigning organisations support previously unsuccessful cases of alleged miscarriage of justice that, subsequently, achieve a successful appeal they contribute to effecting significant changes to the criminal justice system. In this sense, campaigning organisations that contribute to the production of successful appeals that emphasise new 'errors' or 'failings' in the criminal justice process provide the raw material required to effect changes and provide the procedural infrastructure through which all future miscarriages of justice are successfully appealed and remedied.

Despite this, in their critiques of the criminal justice system, campaigning voices have, hitherto, not been very forceful, as they have primarily concentrated upon exceptional cases of wrongful imprisonment. As a result, they have not made the connection that mundane and routine successful appeals are a consequence of exceptional successful appeals that provide the changes to the criminal justice system through which future mundane and routine miscarriages of justice are overturned. They have not been able to comment more broadly on the procedures of the criminal justice system that produce wrongful convictions so mundanely and/or routinely (plea-bargaining, parole deal, time loss rule) which might not feature in the official statistics of successful appeals. Nor have existing configurations of victim support/ campaigning counter-discourse commented upon the forms of harm that accompanies mundane and/or routine miscarriages of justice. This renders critical voices against miscarriages of justice unnecessarily weakened.

Alternatively, organisations that seek to prevent or, at the very least, reduce the occurrence of miscarriages of justice could adopt a policy of incorporating all successful appeals within their gambit and conduct regular reviews or audits of the causes and harmful consequences of miscarriages of justice as evidenced by successful appeals. This would provide for a constant voice on miscarriages of justice to replace the intermittent murmurings that are currently only allowed to speak when high profile cases are overturned through exceptional extra-judicial means. It might lead to more effective changes to address and redress this acute social problem.

6
Academia

Introduction

This chapter turns the analysis of the governmentality of the criminal justice system in response to apparent miscarriages of justice over to the academic sphere. It conducts a general assessment of the forms of academic discourse that were specifically produced in response to the RCCJ, showing that academic voices are generally activated only following successful appeals in exceptional cases. At such times, however, academic discourse on miscarriages of justice is expressed in one of two general voices: on the one hand, academic voices responded to the RCCJ by recommending legislative solutions for the governmental correction of the aspects of criminal justice system that were of public concern. These academic voices against miscarriages of justice did not so much problematise the RCCJ and its outcomes but, rather, recommended practical solutions to apparent limits of the criminal justice system at the time. On the other hand, though, more critical academic voices on the RCCJ generally conceived it, collectively, as a 'failed' 'damage limitation exercise'. It is to these more critical forms of academic counter-discourse on miscarriages of justice that attention is focused to tease out a shared vision of power and reform of the criminal justice system and signal some of its main limitations. In particular, it is argued that the idea that changes to the criminal justice system in response to public crises of confidence are somehow to be regarded as 'failures' indicates a serious theoretical misconception of the intrinsic interrelations of power and knowledge and the due processes of the governmentality of the criminal justice system: changes to the criminal justice system in response to miscarriages of justice need not be conceived in entirely 'negative' terms. On the contrary, the more counter-discourse that is produced about alleged miscarriages of justice which find support in successful appeal cases, then, potentially, the more 'crises' of public confidence in the criminal justice system will be induced. And, in turn, the more problematic aspects of the criminal justice system will, possibly, be subjected to the governmentality processes, with the potential for changes for improvement.

The chapter proceeds in three parts. Firstly, the general academic response to miscarriages of justice is explicated. Secondly, a closer analysis of the forms of critical academic discourse that collectively responded to the RCCJ is conducted, and a shared conception of power discerned. Finally, an analysis of the forms of critical academic counter-discourse that responded to the RCCJ (1993) is undertaken to locate such forms of counter-discourse themselves within the processes of the governmentality of the criminal justice system.

The academic response

Despite the longevity of the miscarriage of justice problem (see Pattenden, 1996: 5–33) and the centrality of high profile miscarriage of justice cases in calls for law reform (Greer, 1994; Naughton, 2001), academic counter-discourse on the subject of miscarriages of justice in England and Wales is not generally produced and/or deployed in any systematic way.[40] Rather, it, too, has tended to be intermittently produced and deployed in response to the public crises of confidence that were induced by particular cases of successful appeal against criminal conviction that were overturned by post-appeal procedures – exceptional miscarriages of justice.

For instance, the Royal Commission on Criminal Procedure (RCCP) was established in response to the public crisis of confidence that surrounded the Confait Affair, which exemplified the need for police accountability, both in the interests of greater reliability of evidence and the enhancement of suspect's rights (Royal Commission on Criminal Procedure, 1981, para, 10.1). In particular, the Fisher (1977) inquiry into the case had been especially critical of the police practices that led to the wrongful convictions of the three youths – Colin Lattimore, Ronald Leighton and Ahmet Salih – for the murder of Maxwell Confait. The whole prosecution, argued Fisher, (1977) was geared simply to providing the case against the boys. In resolving the crisis, the government translated the RCCP's central recommendation into the Police and Criminal Evidence Act (1984) (PACE), which formalised the guidelines on police investigations.[41]

It is, perhaps, interesting to note that whilst the RCCP was sitting, a number of responses were presented by the critical academic community (see, for example, Baldwin & McConville, 1980; Irving & Hilgendorf, 1980). However, specific counter-discourse on miscarriages of justice did not appear again from the academic sphere until the establishment and Report of the RCCJ over a decade later, established is response to the public crisis of confidence (see Colvin, 1994) that followed the exceptional successful appeals of the Guildford Four, the Birmingham Six, and so on. Hillyard's (1994: 69) response to the RCCJ (unintentionally) highlights the intermittent appearance of academic counter-discourse on miscarriages of justice, 'it is some thirteen years since many of us were burning the midnight oil expressing our profound dissatisfaction with the Royal Commission on Criminal Procedure (1981)'. Since the counter-discursive response to the RCCJ, though, the critical community has generally been silent, presumably waiting for the next royal commission or committee of inquiry to 'burn the midnight oils' and 'voice' their dissatisfaction.

An immediate problem with this is that miscarriages of justice are not only an intermittent problem every decade or so or when an exceptional case is 'revealed' or when a royal commission is sitting. On the contrary, miscarriages of justice, as evidenced by successful appeals against criminal conviction – i.e. the number of times that the system itself indicates that it previously got it wrong – are a routine, even mundane feature of criminal justice in England and Wales, occurring an average of 18 times every working day. As such, the existing terrain of academic studies on miscarriage of justice overlooks the scale of the miscarriage of justice problem in England and Wales. It, also, neglects the procedural barriers, obstacles and disincentives that cause wrongful convictions and act against them being overturned. It serves to downplay the existence of, and difficulties faced by, the wrongly convicted in their attempts to satisfy the criteria necessary to overturn their convictions. It, effectively, subjugates the production of counter-discourses on the harmful consequences that are engendered by routine and mundane miscarriages of justice and wrongful convictions that have widespread effects upon both direct and indirect victims from the public gaze (Naughton, 2004a, 2005b).

Another defining characteristic of the most recent counter-discourses on miscarriages of justice to derive from the academic field[42] is that it falls into one of two distinct categories: the 'justice in error' approach or the 'justice in crisis' approach. These approaches were the titles of the two main published collections on the debate about the RCCJ.

Justice in Error, edited by Walker and Starmer (1993) contained 11 contributions which included analyses of police investigative procedures (Coleman et al, 1993), the right to legal advice (Sanders & Bridges, 1983); the right to silence (McElree & Starmer, 1993), prosecution disclosure (O'Connor, 1993), and post-conviction procedures (Mansfield & Taylor, 1993). All of which can be conceived as, primarily, concerned with procedural aspects of the criminal justice process in the interest of reducing inadvertent or unintended 'errors' that might cause miscarriages of justice.

On the other hand, *Criminal Justice in Crisis*, edited by McConville and Bridges (1994) contained 28 contributions from prominent critical socio-legal intellectuals and activists that presented a more sustained collective assault upon the RCCJ from a social justice perspective. That is, they demanded much more than cosmetic reform of the criminal justice system to correct the apparent cause of the miscarriage of justice cases at the centre of the 'crisis'. The call was for fundamental changes to the underlying structures and the operations of the criminal justice process. In addition, despite the ostensible differences in terms of intellectual position and/or subject area, 'all of the papers' that contributed to *Criminal Justice in Crisis* were said in the Foreword to 'reflect a common sense of...betrayal' in the RCCJ in terms of the part it (failed) to play in the reform process (McConville & Bridges, 1994a: xv). This collective conception raises key questions about:

- the evaluative stance and function of critical academic discourse on miscarriages of justice;
- the part of public crises of confidence in the government of the criminal justice system; and,
- the position of the Government in the processes of the governmentality of the criminal justice system and the response to public crises of confidence as conceived by leading critical academics voices.

Without wishing to exaggerate the uniformity of the exponents of critical academic counter-discourse on miscarriages of justice generally, and the complex and contrasting political positioning of the specific critical criminological/socio-legal intellectuals who contributed to *Criminal Justice in Crisis*, the remainder of this chapter explores some of the key conceptualisations of miscarriages of justice and the process of changes to the criminal justice system that were presented therein. As such, this analysis is not an engagement with the forms of socio-legal discourse that were offered by the various contributors to *Justice in Error* or *Criminal Justice in Crisis*. Rather, the aim is to assess the interpretation of some of the foremost academic critics of the criminal justice process and determine the likely success of such forms of critical counter-discourse from the perspective advanced here. In so doing, it is acknowledged that *Criminal Justice in Crisis* came after the publication of the RCCJ, and that not all of the various contributors to be considered actually submitted evidence to the RCCJ or engaged directly with the reform process. Despite this, what the various authors that will be considered have in common is a shared lens though which the crisis in, and changes to, the criminal justice system was viewed and a mutual mode of thinking about the role and rationality of government. The idea is that such an analysis can provide useful insights into critical forms of analysis and perceptions of the processes of the governmentality of the criminal justice system.

Criminal Justice in Crisis and the Royal Commission on Criminal Justice

In her response to the RCCJ, Nicola Lacey's (1994: 40) contribution to *Criminal Justice in Crisis*, for example, conceived miscarriages of justice as intrinsically linked to notions of the abuse of The Government's power. In a similar vein, Bridges & McConville (1994: 3–5) conceived extra-judicial inquiries such as the RCCJ as devices that specifically function in the interests of whichever government happens to be in office at the time of their Report. This view was also echoed by Lacey (1994: 40) in the assertion that:

> ...the very logic of such bod[ies as the RCCJ] is that [they] hope to be judged a success – and success, most obviously, is judged in terms of the acceptance and implementation of its reform proposals. Thus *such bodies always have a clear incentive to 'second-guess' what will find favour with the Government of the day* (my emphasis).

Likewise, the legislative 'corrections' to the criminal justice system that flowed from the RCCJ, i.e. the CCRC, even if they were viewed as generally 'positively' by the critical community as an improvement on the previous provision, were conceived as 'damage limitation exercises', in the interests of reinforcing The Government's 'control' of the criminal justice system (see, for example, Bridges & McConville, 1994: 22–23; also Hillyard, 1994: 74). Celia Wells (1994: 53–54)

summarised her position on the part the RCCJ played in the process as
follows:

> It is unarguable that the criminal justice system is a taken for granted
> part of the apparatus of the state, however defined...[it is] subject to
> government manipulation in support of its claim to authority.

Against such conceptions, this analysis of the relations of governmentality, of government and governed, certainly provides an 'argument'
of a qualitatively different conception of existing forms of power, within
which a polar distinction can be made between 'sovereign' forms of
rule as expressed by the aforementioned critics, and the governmental
rationality that underpins existing exercises of power. To be sure, the
approach of the critical academic community who collectively responded
to the RCCJ in *Criminal Justice in Crisis* epitomises sovereign forms of
authority, when the defining feature of the model of power developed
here conceives power as a relationship between government and governed. Governmental forms of power are exercised via the reciprocal surveillance of aspects of the societal domains for which governmentality
assumes responsibility. This is precisely not about domination but, rather,
about the negotiated outcome of the interplay of dominant forms of
discourse and their counter-discursive opposition.

Moreover, whilst it is true to say that exercises of power under governmentality are intentional, in the sense that government introduces
intended changes to the criminal justice system, it is, simultaneously,
non-subjective (Foucault, 1979b: 95). If power relations *are* intelligible,
it is not, necessarily, due to the State's (as expressed in The Government)
conspiratorial attempt to control the population/the governed but,
rather, because they are imbued, through and through, with 'calculation'. Whilst there is no power that is exercised without a series
of aims and objectives, this does not mean that it results from the
choice or conspiratorial decision of an individual subject or group of
individuals. As Foucault (1979b: 95) famously remarked:

> ...let us not look for the headquarters that presides over (power's)
> rationality...[For]...neither...the groups which control the state
> apparatus, [nor] those who make the most important economic
> decisions direct the entire network of power that functions in a
> society (and makes *it* function)...[Rather]...the rationality of power
> is characterized by tactics that are often quite explicit at the
> restricted level where they are inscribed...tactics which, becoming

connected to one another, attracting and propagating one another, but finding their base of support and their condition elsewhere, end by forming comprehensive systems: the logic is perfectly clear, the aims decipherable, and yet it is often the case that no one is there to have invented them, and few who can be said to have formulated them: an implicit characteristic of the great anonymous, almost unspoken strategies which coordinate the loquacious tactics whose 'inventors' or decisionmakers are often without hypocrisy.

From such a perspective on power, the conception of The Government as the central object or target of critical counter-discourse because it is an apparatus of, and in the position of the management of, the State is displaced. Government (or even The Government for that matter) is, precisely, not *synonymous* with the State 'whose importance is a lot more limited than many of us think' (Foucault, 1991: 103). However, this does not mean that the State is of no significance whatsoever in the discursive interplay of present forms of power. Rather, relations of power, and hence the analysis that must be made of them, necessarily extend beyond the limits of the State. Not only is it impossible for the State to occupy the whole field of power relations, the State can also only operate on the basis of other, already existing power relations. As Foucault asserted, in this sense it is better to view the state as '*superstructural* in relation to a whole series of power networks that invest...knowledge, technology and so forth' (cited Smart, 1988: 123–124 my emphasis). From such a perspective, an alternative reading of mechanisms such as the RCCP and the RCCJ would conceive them as devices through which governmentality attempts to understand and respond to social and legal problems evidenced by exceptional cases of successful appeals which represent official miscarriages of justice, obliging government, and giving it the legitimacy, to intervene in the affairs of the criminal justice system.

If this approach is applied to *Criminal Justice in Crisis*, it is not that The Government discourse is not a powerful *force* in the governmentality processes of the operations of criminal justice system power. Rather, it is to acknowledge that The Government is neither critical academic discourse's only competing discursive force, or necessarily, its most powerful adversary. To be sure, in the interplay of competing criminal justice system discourses, The Government has a stake and a discursive agenda. But, so, too, do other groups, institutions and individuals. All of these various and competing discourses need to be taken into account in analyses of the operations of criminal justice system power – discourse must take account of other, competing, discourses.

For instance, it was not The Government that stood in the way of the long-standing campaign for the abolition of capital punishment in the UK. In fact, the abolition of capital punishment in the UK in the 1960s was largely achieved through The Government of the day's support of the campaign for abolition (see Callaghan, 1997). Indeed, it was not The Government's discourse, but, rather, the power of pro-capital punishment discourse that kept capital punishment firmly in place. It was not until the cases of Bentley, Evans and Ellis exemplified the inherent erroneous nature of capital punishment (i.e. that certain hangings were mistaken and/or certainly inappropriate), and was able to induce public support that abolition was achieved (Christoph, 1962). The same is the case for the introduction of PACE and the establishment of the CCRC. The Government's discourse did not object to the recommendation of the RCCP for the introduction for formalised codes of conduct on police conduct but duly *translated* it into PACE. Nor did The Government's discourse resist the RCCJ's recommendation to establish an extension to the appeals system. On the contrary, it was promptly *translated* by The Government into the CCRC. This is not to paint a picture of an entirely benign or passive Government. It is, rather, to present an alternative account of governmentality: sometimes, legislative interventions by government – such as the abolition of capital punishment, the introduction of PACE (1984) and the establishment of the CCRC – need not be considered by the critical community as wholly repressive but, rather, as intrinsically progressive changes that improve the system, guarding against the possible wrongful conviction of the innocent or reducing the possible harm to innocent victims of wrongful conviction.

Against this, the forms of critical academic counter-discourse against miscarriages of justice that perceived the process in terms of 'a damage limitation' can be said to have misconceived the (admittedly) somewhat paradoxical superstructural position of government. Whilst The Government is the object of counter-discourse, because of its position as facilitator or arbiter in the disposal of public crises of confidence in the governmentality of the criminal justice system, it simultaneously contains its own discursive agenda and is, thus, a potential (often real) discursive opponent in the governmentality of society. Against this, the critical criminological/critical socio-legal interpretations outlined above tended to conflate the two and conceptualised The Government as its only and most powerful competing discursive opponent. However, if the outcomes of extra-judicial governmental devices such as the RCCJ are not of the form desired, this does not, necessarily, signal a 'betrayal' by The Government. It could be as much to do with the success of other competing (counter) discourses in the negotiated struggle to effect changes to the criminal justice system in response to apparent miscarriages of justice.

To continue with the same examples, in the case of capital punishment, there still exists a campaign for its reintroduction in the UK (see Capital Punishment UK, 2006) to which present New Labour Government discourse seems adamantly opposed, but which future Conservative Government discourse might not be opposed (see, for example, Editorial, 2001). Similarly, in the case of PACE, it was police and pro-police discourse that was opposed to, and critical of its introduction, which it regarded as hampering police inquiries, providing too many rights to criminal suspects and too expensive (see, for example, Osoba, 1988). And, in the case of the CCRC, just because there was (to a greater or lesser degree) universal approval to its establishment, that does not imply that it can be simply read-off as a 'successful' 'damage limitation exercise'.

Legislative changes to the criminal justice system could, alternatively, be conceived as the products of historical struggle and the ability of forms of critical counter-discourse that are supported by exceptional successful appeals as evidence of problematics with the existing criminal justice system arrangements, which induced public crises that ultimately yielded governmental intervention and legislative change. In this sense, the forms of counter-discourse that are able to induce public crises of confidence in the criminal justice system should not be viewed as entirely 'negative', but should also be viewed 'positively' for the opportunities to effect changes to the criminal justice system that they provide. To paraphrase Foucault (1980c: 52), it is not possible for criminal justice system power to be exercised without knowledge; it is impossible for knowledge evidenced by real cases not to engender criminal justice system power.

Governmentality and changes to the criminal justice system

To demonstrate a collective misconception of extra-judicial governmental devices such as the RCCJ, and a lack of reflexivity in the interplay of criminal justice system power, this section considers a number of disparate demands and criticisms of the Report of the RCCJ that were expressed in *Criminal Justice in Crisis*. Without wishing to present a 'straw' conception of the forms of counterdiscourse that appeared in *Criminal Justice in Crisis*, the examples to be considered were fairly arbitrarily selected and are representative of the general and collective approach to the relations of power to which all of the authors were said to have subscribed. The attempt is to provide an alternative and reflexive understanding of the relations of power and resistance, of discourse and its counter-discursive opposition. The hope being that this can contribute to the future production and deployment of counter-tactics and strategies that might more effectively engage with predominant criminal justice system discourse on behalf of the governed. In particular, the foregoing analyses of the relations of power between government and governed indicates that those actively engaged with the improvement of the criminal justice system should be encouraged to seek out cases that exemplify 'errors' that can feed back into the criminal justice system in the interests of reducing the occurrence of such 'errors' in the future.

Contrary to this, various contributors to *Criminal Justice in Crisis* raised a number of disparate demands and criticisms pertaining to what were perceived as the 'failures' of the Report of the RCCJ from a more theoretical or structural perspective. For Bridges & McConville (1994: 50), for example, the major problem of the Report of the RCCJ was that it 'failed' 'to provide a clear statement of the basic values which the criminal justice system should seek to uphold and a consistent, comprehensive account of the workings of that system'. Similarly, for Lacey (1994: 30), the RCCJ was a 'missed opportunity' to look critically at the 'structural factors which gave rise to many of the particular problems in the administration of criminal justice... and the basic assumptions, values and goals which ought to inform criminal justice practices'. For Maher (1994: 59), the main problem with the RCCJ was that it did not consider 'concepts such as individual rights of suspects and other persons in the criminal process; or ideas such as process or intrinsic values.' For Brogden (1994: 152), the major 'failing' of the RCCJ was that it 'was not required to investigate what has been a major area of contention for two decades, police powers of stop-and-search.' For Singh (1994: 172) 'the RCCJ should have used the opportunity presented to it to reconsider the purpose of arrest and detention...by failing to consider the variety of reasons which may underlie the police decision to arrest and detain, the Commissioners have implicitly endorsed the police practice of using these powers for the purpose of inflicting summary punishment.' For Cape (1994: 186–187): 'The failure [of the RCCJ] to take account of the structural imbalance between the two parties [defence and prosecution] leads to a complete failure to deal with an issue that is fundamental both to police detention and to the provision of defence services at the police station; that is, what is the true purpose of police interrogation of suspects.' In addition, Hillyard (1994) criticised the 'failure' of the RCCJ to improve the treatment of the Irish community. Boothman (1994: 96) argued that the Commission's recommendations would actually serve to further discrimination and more deeply institutionalise racism within the criminal justice system. And, Hodgson (1994: 200) was critical of the RCCJ's 'failure' to thoroughly evaluate the function of the criminal defence lawyer.

Such demands, despite the validity of their divergent critiques, misconceive the specific *conditions* of governmental intervention into the criminal justice system and the relations of power and resistance within the processes of governmentality of the criminal justice system – cases need to be found to support issues. Moreover, the evaluative stance of such analyses is couched too much in terms of 'success' or 'failure', which produces a totalising all or nothing feel. Governmentality, on the other hand, is precisely not about 'success' or 'failure'. On the contrary, governmentality, as a process, is always on-going, 'unfinished' (cf Mathiesen, 1974); in a state of continual contestation, negotiation and renegotiation in its management or arbitration of competing discourses (cf Foucault, 1980a). This is not to suggest that effecting changes to the criminal justice system is easy or that real opportunities to alter the course of the criminal process and reorient it around issues of social justice arise all that often. But, it does emphasise the need for a constant, as opposed to an intermittent, engagement with specific problems such as of miscarriages of justice, for example, that actively pursues cases to support campaigns for criminal justice system improvement.

This indicates that if the object is the improvement of the procedures for dealing with Irish criminal suspects, for example, critical counter-discourse needs to be produced about a case(s) that specifically exemplifies the mistreatment of Irish suspects and is able to induce a public crisis of confidence in this particular aspect of the existing criminal justice system. If a crisis is successfully induced, the remit or 'terms' of the extra-judicial inquiry that will, more than likely, be established in governmental response need to be framed to address this particular and specific criminal justice system problem. In this process of agenda setting, other discursive forces will come into play with their own competing, and, in many instances, conflicting discursive agendas, interpretations and supporting evidence. This stage in the disposal of public crises is crucially important, as the public perception of the problem to be addressed and, hence, in need of legislative correction will determine the possible success of the governmentality process. This is the point at which the assumptions, parameters and possibilities of change are set. As George (1991: 76) has argued, a way to 'guarantee a debate':

> ...is to shift the framework of debate in such a way that any conclusion reached within it is in accord with one's views. Whether one wins or loses particular debates conducted within such a shrewdly chosen framework is then largely irrelevant, since the very act of debating will strengthen those presuppositions that are ultimately of greatest concern.

An example of this analysis can be derived from an analysis of Winter's (1994) critique of the RCCJ. In particular, Winter (1994: 80) stated that when the RCCJ was announced 'we' (the Britain and Ireland Human Rights Project (BIHRP)):

> ...wrote to the then Home Secretary asking him to extend the Commission's terms of reference to include Northern Ireland...The terms of reference would not be expanded, we were informed...We went ahead and submitted evidence to the Commission anyway, convinced that the fact that so many miscarriages of justice involved cases concerned with the conflict in Northern Ireland.

Winter (1994) is almost certainly correct on the significance of the exceptional successful appeals of 'Irish' cases and the establishment of the RCCJ. At the same time, she demonstrates well the importance of the terms of reference of such governmental devices for the subsequent disposal of public crises of confidence. This raises the question of the strategy of the BIHRP to submit their evidence 'anyway', despite being informed that the 'terms' would not be expanded. At this stage, once the terms had been established, it might have been more tactical for critical researchers to shift their focus to research that exemplified the failings in the criminal appeals procedure in the interests of more fruitful corrective recommendations on the criminal appellate framework. As it was, critics continued with their own disparate agendas, which they had been informed were outside of the terms of reference of the RCCJ and which, therefore, inevitably failed.[43]

Another example of this analysis can be derived from Boothman's (1994: 91) contribution to the critique of the RCCJ, which noted that the Institute of Race Relations (IRR) was 'disturbed' that:

> ...race did not gain a mention in the Royal Commission's terms of reference...Yet...there was a considerable body of research on race and criminal justice which at the very least suggested a serious problem...and a number of the most serious miscarriages of justice that had lead to the Commission being established had in fact involved black defendants.

As with Winter (1994), Boothman (1994) is, undoubtedly, correct on the significance of 'race' and discrimination in the criminal justice process. So much has been officially acknowledged as a consequence of the Stephen Lawrence Affair. In particular, the Stephen Lawrence Affair formally established the phenomenon of institutional racism with the Metropolitan Police Force (see Macpherson, 1999), which has long been alleged by the critics in the UK (for details see Guardian Unlimited, 2006). But, how was such acknowledgement achieved? It was certainly not achieved by submitting critical counter-discourse on 'racial' discrimination to an extra-judicial governmental inquiry that was perceived to be primarily a review of the law on criminal appeals. On the contrary, it was achieved through a specific case that exemplified structural racism within the criminal justice system that was able to induce a public crisis of confidence in the governmentality of the criminal justice system in its treatment of suspects, defendants and victims in the context or 'terms' of 'race'. In keeping with the analysis developed above, the Stephen Lawrence Inquiry was established in response to the public crisis of confidence that the case induced (see, The Law Commission, 2001).

It is within this context that the aforementioned criticisms of the RCCJ should be assessed. They say as much about the (mis)understandings of such forms of critical counter-discourse of the processes required to effect changes to the criminal justice system as they do about the success of other competing discourses – discourse not only has to take account of other discourse, it must also take account of itself.

Conclusion

This chapter discerned two types of academic voice in intermittent response to miscarriages of justice: a voice that closes the circle on the governmentality of criminal justice system by fully participating in the recommendations of extra-judicial enquires and a voice that is essentially critical of such an engagement. In focusing on this latter, more overtly critical, expression of the academic voice, it was demonstrated that the critical academic counter-discourses that were presented in *Criminal Justice in Crisis*, the primary critical academic text on miscarriages of justice in collective response to the RCCJ, generally misconceived the relations of power and resistance in the processes of governmentality of the disposal of public crises of confidence in the criminal justice system.

Phenomena such as exceptional successful appeals are intrinsically connected to specific forms of critical knowledge that exemplify problematic aspects in the existing legislative framework of the criminal justice system. If such counter-discourse is able to induce a public crisis of confidence in the criminal justice system then it signifies a problematic moment in the governmentality of the criminal justice system. In these processes, the utility of the public crisis of confidence is to identify and to prioritise the most problematic aspects of the existing criminal justice system as part of the broader surveillance or visualisation of the criminal justice system in the interests of the governed. This provides the necessary force to forms of counter-discourse required to operationalise interventions under the rubric of governmentality. In response, the processes of governmentality domesticate the crisis by following the recommendations of royal commissions and committees of enquiry through legislative changes to the criminal justice system, transforming a 'negative' public crisis of confidence in the governmental authority of the management or rule of the criminal justice system into a 'positive' reaffirmation of such governmental rationality.

This governmental rationality, however, is not a conspiratorial, abusive, control of the criminal justice system for its own ends, as conceived by the forms of critical academic discourse in *Criminal Justice in Crisis*, but a rationality that operates to change the criminal justice system when the appropriate *conditions* for governmental intervention are present. Accordingly, extra-judicial governmental inquiries such as the RCCJ should not merely be conceived merely as 'damage limitation exercises' but, rather, as, also, potentially representing an arena within which an enactment in the power struggle between dominant forms of criminal justice system power and its critical counter-discursive opposition takes place. And, the success of the governmental *translation* of the recommendations of extra-judicial inquiries into corrective criminal justice system legislation that disposes of public crises can be conceived as representing an episode in the on-going negotiated management of the governmentality criminal justice system.

As such, public crises of confidence in the criminal justice system need not be seen as entirely 'negative' events either, nor, necessarily, as a sign of a Government in terminal 'crisis'. On the contrary, states of public 'crisis' should not only be welcomed, the inducement of public 'crises' of confidence in specific 'errors' or apparent shortcomings of the criminal justice system should be a primary task of critical counter-discourse against the way things are. They are a necessary prerequisite *condition* for effecting changes to the criminal justice system. But, when such opportunities arise, they should not be squandered. They should be recognised and exploited for the fundamental changes that they can help to bring about.

7
Human Rights

Introduction

In addition to the specific academic voices on miscarriages of justice that articulate opposition at intermittent intervals in response to exceptional successful appeal cases, a further discernable voice exists that straddles the academic and campaigning spheres, coalescing around a central concept of compliance with enacted human rights. To be sure, from the perspective constructed here, human rights can be viewed as inherent to governmentality, to the shift from sovereignty to governmental modes of society, and a defining rationality in the relations and exercise of bio-power in modern rule of law societies. As the concept of human rights specifically relates to miscarriages of justice, it is claimed that as many as 3,000 people are currently imprisoned in England and Wales who are innocent. This estimate is said to have been reported in a Home Office bulletin, appeared in Prison News, was confirmed by a prison governor and broadcast as accurate on several occasions by the British Broadcasting Company (BBC) (The Portia Campaign, 2006; Watkins, 2001). More recently, it was confirmed by a senior representative from the Parole Board in a 'Chatham House Rules'[44] meeting with the organisation Progressing Prisoners Maintaining Innocence (PPMI)[45] that there are currently many thousands of prisoners maintaining innocence in England and Wales. Leaving aside the various reasons why a prisoner may maintain innocence when they are not (Naughton, 2006c; Brandon & Davies, 1973: 21–22) and, therefore, the fact that not all prisoners maintaining innocence will be innocent (McGraw, 2006), clearly these are matters that are appropriate for human rights discourse. Governmental rationality on miscarriages of justice and the possible wrongful imprisonment of the innocent is not confined to a pursuit of factual innocence of victims of wrongful convictions/imprisonment. On the contrary, it is grounded in a notion that any breach of enacted human rights signals an illegitimate exercise of governmental power and is, therefore, unlawful. A clearer understanding of this can contribute to the reorientation of definitions of miscarriages of justice away from exceptionalist understandings to include all successful appeals, whatever their cause and from whichever appeal route they derive.

Nevertheless, at this stage in its articulations, the existing human rights voice has not capitalised on the promise of the Human Rights Act (1998) (HRA) and problematised claims of wrongful imprisonment on the scale indicated by the official data on prisoners maintaining innocence. Nor has it considered the victims in routine and/or mundane successful appeals as miscarriages of justice, many of whom will have spent a period of incarceration. On the contrary, successful appeals have tended to be seen as an indication that legal rights and freedoms are being upheld, and that the system is actually fulfiling its human rights obligations against miscarriages of justice by providing mechanisms for overturning them as and when they occur. Accordingly, the existing human rights voice can be conceived to suffer the same definitional limitations as the voices bound up with the governmentality of the criminal justice system in response to certain successful appeals. It is, primarily, directed towards victims in exceptional cases of successful appeal that failed to be overturned through routine and/or mundane means. Hence, the number of victims of miscarriages of justice and/or wrongful convictions and/or wrongful imprisonment and the harm that they experience that can be calculated from the existing human rights voice is also extremely limited.

It is acknowledged that no system of criminal justice can work from an assumption that it mundanely and/or routinely gets it wrong, and that the system (any system) *must* operate on the basis that its verdicts are for the most part sound. Despite this, the sheer number of claims of innocence by prisoners, coupled with the number of successful appeals that are currently occurring indicates a scale of miscarriages of justice that is at odds with the general spirit of the HRA and the Articles therein, which limit the lawful restrictions and/or abuses from the Act. From such a qualified frame of reference, this analysis proceeds by firstly drawing out from the recent literature on the HRA an image of the limited scope of the current human rights voice. Secondly, extending previous arguments, a more adequate application of the HRA is envisaged to show, in a provocative and illustrative fashion, how the current scale of victims of miscarriages of justice that can be inferred from the official statistics on successful appeals and prisoners maintaining innocence could be said to contravene almost every Article. This exposes the limits of existing forms of human rights counter-discourse, extending the contribution of human rights discourse in the surveillance of the criminal justice system to redress miscarriages of justice. In this sense, there is a requirement for the criminal justice system to at least think the unthinkable and to consider the conditions for performing the unperformable by taking the problems of miscarriages of justice and the wrongful imprisonment of the innocent seriously.

Existing invocations of the Human Rights Act (1998)

The HRA was passed by Parliament in 1998, and came into force in October 2000. It gives further effect to rights and freedoms guaranteed under the European Convention on Human Rights. It has been invoked in one of two distinct ways. On the one hand the human rights voice has referred to the HRA and spoken in the interests of overturning potential exceptional miscarriages of justice in the narrow confines of already convicted prisoners. Alternatively, the human rights voice has used the HRA in the general interests of the welfare of the prison population, introducing a broader definition of what would constitute a miscarriage of justice from the human rights perspective. In July 1999, for example, five law lords were called upon to decide whether prison inmates had the right to talk to the media. Under Article 10 of the ECHR, Freedom of Expression,[46] Ian Simms and Michael O' Brien (who would later achieve a successful appeal as one of the Cardiff Newsagent Three) challenged The Prison Rules' stipulation that journalists should be allowed to visit prisoners only on condition that they sign an undertaking not to disclose or publish any information obtained during the visit. Finding in favour of Simms and O'Brien the judges invoked the human rights voice and said that prisoners who protested their innocence often had no other means of searching out the fresh evidence needed to have their cases reconsidered by the CACD. As such the Home Secretary's ban on journalists was determined to be 'an unlawful interference with free speech' (see Regina v. Secretary of State for the Home Department *ex parte* Simms (A.P.) Secretary of State for the Home Department *ex parte* O'Brien (Consolidated Appeals)).

This would seem to indicate that the treatment of prisoners within England and Wales, whether legitimately imprisoned or potential victims of wrongful convictions, currently complies with Article 10 of the ECHR/HRA. In March 2002, however, John Hirst had to win a further legal challenge under Article 10 for the right to speak to journalists on the telephone (Hirst v Secretary of State for the Home Department [2002] 1 WLR 2929). In a similar vein to the earlier ruling, Mr Justice Elias invoked the human rights voice and gave the reason for the judgement on the following grounds:

> News is perishable, and news stories have to be put together within a very short space of time. Concern over certain aspects of prison conditions, for example, will often arise from some specific event. The journalist must catch the tide or the impact of the story will be lost…It will frequently be too late for information to be obtained by written communication; the prisoner has to be contacted and there has to be time for the reply (Hirst v Secretary of State for the Home Department [2002] 1 WLR 2929: Para, 21).

In line with the processes inherent to the governmental project, it would seem that the matter of a prisoners' right to freedom of expression is a multifaceted one, where each of those facets must be obtained individually through successful legal challenge. Moreover, it would seem that the right of prisoners to express themselves to the media, either by written communication or by telephone is deemed to be lawful if it serves the general interests of overturning potential miscarriages of justice and/or wrongful convictions. It is interesting, then, that convicted prisoners are not allowed to vote. This was reported in April 2001 when the high court upheld a ban on convicted prisoners having the right to vote which had been also challenged under Article 10 of the HRA, and had the support of Martin Narey, the then director general of the prison service (see Dodd & Milne, 2001). In the judgement, Lord Justice Kennedy reiterated the Government's policy as follows: 'As the home secretary said, parliament has taken the view that for the period during which they are in custody convicted prisoners have forfeited their right to have a say in the way the country is governed' (cited Dodd & Milne, 2001). In March 2004, John Hirst took the case to the European Court of Human Rights. It ruled that the British government was in breach of the European Convention on Human Rights. The British government appealed to the European Court's Grand Chamber, which upheld the ruling 6 October 2005. At the time of writing, prisoners in Britain remain unallowed to vote but the Lord Chancellor said that there would be a review and that some categories of prisoner might be allowed to vote (Dyer, 2004; BBC News, 2005). This indicates that the wrongly imprisoned are still denied a crucial aspect of the freedom of expression, which can be conceived as an intrinsic element of Article 10 in a liberal democratic society. It also seems counter to the judgements in the two successful challenges brought under Article 10 which emphasised the importance of the rights of communication and democratic participation of prisoners who might be innocent for the contribution that they might make in the interests of justice. As things currently stand, then, unless and until prisoners are allowed to vote, alleged victims of miscarriages of justice who receive long term prison sentences will not receive appropriate attention from politicians who tend to engage only with vote enhancing activities.

More recently, in November 2002, Richard Roy Allan was successful in a challenge against the United Kingdom in the European Court of Human Rights at Strasbourg under Articles 8 (Privacy), and 6 (Fair Trial) of the HRA. It was ruled that the police had acted unlawfully in recording his conversations by audiotape and on video and in using a police informant as a means of conducting 'surreptitious interrogation, circumventing the protections for a suspect who has availed himself (sic) of legal advice and exercised the right to silence' (see Allan v The United Kingdom, 2002). On this issue, there has been widespread condemnation that the police practice of 'bugging' conversations between suspects and their solicitors is a breach of Article 8 of the HRA, which provides for the right to consult a lawyer in private, and could be a cause of miscarriages (see Gibb, 2002).

In terms of attempts to ensure the welfare of convicted prisoners, in July 2002 the European Court of Human Rights ruled that the human rights of Lawrence Conners and Okechukwiw Ezeh, for example, had been breached in contravention of Article 6 of the HRA (Fair Trial) after both had extra days added to their sentences in disciplinary hearings. The effect of the ruling is that prison governors are likely to lose the authority to act as 'judge and jury' in internal hearings relating to alleged breaches of prison disciplinary regimes and prisoners will be allowed the right of legal representation (Ezeh and Conners v The United Kingdom, 2003).

In addition to these specific cases, it has been widely speculated that overcrowded and squalid conditions in prisons in England and Wales (see, for example, Owers, 2006: 5)[47] may be a breach of prisoners' general human rights (see, for example, Morris, 2002). The HRA has been invoked in the context of 'deaths in custody' (Liberty, 2001). The HRA has been invoked in an application for a judicial review following claims that the 2,900 teenagers aged between 15 and 17 in prison in England and Wales is 'brutal, inhumane and illegal' (see Leppard, 2002). And, the HRA has been invoked in the area of prisoners' disability rights (see Prasad, 2002; also Prison Reform Trust, 2006).

The foregoing examples indicate that the human rights voice has liberally invoked the HRA, but only in one of two very limited contexts: in the name of allowing convicted prisoners the rights and freedoms to overturn possible injustices/miscarriages of justice; alternatively, in the context of ensuring the legal welfare of prisoners who may be denied the rights and/or freedoms that are available to the citizenry as a whole. The above examples also illustrate the force of the human rights voice when it speaks. When successful rulings are achieved under the HRA, individual victims of miscarriages of justice, or injustice in the treatment of convicted prisoners generally, it is officially acknowledged that they have been illegally harmed in some way. The effect also induces changes to problematic aspects of the criminal justice system to reduce the possibility of others being harmed in the same way. In the same way that campaigning organisations can be seen as engaged in a systematic surveillance of a range of alleged failings of the criminal justice process, concerns about human rights abuses, represent an on-going watchdog role as part of the governmental project, holding government to account for apparent transgressions from enacted human rights legislation.

However, the human rights voice has not yet been invoked to speak about the current scale of successful appeals in England and Wales, nor the extent of harm to victims of miscarriages of justice that such a scale of successful appeals implies. Indeed, from a conventional human rights perspective successful appeals are not miscarriages of justice at all. On the contrary, as Pattenden (1996: 57) in the most extensive existing research on appeals against conviction and sentence in England and Wales asserted, the foremost function of an appeal against criminal conviction is to satisfy the guaranteed right in enacted national and international human rights legislation, which is open to everyone convicted of a criminal offence, providing the right to appeal against that conviction to provide redress. From such a perspective, successful appeals are not viewed negatively as indicators of a systemic failure, but positively as a sign that the appeals system is fulfiling its 'function'. The problem with this is not that successful appeals *per se* indicate judicial 'failure'. On the contrary, to repeat, it is inevitable that there will be judicial 'mistakes' and/or 'errors' and that there will be some miscarriages of justice. The problem is that the current scale of miscarriages of justice that the official statistics on successful appeals infers can be conceived as in contravention, not only with the spirit of the HRA, but also with almost every Article of the Act!

The unlawfulness of the current scale of successful appeals against criminal convictions?

In addition to stating the rights and freedoms provided to individuals in England and Wales, the Articles of the HRA also provide for occasions of lawful contravention. Essentially, these lawful contraventions relate to the lawful arrest and/or detention of persons guilty or suspected of criminal offences, to the maintenance of order, and the general promotion of the rule of law. At the same time, however, the HRA determines the limits upon what might constitute a possible lawful contravention of the Act. These limits are spelt out in Schedule 1 through Articles 17, Prohibition of Abuse of Rights, and 18, Limitation on use of Restrictions on Rights, which state that:

> Nothing in this Convention may be interpreted as implying for any State, group or person any right to engage in any activity or perform any act aimed at the destruction of any of the rights and freedoms set forth herein or at their limitation to a greater extent than is provided for in the Convention (HRA, 1998, Article 17).

And, that:

> The restrictions permitted under this Convention to the said rights and freedoms shall not be applied for any purpose other than those for which they have been prescribed (HRA, 1998, Article 18).

The current scale of victims of miscarriages of justice that can be inferred from the official statistics on successful appeals, coupled with official data that thousands of prisoners are currently maintaining innocence, can be conceived as excessive and, therefore, in direct contravention of Article 17 and Article 18 of the HRA. In direct contravention of Article 17, those engaged in the conviction of victims of miscarriages of justice who overturn their convictions and the treatment of prisoners maintaining innocence, whether intentionally or unintentionally, are engaged in activities limit the rights and freedoms of victims of miscarriages of justice and prisoners maintaining innocence to a greater extent than is provided for in the HRA, conceivably acting to 'destruct' the rights and freedoms set forth in the HRA. In direct contravention of Article 18, the number of prisoners maintaining innocence added to the official statistics on successful appeals indicates a scale of victims of miscarriages of justice that can be conceived as violations to the rights and freedoms of the HRA that are not permitted. Furthermore, as there has been no governmental intervention whatsoever into the problem, such violations can be conceived to be currently being applied for purposes other than those for which they have been prescribed. To illustrate this, I draw from the literature on successful appeals and consider the lawful restrictions to the various remaining Articles of the HRA provided in Schedule 1 in chronological order.

The rights and freedoms provided by the HRA commence with *Article 2, The Right to Life*, with the following statement:

> Everyone's right to life shall be *protected* by law. *'No one shall be deprived of his (sic) life intentionally* save in the execution of a sentence of a court following his conviction of a crime for which this penalty is provided by law (s. 1 my emphasis).

In terms of lawful restriction or contravention of the right to life, Article 2, s. 2 states that:

> Deprivation of life shall not be regarded as inflicted in contravention of this Article when it results from the use of force *which is no more than absolutely necessary* (my emphasis)

There are a number of issues here that need to be unpacked. Firstly, the HRA would seem to intrinsically assume that law in England and Wales serves only, and always, in the interests of the *protection of life*. This assumption entirely attunes with, and might seem completely credible from, the standpoint of popular perceptions of miscarriages of justice in England and Wales, i.e. that they are exceptional and small in number and that safeguards exist to remedy them should they occur. But, as the foregoing analyses have sought to show, the various laws in England and Wales that govern the treatment and resolution of miscarriages of justice do not take appropriate or adequate account of the extensive scale of miscarriages of justice that can be inferred from the official statistics on successful appeals and their harmful consequences. Nor, therefore, the possible harm to the life of victims of miscarriages that law can, itself, pose.

By definition, 'deprivation' of life can also refer more generally to any action that might 'prevent', 'hinder' or interfere with the fulfilment or 'enjoyment' of an individual's life (Collins Concise Dictionary, 2000: 300). As such, any miscarriage of justice that might serve to dispossess or detrimentally impact upon an individual's life can, also, be conceived as being in contravention of Article 2. It is in this context that victims of miscarriages of justice bear testimony that the (mis)application of law can be conceived as a threat to their lives. As this relates to exceptional miscarriage of justice cases, this can be illustrated in the high profile wrongful imprisonment cases of the Birmingham Six, Guildford Four, Maguire Seven and Bridgewater Four, who together spent over 100 years of wrongful imprisonment.[48] A more mundane example is the case of David Jones who was wrongly accused and charged, but not convicted of, a paedophile offence, with significant impacts on his personal and professional life. What these examples show is that a range of harm is caused to victims of miscarriages of justice from whichever appeal court they derive that has a detrimental effect upon the enjoyment and/or fulfilment of their lives, however defined.

In the recent literature on successful appeals there are various examples in which there were judicial declarations, and, therefore, official acknowledgement, that the convicting evidence in certain cases of miscarriages of justice was unlawfully obtained through treatment that amounted to torture, thus, in direct contravention of *Article 3 of the HRA, Freedom from Torture, Inhuman and Degrading Treatment*. For example, quashing Keith Twitchell's conviction in the CACD Lord Justice Rose said that the case was:

> ...yet another appeal arising from the lamentable history of the...West Midlands serious crime squad (within which) a significant number of police officers...some of whom rose to very senior rank, behaved outrageously, and in particular extracted confessions by grossly improper means, amounting in some cases to torture (R v Twitchell [2000] 1 Cr App R 373).

Other examples of relatively recent successful appeals that all aptly demonstrate the contravention of Article 3 in the conviction of exceptional victims of miscarriages of justice within England and Wales include those of Patrick Molloy (see Regan, 1997b), Derek Treadaway (R v Treadway [1996] EWCA Crim 1457) and George Lewis (see Weaver, 1998) (discussed in more detail in the next chapter). But, this too, is not only an exceptional matter. In addition to these exceptional examples of successful appeals, there is evidence to suggest that Article 3 of the HRA is also routinely and/or mundanely contravened. This recently emerged following an inspection of a range of places of detention in England and Wales in April 2002 by the European Committee for the Prevention of Torture and Inhuman or Degrading Treatment or Punishment (CPT).[49] The CPT's delegation, which was the first to visit Wales and to examine the treatment of persons held in a military establishment in the United Kingdom, inspected 12 places of detention in England and Wales (European Committee for the Prevention of Torture and Inhuman or Degrading Treatment or Punishment, 2002).

Following its inspections, the CPT reported that whilst the establishments that were visited in London were found to be 'satisfactory', all of those visited in Wales were found to be in contravention of Article 3. It transpired that a number of those interviewed separately at both Parc Prison (Bridgend) and Hillside Secure Centre (Neath) informed the CPT that they had been ill-treated by police officers. Allegations included abuse at the time of arrest and in police cells, including being punched and kicked. Moreover, the CPT's inspection of Cardiff Central Police Station found its cells were 'dirty and poorly ventilated', with the effect that the people held there were also being treated in contravention of Article 3 (see Eden, 2002). In a consideration of the CPT's visit to England and Wales, however, it must also be noted that the CPT only inspected a very small sample of all the places of detention within England and Wales. Taking prison establishments as an example they inspected only four prisons (three in England and one in Wales) out of a total of 138[50] prison establishments in England and Wales (HM Prison Service, 2002). As such, even the CPT's finding of 'satisfactory' treatment in establishments in London must be treated with extreme caution, as not all London establishments were visited. There is also the possibility that the establishments that were visited in London by the CPT could have been 'staged' to present a 'satisfactory' image to the visitors. Such a phenomenon is widely acknowledged to occur in other areas of social life which encounter periodic public scrutiny or review, such as the field of education with its Ofsted inspections and reports on school performance (see, for example, Carvel, 1999b; Younge, 2000). It is possible to argue that as it was the CPT's first visit to Wales, the establishments that were visited might have been unprepared or not known what to expect, and hence failed to present the required image.

In saying this, however, it must be emphasised that there is no real value in separating England from Wales in terms of the treatment of those held in places of detention, as all of the establishments, whether in England or Wales come under, and are covered by and subject to the same penal and governmental guidelines, Standards and Performance Indicators (see, for example, Prison Service Standards Manual, 2000). Accordingly, whether a particular establishment that is identified to be in contravention of Article 3 of the HRA is geographically located in England or in Wales it represents an unlawful violation of the Act by the criminal justice system that collectively governs England and Wales. As such, the CPT's finding that Article 3 of the HRA was being contravened in terms of the general treatment of prisoners within the jurisdiction of England and Wales is highly relevant to the specific issue of the treatment of victims of miscarriages of justice who receive custodial sentences and prisoners maintaining innocence who may never achieve a successful appeal. It indicates that victims of miscarriages who are wrongly imprisoned within England and Wales are also likely to be specifically denied Article 3 of the HRA during their wrongful imprisonment.

The rights and freedoms provided by *Article 4 of the HRA, Freedom from Forced Labour*, are also particularly relevant to an analysis of the thousands of prisoners who are currently maintaining innocence in England and Wales. As the law currently stands, Rule 31(1) of The Prison Rules (1999)[51] requires that convicted prisoners, male and female, do 'useful' work for up to ten hours a day. This work can take a variety of forms in industrial workshops and/or agricultural units, and includes the production of goods and services needed by prisons, as well as for sale in the local community. Alternatively, prisoners can work within the prison in cleaning, catering, and general building and maintenance work. In return prisoners receive around £7 per week, depending upon resources, the amount and type of work available and the level that the prisoner has reached on the 'Incentives and Earned Privileges Scheme' (IEPS) (for how this applies to male and young male convicted prisoners see Prisoners Information Book, 2002: 119–121; for women and young females see Prisoners Information Book, 2003: 118–120).

Significantly, any non-compliance by a convicted prisoner with the requirement to work invokes disciplinary procedures under Rule 51 (21–23) against the offending prisoner (The Prison Rules, 1999, Rule

51(21–23)). If found to be guilty of an offence against discipline the governor may impose a range of punishments including: a caution; loss of facilities (privileges) for up to 42 days (21 for prisoners under 21); stoppage of up to 42 days earnings (21 for prisoners under 21); cellular confinement for up to 14 days (seven days for prisoners under 21); and, up to an additional 42 days in custody (The Prison Rules, 1999, Rule 55).[52, 53]

Crucially, if a prisoner is found guilty of more than one disciplinary offence they can be punished for each one with punishments running consecutively (except that the total number of additional days added to a prisoners sentence must not exceed 28 for any one incident) (for male prisoners and young male offenders see Prisoners Information Book, 2002: 75–86. For female prisoners and young female offenders see Prisoners Information Book, 2003: 71–86).

As the law stands for unconvicted prisoners awaiting trial, The Prison Rules provides the following 'Statement of Principle': 'Unconvicted prisoners are presumed to be innocent. Subject to the duty to hold them and deliver them to court securely and to the need to maintain order in establishments, they will be treated accordingly' (for how this applies to male prisoners and young male offenders see Prisoners Information Book, 2002: 19; for how this applies to female prisoners and young female offenders see Prisoners Information Book, 2003: 19). In other words, it is not compulsory for unconvicted prisoners to labour. Nonetheless, the unconvicted are still subject to the discourse to labour through the following incentive:

> As an unconvicted prisoner you do not have to work in prison. If you are willing to work but there is no work available, you will be given a small amount of money each week to cover basic things you may need to buy from the prison shop. If you are offered work and you refuse it, you may not get any money from the prison, and the prison does not have to offer you any more work (for how this applies to male prisoners and young male offenders see Prisoners Information Book, 2002: 29; for how this applies to female prisoners and young female offenders see Prisoners Information Book, 2003: 29).

In such a context, it is not difficult to argue that prisoners, whether male or female, young or 'old', whether convicted or unconvicted, and/or whether actually guilty of the criminal offences for which they were convicted are, in effect, *forced* to labour. A failure to comply with the compulsory requirement to labour does not only engender extra punishment, it prevents prisoners the ability to purchase the necessary items that might provide some basic quality of life. The question is, does this coerced labour of convicted (and even unconvicted) prisoners constitute the contravention of Article 4 of the HRA? On this matter, s. 3(a) of Article 4 states that:

> For the purpose of this Article the term 'forced or compulsory labour' shall not include: (a) any work required to be done in the ordinary course of detention imposed according to the provisions of Article 5 of this Convention or during conditional release from such detention.

This lawful restriction to Article 4 seems entirely reasonable from the common-sense perspective of popular perceptions of the scale of the miscarriage of justice phenomenon. From such a perspective there is a certain accepted inevitability that any human system will produce some wrongful convictions. Accordingly, there is a corresponding accepted inevitability that some wrongful conviction victims will consequentially suffer a denial of their rights and freedoms. The legitimacy of such a perspective is grounded in the belief that only very few people will inevitably be denied the rights and freedoms that are provided to the citizenry of England and Wales. It is also grounded in a belief that when such a denial is known about the situation will be speedily rectified and the miscarriage of justice victim will be appropriately and adequately compensated for the harm caused. So much is also an explicit requirement of the HRA, manifest in the mechanisms for the fast-track remedy of miscarriages of justice (s. 4 and s. 5) and their compensation (s. 8) should they occur. However, the denial of rights and freedoms on the current scale within England and Wales as indicated by the number of prisoners maintaining innocence and the estimated 3,000 victims of wrongful imprisonment can be conceived to present new dilemmas to the continued legitimacy of current criminal conviction and penal practices. It can also, therefore, be conceived as an indicator that Article 4 is also contravened by England and Wales' criminal justice system. Bringing the matter within a rubric of 'state crime', if the present legislative provision is incompatible with the stated aims of the criminal justice system, it can, reasonably, be said to be 'unlawful' on its own terms, and, therefore, incompatible with the HRA (1998, s. 4) (cf. Green, 2002: 76).

Under Article 5 of the HRA, Right to Liberty and Security, s. 1 it is stated that: 'Everyone has the right to liberty and security of person. No one shall be deprived of his (sic) liberty.' The HRA, however, does provide a number of possible lawful restrictions to Article 5 including: '(a) the lawful detention of a person after conviction by a *competent court*...(c) the lawful arrest or detention of a person effected for the purpose of bringing him (sic) before the *competent* legal authority on *reasonable suspicion* of having committed an offence or when it is reasonably considered necessary to prevent his (sic) committing an offence or fleeing after having done so' (HRA, 1998, s. 1 my emphasis). A dominant theme of England and Wales' lawful non-compliance with Article 5, then, relates to the twin notions of the 'reasonable' suspicion of a suspect's criminality and, then, the 'competence' of the judicial proceedings against the suspect. As this relates to miscarriages of justice, the notion of reasonable suspicion is immediately called into doubt. If the suspicion and subsequent conviction of a suspect of a criminal offence was entirely 'reasonable', understood in the straightforward sense, then miscarriages of justice and/or wrongful convictions would, indeed, be in line with popular perceptions, i.e. exceptional and small in number.

As for the 'competence' of England and Wales' legal authority, this too has, arguably, been undermined by exceptional miscarriage of justice cases that highlight the very *incompetence* of many criminal trials to decipher and decide upon, for example, competing and opposing expert scientific evidence. The cases of the Birmingham Six, the Guildford Four, the Maguire Seven, the Bridgewater Four are relevant to this discussion, as are the cases of Judith Ward and Stefan Kiszko. More recently, the cases of Sally Clark, Angela Cannings, Kevin Callan, Sheila Bowler and Patrick Nicholls, to name but a few, have continued to raise concerns about the limitations of forensic scientific expert evidence and the likelihood that they had been convicted of murder and given life sentences when no crime had even occurred (see Naughton, 2005). All of which not only calls into question the reliability of scientific evidence in criminal trials, but also the competence of criminal trials by jury in determining cases which hinge upon expert scientific evidence. In response to the challenge that such cases presented to the forensic science community, two inquiries into the state of forensic science in England and Wales that have reported – the RCCJ (1993) and the House of Lords Select Committee on Science and Technology (1993) (CST). The general conclusion of both the RCCJ and the CST was that, although forensic science had experienced a bad press following the success of some of the aforementioned exceptional cases, these were exceptions to the general rule of reliable (truthful) forensic practice.

In sharp contrast, Erzinclioglu's (1998, 2000, 2001) researches drew from over 20 years as a practising forensic scientist. In them, he argued that the debate about forensic science has been concerned mainly with individual cases of miscarriages of justice, when the real problem lies with a system that allows such injustice to occur in the first place and with such frequency, i.e. a structural problem. For Erzinclioglu (1998, 2000, 2001), there are several interrelated problems, which, in combination, produce a system that invites malpractice, with the inevitable consequence that miscarriages of justice will occur. The recent literature on successful appeals contains a range of critical researches on aspects of expert scientific evidence and their potential to cause wrongful convictions that may never be overturned. For example, Norman's (2000, 2001, 2001a, 2001b) and Norman and Fryer's (2002) researches cast doubt upon the scientific evidence upon which dozens of criminal convictions were obtained against women for the murder of their children, when the most likely cause, and which counter-scientific evidence suggests, seems to be 'cot death' or Sudden Infant Death Syndrome' (SIDS) (see also Coulter, 1996; Sweeney & Law, 2001; Arthur, 2002; Morgan, 1992). In a similar vein, Robins (2000), Burrell (2000), Mega & Syal (2001) and Panorama (2001) all reported a series of cases that revealed serious flaws in the fingerprint system which have led to unsafe criminal convictions. In addition, Ingrams (2002) was critical of the supposed 'incontrovertible' proof of DNA evidence when presented in court, despite the lack of public and judicial understanding of what he termed the 'mysteries of DNA'. Thus, despite the fact that expert scientific evidence is intended to resolve adversarial disputes in the interests of justice (a truthful judicial outcome), miscarriages of justice that are caused by expert scientific evidence are commonplace.

In addition to the notions of reasonable suspicion and judicial competence, Article 5 s. 4 of the HRA further contains the following important right of appeal for those who might be wrongly imprisoned of criminal offences: 'Everyone who is deprived of his (sic) liberty by arrest or detention shall be entitled to take proceedings by which the lawfulness of his (sic) detention *shall be decided speedily by a court and his (sic) release ordered if the detention is not lawful'* (my emphasis). At first sight, s. 4 of Article 5 seems acutely circular in that the lawfulness of a criminal conviction will be determined by the same law that delivered the previous prison sentence and if that previous prison sentence is determined to be unlawful then the person who was unlawfully imprisoned will be released according to law! Despite this, s. 4 of Article 5 presents a number of possible challenges to existing appeal practices and procedures. For instance, a recent precedent that was established by a challenge under s. 4 of Article 5 of the HRA by patients compulsorily detained in psychiatric hospitals under the Mental Health Act (1983) (MHA) might also be highly relevant to the current post-appeal procedures of the CCRC, and the continued legislative viability of the CAA (1995) which established the CCRC. In one of the most significant rulings to emerge under the HRA, it was declared that patients had the right to *speedy* appeal hearings against their detention under the MHA (1983) to protect their liberty in case they were being unfairly detained. Moreover, that the government had, indeed, breached the human rights of thousands of people by not providing prompt reviews of their detention by independent tribunals (KB & Ors, R (on the applications of) v Mental Health Review Tribunal [2002] EWHC 639 (Admin)). As such, there is the potential, at least, that a corresponding challenge could also be made under Article 5 s(4) of the HRA against the delays in the procedures of the CCRC in referring cases back to the CACD. As James (2002a: 5) noted, when assessing an appellate procedure, it is essential to do so in the context of its ability to grant fast and fair resolutions to those cases where justice 'failed' the first time around. In attempting such a challenge, however, an immediate problem that emerges is that neither the DCA, nor the Court's Service collect or publish information for the average time taken from an application to the CCRC to a hearing of the appeal in the CACD.

Accordingly, in an attempt to arrive at an estimate of the average time taken for miscarriages of justice to be quashed at the post-appeal stage of the process, Table 7.1 (below) draws from the CCRC's published results of cases referred back to the CACD and their outcomes. It provides an analysis of a sample of ten cases which were randomly considered out of the 36 cases that were successfully quashed following a referral back to the CACD by the CCRC between April 1997, when the CCRC started handling case work, and October 2001 (see Table 2.1 above). And, it determines an average time of almost four years (three years and nine months) for meritorious cases to be quashed through the post-appeal procedures of the CCRC.

The delays represented in Table 7.1 can be conceived to compound the subjective harmful consequences of victims of exceptional wrongful convictions. They also compound the more objective harmful

Table 7.1 Average time taken from application to Home Office or Criminal Cases Review Commission to quash criminal conviction in meritorious cases

Name	Date Convicted	Appeal History	Date applied to Home Office or CCRC*	Date referred by CCRC	Date conviction quashed by CACD	Time from application to Home Office or CCRC to quashed conviction	Average time from application to Home Office or CCRC to quashed conviction
James Hester	20 July 1995	Leave to appeal refused 28 March 1996	Home Office April 1996	7 April 1998	3 December 1998	24 Months	
Danny McNamee	27 October 1987	Appeal dismissed 18 January 1991	Home Office September 1994	7 July 1997	17 December 1998	51 Months	
Mary Durham	12 June 1989	Leave to appeal refused 24 July 1990	Home Office 17 June 1996	28 January 1999	16 July 1999	72 Months	
Trevor Campbell	12 March 1985	Refused by single judge 27 February 1986 and by full court 27 June 1986	Home Office 17 June 1996	21 January 1999	14 October 1999	40 Months	
Keith Twitchell	26 February 1982	Not provided	Home Office January 1991	7 January 1998	26 October 1999	105 Months	
Michael O'Brien	20 July 1998	Dismissed 16 March 1990	Transferred from Home Office to CCRC April 1997	20 October 1998	7 December 1999	32 Months	

Table 7.1 Average time taken from application to Home Office or Criminal Cases Review Commission to quash criminal conviction in meritorious cases – *continued*

Name	Date Convicted	Appeal History	Date applied to Home Office or CCRC*	Date referred by CCRC	Date conviction quashed by CACD	Time from application to Home Office or CCRC to quashed conviction	Average time from application to Home Office or CCRC to quashed conviction
Ellis Sherwood	20 July 1998	Dismissed 16 March 1990	June 1997	20 October 1998	7 December 1999	30 Months	
Darren Hall	20 July 1998	Dismissed 16 March 1990	June 1997	20 October 1998	7 December 1999	30 Months	
John Kamara	December 1981	Leave to appeal refused in 1983	Transferred from Home Office to CCRC in April 1997	26 April 1999	31 March 2000	35 months**	
William Gorman	4 December 1980	Not provided	Home Office 16 December 1996	30 July 1998	7 October 1999	34 Months	
							45.3 Months

Source: Criminal Cases Review Commission (2002b) 'Results of Cases referred to the Court of Appeal' website: http://www.ccrc.gov.uk retrieved 3 May 2002. * Prior to the establishment of the CCRC under the Criminal Appeal Act (1995) the decision of whether to refer a case that had exhausted its appeal rights back to the CACD lay with the Home Secretary, and C3 Division, the Criminal Cases Unit in the Home Office. Following a recommendation by the Royal Commission on Criminal Justice (1993) the CCRC was established on 1 January 1997 and started handling casework on 31 March 1997. In April 1997, all the cases under review by C3 were transferred from the Home Office to the CCRC. ** The calculation for the case of John Kamara is a minimum calculation from April 1997 when transferred to the CCRC from the Home Office to 31 March 2000 when his conviction was quashed, as the date of his application to the Home Office was not provided.

consequences of miscarriages of justice to society as a whole by, for example, increasing the financial burden of justice in 'error' (explicated in the next chapter). Moreover, as James et al's (2000: 143–146) research showed, as the CCRC deal with a daily intake of around four applications against a best disposal rate of two this has resulted in delays and backlogs in the post-appeal processes of the CCRC which can be conceived to be in contravention of Article 5 s. 4 of the HRA, and also, possibly, Article 6, as the CCRC is failing in its task of providing fast and fair resolution to victims of exceptional miscarriages of justice.

Under *Article 6 of the HRA, Right to a Fair Trial*: 'Everyone is entitled to a fair and public hearing within a reasonable time by an independent and impartial tribunal' (s. 1). The conventional trend to focus on exceptional cases of wrongful imprisonment serves to support the notion that, on the whole, England and Wales' criminal process is fair in that it supports the impression (perception) that miscarriages of justice are uncommon. But, if the critical gaze also considers routine and/or mundane successful appeals, as well as exceptional ones, any notion of 'fairness' quickly evaporates, in a system where there are thousands of successful appeals which are overwhelmingly determined on points of law (see, RCCJ, 1993; Brandon & Davies, 1973). On this matter, James's (2002a) research into the possible implications of the HRA for potential applicants at the post-appeal stage of the CCRC is highly significant. In particular, James (2002a: 7–8) distinguished two roles for the CCRC. On the one hand, the CCRC can be regarded as a preliminary or advisory stage of the CACD, a gateway to the CACD which can be conceived to make no legally binding decisions as it is the CACD that is the ultimate arbiter of rights under Strasbourg jurisprudence. On the other hand, however, when the CCRC makes the decision to *reject* applications, it is, in fact, determinative of the applicants' rights, and should thus be considered in the role of tribunal. At such times, a range of current practices of the CCRC can be conceived to undermine the 'fairness' of the criminal process, and, therefore, as a contravention of Article 6 of the HRA. For example, the CCRC's lack of effective mechanisms for the reception and reconsideration of fresh evidence could be conceived as a breach of Article 6 on the grounds that it does not provide a suitable forum for the hearing of fresh evidence. Further, the CCRC's act of appointing the same police force to reinvestigate complaints against it could be said to conflict with the notions of independence and impartiality under Article 6. Moreover, the current availability and limits of post-appeal funding present a situation within which applicants cannot prepare a proper post-appeal defence case to the CCRC or put their case forward in person, which can also be conceived as contrary to Article 6 (for details of these examples see James, 2002a: 6–7).

A further important feature of Article 6 of the HRA to this analysis is stated at s. 2: 'Everyone charged with a criminal offence shall be presumed innocent until proved guilty.' Against this, there is widespread evidence that many victims of miscarriages of justice within England and Wales were the victims of a criminal process that can be conceived as one which very much reverses s. 2 of Article 6 by regarding them as guilty until proven innocent (see, for example, Norton-Taylor, 2001; Woffinden, 2000a; Hinsliff & Bright, 2000; Wadham, 2001; Hopkins, 2001). Indeed, from the critical literature on miscarriages of justice the very raison d'être of many criminal prosecution cases within England and Wales' adversarial system of criminal justice can be conceived as the construction of cases upon a working assumption of guilt (see, for example, Green, 1997; McConville et al, 1991; Woffinden, 1987).

Under *Article 7 of the HRA, No Retrospective Penalties* s. 1 states:

> No one shall be held guilty of any criminal offence on account of any act or omission which did not constitute a criminal offence under national or international law at the time when it was committed. Nor shall a heavier penalty be imposed than the one that was applicable at the time the criminal offence was committed.

On the face of it, a right or freedom that revolves around the relative justness of law and the limitation of retrospective punishment seems entirely reasonable and consistent with the judicial rationale and existing practices of England and Wales' criminal process. Once again, however, in the context of the official statistics on successful appeals and prisoners maintaining innocence, this right, arguably, calls into question the continued legitimacy of a range of legislation that underpins existing criminal conviction practices. The legitimacy of such legislation is, arguably, grounded in an assumption and perception that the criminal justice system is a human system that can *sometimes* get it wrong. It is not grounded in an assumption that the system routinely and mundanely gets it wrong, with the consequences that thousands (possibly tens of thousands) of people directly suffer, and many millions more (the rest of the population) suffer indirectly in numerous ways (discussed in detail in the next chapter). As stated, it is acknowledged that the criminal justice and penal systems have to work under a presumption that court verdicts are on the whole correct. The current scale of miscarriages of justice and prisoners maintaining innocence does, however, at the very least, raise the question: is it legitimate to continue with a criminal justice process and a form of punishment that routinely and mundanely gets it wrong every day, month and year?

An analysis of victims of miscarriages of justice whether wrongly imprisoned or not, also verifies that *Article 8, Right to Respect for Private and Family Life*, is not only contravened in exceptional circumstances, it is also routinely and mundanely contravened. It is stated that 'everyone has the right to respect for his (sic) private and family life, his (sic) home and his correspondence' (HRA, 1998, Article 8 s. 1; s. 2). Yet, every person who is successful in their appeal against their criminal conviction is testimony to the fact that, to a greater or lesser degree, the 'privacy' of his/her family life, however defined, was, in effect, *disrespected*. In the case of the wrongly imprisoned, this can take the form of many years of wrongful imprisonment with the consequence of absence from a partner and/or during a child's upbringing can damage family and friendship relations. Frank Johnson (Bird, 2002; Hopkins, 1999, 2002), for instance, wrongly imprisoned for 26 years, claims that his life was 'ruined', his wife left him, he did not see his children and he lost all contact with his past life (see Hill, 2002c). These matters are only compounded for prisoners maintaining innocence who are victims of the 'parole deal' and who may never be released to rejoin their families or friends (Naughton, 2004b, 2005e, 2006b). In the case of victims of miscarriages of justice who are not imprisoned they, too, experience breakdown of family relations, harm to reputation and/or standing within his/her community. The case of Gavin Mellor, who lost a challenge under Article 8 of the HRA to donate his sperm for the artificial insemination of his wife in the hope she might become pregnant and they could start a family, highlights another issue relating to the right provided by Article 8 that is generally denied to prisoners within England and Wales, which by association is also specifically denied to thousands of victims currently estimated to be wrongly imprisoned (see R v Secretary of State for the Home Department *ex parte* Mellor [2001] EWCA Civ 472). This relates to the specific issue of victims of wrongful imprisonment because they, too, will be denied the same right to start a family during their wrongful imprisonment, further compounding the potential harmful consequences.

Article 12 of the HRA, Freedom to Marry and Found a Family, would seem to be closely related to those provided under Article 8 – respect for private and family life. To show that Article 8 was denied to convicted prisoners, including those wrongly convicted, the case of Gavin Mellor who was not allowed to donate the necessary sperm for his wife IVF treatment was cited. Mellor's case is also evidence of the contravention of Article 12 for all prisoners including wrongly convicted prisoners 'to found a family'.

As for the right to marry, a feature of many exceptional wrongful imprisonment cases is that the victims who were married at the time of their wrongful imprisonment experienced a detrimental impact upon their marriages. It is widely reported that the marriages of Paddy Hill (see Hattenstone, 2002) and Gerry Hunter (see Geffen, 1999) (both Birmingham Six), Michael O'Brien (Cardiff Newsagent Three) (see Hill, 2001a) and Eddie Browning (see Linder, 1997) all broke-down, either during or as a direct consequence of their wrongful convictions and imprisonment. An additional consequence of wrongful imprisonment is that during their time spent in prison many victims are denied the opportunity to meet a prospective partner whom they may wish to marry and found a family with. Indeed, an analysis of exceptional successful appeals shows that victims of miscarriages of justice who were not married at the time of their wrongful imprisonment do not, as a rule, marry during their wrongful imprisonment. For example, Andrew Evans did not marry during his 25 years of wrongful imprisonment; nor did Michael Hickey during his 17 years of wrongful imprisonment; nor did Vincent Hickey during his 17 years of wrongful imprisonment; nor did Stephen Downing during his 27 years of wrongful imprisonment; nor did John Kamara during his 20 years of wrongful imprisonment. Accordingly, the contravention of Article 12 can be conceived as a profound feature of wrongful imprisonment, as it either detrimentally impacts upon the victims who are married or denies many the opportunity to meet a potential spouse to marry and found a family whilst wrongly imprisoned.

According to *Article 14 of the HRA, Prohibition of Discrimination*:

> The enjoyment of the rights and freedoms set forth in this Convention shall be secured without discrimination on any ground such as sex, race, colour, language, religion, political or other opinion, national or social origin, association with a national minority, property, birth or other status.

In assessing Article 14, Box's (1983) classic analysis of the composition of England and Wales' prison population is highly insightful. Of particular relevance Box (1983: 2) revealed that:

> For every 100 persons convicted of...serious crimes, 85 are male. Amongst this convicted male population, those aged less than

30 years, and particularly those aged between 15 and 21 years are over-represented. Similarly, the educational non-achievers are over-represented – at the other end of the educational achievement ladder there appears to be hardly any criminals, since only 0.05 per cent of people received into prison have obtained a university degree. The unemployed are currently only 14 per cent of the available labour force, but they constitute approximately 40 per cent of those convicted. Only 4 per cent of the population are black, but nearly one-third of the convicted and imprisoned population are black. Urban dwellers, particularly inner-city residents, are over-represented.

More recently, Pantazis (1998) drew from a national survey of prisons conducted by the Home Office in 1991 and confirmed Box's (1983) findings on the inequality of the prison population as it consists mainly of young poorly educated males, within which those from ethnic minority backgrounds were overrepresented. In particular, the main findings of the national survey were that:

- 96 per cent of the prison population were men, whereas within the general population the number of men and women are roughly equal;
- approximately 40 per cent of the prison population were under 25, compared to 16 per cent of the general population;
- 41 per cent of male prisoners were from partly or unskilled occupations, against 18 per cent of the general male population;
- 15 per cent of male prisoners identified themselves as either black or Asian, when less than 5 per cent of the total general population come from those ethnic groups; and,
- 40 per cent of male prisoners under the age of 25 left school before the age of 16, compared with 11 per cent of the general male population.

From such research findings, it would be possible to conceive that Article 14 of the HRA is routinely contravened by England and Wales' criminal justice system, as the prison population is not comprised of a representative cross-section of the population as a whole. On the contrary, people from a certain 'sex' – *male* – with a certain 'property status' or 'social origin' – *working class* – within which people – *men* – and from 'national minority' groups of 'race', 'colour', 'language' and/or 'religion' are all over represented. In an attempt to determine the extent to which the inherent discrimination that is evident in the general prison population is applicable to victims of wrongful imprisonment, Table 7.2 (below) presents details of 20 of the most prominent wrongful imprisonment cases between 1997–2002.

Table 7.2, then, demonstrates that victims of wrongful imprisonment are generally men who were under 30 at the time of their wrongful conviction, were either unemployed or in manual or low skill occupations, within which men from ethnic minority groups are vastly overrepresented against their number in the general population. This rudimentary analysis requires deeper exploration, but it does seem to indicate that Article 14 of the HRA would seem, also, to be routinely contravened by England and Wales' criminal justice system in terms of the specific context of wrongful imprisonment.

Conclusion

The foregoing analysis has attempted to illustrate, albeit in a provocative mode, that the current scale of miscarriages of justice, as inferred from the number of successful appeals, together with the thousands of prisoners maintaining innocence, can reorientate the existing human rights voice to cover a scale of denial of legal rights and freedoms that has not previously been acknowledged and/or articulated. Although the HRA recognises that miscarriages of justice can occur and provides legislation for their speedy remedy and compensation, it also limits and prohibits the abuse of the lawful transgressions or contraventions from the Act. From this perspective, the number of victims in cases of successful appeals can be conceived as excessive excursions from, and, hence, contrary to the HRA, and an indication of an excessive amount of harm to victims of miscarriages of justice; the current scale of wrongful convictions is incompatible with almost every Article of the HRA, covered by Schedule 1.[54] This not only presents a challenge to existing perceptions of the scale of the harm to victims of miscarriages of justice, it also presents a different set of moral and ethical implications for analyses of human rights and victims of miscarriages of justice. The sheer number of victims of miscarriages of justice, whether imprisoned or not, would seem to indicate that a judiciary that produces so many wrongful convictions as indicated by the number of successful appeals and the estimated number of cases of wrongful imprisonment is incompatible with, even in unlawful violation of, the HRA. The forcefulness of this critique is further strengthened in the context of the estimated 3,000 victims of wrongful imprisonment in

Table 7.2 Composition of wrongful imprisonment victims by sex, age, occupation and ethnic status/appearance* in 20 of the most prominent cases between 1997–2002

Name	Sex	Age when wrongly convicted	Occupation	Ethnic Status/ Appearance*	Years spent wrongly imprisoned
1. Alex Allan	Male	29	Welder		7
2. James Reith	Male	27	Unemployed		2
3. Andrew Evans	Male	17	Unemployed		25
4. Peter Fell	Male	21	Hospital Porter		17
5. John Robert	Male	19			15
6. Jeremy Bamber	Male	23	P/T Farm Worker		
7. John Kamara	Male	24		Described as 'Black'	20
8. Michael O' Brien	Male	22			10
9. Ellis Sherwood	Male	20			10
10. Darren Hall	Male	20			10
11. Raphael Rowe	Male	19		Described as 'Black'	10
12. Randolph Johnson	Male			Described as 'Black'	10
13. Michael Davis	Male			Described as 'Black'	10
14. Michael Hickey	Male	17			17
15. Vincent Hickey	Male	24			17

Table 7.2 Composition of wrongful imprisonment victims by sex, age, occupation and ethnic status/appearance* in 20 of the most prominent cases between 1997–2002 – *continued*

Name	Sex	Age when wrongly convicted	Occupation	Ethnic Status/ Appearance*	Years spent wrongly imprisoned
16. James Robinson	Male	46			17
17. George Lewis	Male	21		Described as 'Black'	5
18. Sheila Bowler	Female	62	Piano Teacher		4
19. Stephen Downing	Male	17	Cemetery Worker		27
20. Mohammed Patel	Male	31	Accountant	Indian	2 Years 4 Months

Source: Compiled from the archives of the INNOCENT: <http://www.innocent.org.uk> 30 November 2006.* The analysis of 'Ethnic Status/Appearance' is a crude one based on the description of 'colour' or ethnicity of the wrongly imprisoned victims as reported in the case study literature. Hence, it takes no account of the possible ethnic minority groups that might feature who might be white, e.g. Irish. This serves the illustrative purposes here, however, as six out of 20 (30 per cent) were described other than 'white'. Thus, indicating the overrepresentation of those from ethnic minority groups.

England and Wales and the thousands of prisoners currently maintaining innocence, refusing to comply with the requirements of the penal regime, and who may never be released.

The object of this analysis is not to require or demand that the criminal justice system proceed on the basis that its findings are unsound and that convicted criminals and/or prisoners are innocent. However, the current scale of miscarriages of justice and prisoners maintaining innocence does raise significant human rights issues for the judiciary, the penal system and the CCRC, which, despite the difficult nature of the analysis, cannot be ignored. These matters not only need to be considered in depictions of the scale and consequences of miscarriages of justice they also need to be addressed by a system that so mundanely produces them.

8
Zemiology

Introduction

In the last chapter, the human rights voice was adjusted to accommodate all successful appeals and the phenomenon of prisoners maintaining innocence to more fully capitalise upon the promise of the limitations to the lawful restriction of rights and the prohibition of the lawful abuse of rights as proscribed by the HRA. In so doing, a qualified construction of the human rights voice was shown to extend existing voices on the harmful consequences to victims of miscarriages of justice to cover a scale of denial of individual rights and freedoms not previously conceived and/or appropriately responded to. However, even though such an enhanced human rights voice would extend the existing surveillance of miscarriages of justice in the interests of the governed, it would still entail significant limitations. In particular, even if the human rights voice did capitalise on the full potential of the HRA it would still tend to construct the harmful consequences of wrongful convictions at the level of the individual and in terms of the denial of legally defined rights and freedoms. From such a limited frame of reference, even if an individual suffered loss of life, which would appear to be in moral contravention of Article 2 of the HRA, if that loss of life were legally proscribed then the human rights voice would not conceptualise harm. Another major limitation with any voice constructed from the perspective of the HRA would be that it would be largely silent about many other forms of harm that are engendered by miscarriages of justice and wrongful convictions that impact upon secondary victims and/or the citizenry as a whole.

To extend the gaze of the governed on the harmful consequences of miscarriages of justice still further, this chapter attempts to provide an even more adequate depiction of the *trails of harm* that they leave behind, not only to the direct victims but also forms of harm more holistically conceived to secondary or 'indirect' victims. In so doing, this chapter considers the potential of the emerging *zemiological* perspective on questions of crime and punishment. Whilst welcoming the contribution of this approach, and indeed seeking to contribute to it, I also want to flag up the limitations in the zemiological account itself, in particular, its tendency to shift notions of 'crime' and 'harm' entirely outside legal parameters. It is argued that such a move would only deprive a zemiological voice on miscarriages of justice of the discursive force to impact upon effective changes to the systems with which it finds fault.

Conceptual and methodological issues

Zemiology (from the Greek, *zemia*, harm or damage) is an emerging academic perspective within critical criminology and socio-legal studies that was born out of a frustration with criminology's failure to challenge state definitions of 'crime' and 'victim' (Sanders, 1999: 5). In essence, zemiology is an outgrowth of the research program outlined by Sutherland (1940, 1983) and Schwendinger and Schwendinger (1975: 132–138) which argued that criminologists should concern themselves with 'social injury' and/or 'public wrong', and that definitions of 'crime' should revolve around violations of human rights; indeed, that critical criminologists should be 'defenders of human rights' (see also Green & Ward, 2000: 104). The zemiological approach attempts to attain a more holistic understanding than is available in conventional criminological and socio-legal discourses of the range of serious *harms* that are engendered by social and political decisions and/or structures in the interests of social justice (Gordon et al, 1999). In particular, zemiology argues that undue attention is given to many events and incidents that are defined as 'crime', which serves to distract attention from other events and incidents which often involve a comparable and even increased amount of serious harm to victims. For instance, whilst there is an annual average of over one million recorded workplace injuries in Britain, a restriction to the term 'crime' means that only 1,000 or so that are successfully prosecuted each year are available to critical analysis. These are enormous differences that minimise and marginalise the extent of the harm caused by injuries at work, and reveal profound implications in terms of what can be done with such data conceptually, theoretically *and* politically (Tombs, cited Hillyard & Tombs, 2004: 13; see also Pearce & Tombs, 1992).

There is a utility in the zemiological approach in this attempt to reconfigure definitions of miscarriages of justice to include all successful appeals and provide a more adequate depiction of miscarriages of justice and the harm that they engender (see, also, Naughton, 2003, 2004a). In a similar way to the zemiological analysis of workplace injuries, this book is, in large part, concerned to demonstrate that existing conceptions of miscarriages as exceptional occurrences that amount to a handful of cases each year are similarly inadequate. To be sure, existing analyses of the harmful consequences of miscarriages of justice have largely derived from autobiographical and/or biographical accounts of single cases of high profile exceptional successful appeals that were the products of post-appeal procedures (for example, Kee, 1986; Mullin, 1986; Callaghan & Mulready, 1995; Hill & Hunt, 1995; Hale, 2002). From such sources, the harmful experiences and/or consequences of miscarriages of justice are constructed as highly individualised accounts, which can be conceived to be not sufficiently zemiological. They give no sense of the scale of the problem inferred by the recorded statistics of successful appeals in England and Wales that amount to many thousands of cases each year. They, therefore, also omit the harmful consequences that occur in the most apparently mundane of successful appeals at the Crown Court from magistrates' courts and the routine appeals that are successful at the CACD that often entail a comparative amount of harm with exceptional cases. Moreover, where existing analyses have considered the harmful consequences of miscarriages of justice they have generally done so in the very narrow confines of the individual victims. This, in turn, illustrates the need for a *rethink* on how miscarriages of justice and the victims of miscarriages of justice are conceptualised and defined, and how the harm of miscarriages of justice is measured and quantified: 'What one measures, and how one measures it, makes an awful lot of difference to what one finds and the range of...responses that then appear to be "feasible"' (Hillyard & Tombs, 2001: 13). From this perspective, a zemiological approach can be *applied* to the terrain of miscarriages of justice to produce a more comprehensive voice and/or set of analyses of the harm that accompanies the possible scale of miscarriages of justice that can be inferred from the official statistics of successful appeals. This will provide a more comprehensive and accurate picture of the vicissitudes of miscarriages of justice and, hence, represent the constitution of a more *forceful* counter-discourse, bringing zemiology into unity with the Foucauldian inspired attempt to construct a regime of truth on miscarriages of justice.

Before proceeding with the application of a qualified zemiological voice to the terrain of successful appeals, however, it is important to consider the unique *methodological issues* that the zemiological approach raises. This is because the fundamental notion behind zemiology, namely 'harm', inevitably carries a certain degree of vagueness, subjectiveness, and/or a possible multiplicity of reference. For instance, in the most obvious reference, the 'physical harm' of a miscarriage of justice can be fairly straightforwardly defined, demonstrated and quantified. A black eye (without complications) can be conceived as qualitatively and quantitatively less harmful than the loss of an eye, a bruised arm (to a person who is not haemophilic) is less harmful than a fractured one, and so on. Similarly, the financial harm of miscarriages of justice can be relatively unproblematically analysed in the cost/benefit mode, presenting methodological issues that are fairly well recognised and able to be accounted for.

However, the forms of social and psychological harm that are engendered by miscarriages of justice present an entirely different set of methodological concerns. Whilst an extensive range of social and psychological harms can be conceptualised in the abstract, few harms apply equally to all victims of miscarriages of justice, whether primary or secondary victims. Miscarriages of justice are qualitatively and quantitatively different, as are the social circumstances and psychological dispositions of miscarriage of justice victims. Single men who are victims of miscarriages of justice, for example, are likely to experience harm in very different ways, and possibly to a lesser extent than, say, a married father of five children, whose wife and children will also experience a whole range of social, psychological and/or financial harms. Similarly, a miscarriage of justice for drink driving which incurs a penalty of 12 month loss of driving licence can be conceived as qualitatively and quantitatively less harmful than a miscarriage of justice for a paedophile offence which incurs a custodial sentence and potentially permanent damage to reputation. Even if such an offence is successfully appealed there is the potential that the appellant will always be perceived as a paedophile – for some 'there is no smoke without fire'.

This indicates the need for a zemiological continuum of harm, whereby it needs to be acknowledged that the associated social and/or psychological harm(s) experienced by victims of miscarriages of justice, for example, may differ from person to person, i.e. different people may experience the psychological harm of ten years wrongful imprisonment differently. To follow the same example, the psychological harm of a miscarriage of justice for drink driving can, probably, (but not necessarily), be conceived as qualitatively and quantitatively less harmful than a miscarriage for paedophilia. Accordingly, what follows does not claim that the social and psychological harmful consequences unearthed by this analysis are universally valid and/or representative for all victims of miscarriages of justice. Rather, examples of social and/or psychological harm are provided to give some indication (insights) of likely forms of harm that might be experienced as a consequence of miscarriages of justice in the interests of extending existing understandings.

The wider harms of miscarriages of justice

The newness of the zemiological project means that the most significant attempt to date to provide a definitional framework was presented in two work-in-progress conference papers by Paddy Hillyard and Steve Tombs (1999, 2001), which were later reworked and published in an edited collection of a range of critical theoretical and empirical analyses of forms of harm currently omitted by the 'mainstream' criminological gaze (Hillyard et al, 2004). Acknowledging the inherent problem with a zemiological approach in terms of its broadness and its all encompassing nature (discussed below), Hillyard and Tombs (2004: 19–21) marked out, tentatively, a range of types of harms along the following four lines, all of which resonate with this analysis of the wider harms of miscarriages of justice:

- social harm: would encompass notions of 'autonomy, development and growth, and access to cultural, intellectual and informational resources generally available in any given society' (Hillyard and Tombs, 2004: 20, 1999: 9).
- psychological harm: 'would cover any psychological or emotional distress arising from events and behaviours outside of an individual's...control' (Hillyard and Tombs, 2001: 11, 2004: 20).
- physical harm: 'would include...assaults, illness and disease, lack of adequate food, shelter, or death, torture and brutality by state officials (Hillyard and Tombs, 2004: 19, 1999: 9).
- financial harm: 'would incorporate...misappropriation of funds by government (Hillyard and Tombs, 2004: 19–20, 1999: 9).

To illustrate some of the various forms that each of the types of harm can take, the remainder of this section draws from the literature on successful appeals. However, there has been an almost total neglect of, and, hence, a general absence of information about, the harm caused to victims in mundane and/or routine miscarriages of justice, that is, victims who are routinely successful in appeal in either the CACD or mundanely the Crown Court. So, whilst statistical data on the *number* of victims that are routinely wrongly convicted each year is available, the available information of the *harm* to victims of miscarriages of justice has, largely, been restricted to biographical accounts of victims in exceptional cases. This impacts upon the analysis developed here by restricting it to an exploration of the available material, largely on exceptional cases. This is not to imply that the exceptional cases that are cited are necessarily exceptional from a zemiological perspective. On the contrary, there is enough available evidence to suggest that the harm caused to victims in mundane and routine cases of successful appeal against criminal conviction is often comparable with the victims in high profile cases. For instance, the general social and psychological harm to victims of miscarriages of justice for paedophilia, which may or may not incur a custodial sentence, and the knock-on effects to their families/friends/communities has been well documented (see, for example, False Allegations Support Organisation, 2006). Moreover, the small amount of evidence that exists about successful appeals against miscarriages of justice in Magistrates' Courts illustrates the far-reaching harmful consequences of wrongful convictions for routine criminal offences such as drink-driving offences – victims lose jobs, go to prison, some even attempt to commit suicide (Ford, 1998a). With this in mind, what follows is, in part, an attempt to *initiate* a systematic project on the harmful consequences to victims of routine and mundane miscarriages of justice. To be sure, this contribution is not exhaustive. The strategy is to provide insights of some of the more prominent forms of social, psychological, physical and/or financial harm that victims of exceptional miscarriages of justice might experience to both enhance existing critical voices and encourage further research into routine and mundane cases.

Social harm

A range of forms of *social harm* to the direct victims of miscarriages of justice was accounted for in the previous chapter that reorientated the human rights voice to speak of the widespread contraventions of the HRA. In addition to the forms of politico-legal harm, a zemiological voice would emphasise additional forms of social harm felt by the individual victims of miscarriages of justice as it can also relate to being deprived of a partner's support. Social harm from such a perspective can also relate to a parent's absence during a child's upbringing, which can have associated impacts upon both the absent parent and the child's health and life-chances. Symmetrically, it can also have profound impacts upon the families and friends of the direct victims of miscarriages of justice. Furthermore, it can also relate to the victims of the criminal offences for which the wrongfully convicted were wrongfully convicted, and to their families and friends, too.

Examples of all of these various aspects of these additional forms of social harm that miscarriages of justice engender can be found throughout the counter-discourse against miscarriages of justice, but has, hitherto, not been emphasised and/or capitalised upon and, hence, has had little impact. For instance, a zemiological voice on the forms of *social harm to the direct victims of miscarriages of justice* would extend existing notions of the denial of legally provided human rights and freedoms. Legally grounded analyses do not provide an appropriate or adequate depiction of the range of the social harmful consequences that victims of wrongful conviction experience. Further, for married victims with children the social harm of wrongful imprisonment can be conceived as the most socially harmful in the sense that the impacts are more widely felt. For example, almost a decade after his successful appeal Paddy Hill (Birmingham Six) declared: 'Me, I died in prison, inside' (cited Hattenstone, 2002), thus indicating that he will probably never get over the social harmful effects of his 16 years of wrongful imprisonment, during which his wife divorced him and his children grew up in children's homes without him. Similarly, during Gerry Hunter's (also Birmingham Six) arrest he was violently and brutally assaulted and his home was vandalised. And, during his 16 years of wrongful imprisonment he also had no chance to take part in the care of his children, the youngest of whom was four years old when he was arrested, and his wife and children had to live at subsistence level supported by state benefits (which need to be included in the wider financial costs of miscarriages of justice to the population as a whole) because he was unable to provide for them (see Geffen, 1999). When Michael O' Brien (Cardiff Newsagent Three) was wrongly imprisoned his son was three years old, his wife was eight months pregnant with their second child, and he had recently renewed a relationship with his alcoholic stepfather after years of conflict. In terms of social harm, during his ten years of wrongful imprisonment, he was also absent from his son's life, his second child, a daughter, suffered a 'cot-death' when she was two months old, his wife left him, and his father, reported to have been broken by his son's wrongful imprisonment, drank himself to death (see Hill, 2001a).

In addition to such forms of social harm, which might be termed immediate social familial loss, another form of social harm experienced by many victims of miscarriage of justice is the stain on their reputations, despite a successful appeal. As Annette Hewins, who was successful in a routine appeal in the CACD in February 1999 for an arson attack that killed three people, asserted:

> I was exonerated by the courts but not in the community in which I live. That won't happen until the investigation is officially reopened and the killer is caught...until...[the] murderer is found...I will carry the stigma. Injustice doesn't cease just because you walk free from the court of appeal (cited Roberts, 1999).

To be sure, a feature of many miscarriages of justice are the 'whispering campaigns' about the guilt of the victims that continue long after the victims have achieved a successful appeal (for further examples see Dyer, 1997; White, 1997; Editorial, 1998b, 1998c). These brief examples give an insight into the likely forms of social harm to victims of wrongful convictions. One form of social harm that almost all victims of wrongful imprisonment are likely to share was summed up by Gareth Peirce (cited Gillan, 2001) in the following terms: 'They [victims of wrongful imprisonment] come out with no money and no counselling. They have no references, it is difficult to open a bank account, and you can't get a mortgage. They have no GP. [They] don't belong' (see also, Dudley, 2002).

In addition to the harms experienced by the individual victims of miscarriages of justice, there are profound *social effects upon the families and friends of the victims*. In some cases the harm caused in terms of the anger, anguish, pain, suffering and sheer frustration of the family and friends of the wrongly convicted can be just as severe as the people they support, and can have profound and long-lasting effects upon their own lives. For example, Ann Whelan, the mother of Michael Hickey one of the Bridgewater Four, was singled out following the successful appeal in the Bridgewater case for the 19 years that she had campaigned tirelessly and relentlessly for their release (Leonard, 1997). Prior to the wrongful conviction of her son, for his alleged part in the murder of Carl Bridgewater, Ann Whelan had no interest in the criminal justice system. Her son's conviction, however, changed everything and will probably define the remainder of her life, as well as the life of her son. A letter to *The Times* in July 1998 suggests that her campaign is far from completed. She complained that in the 12 months since the quashing of the Bridgewater convictions nothing had been done to bring to account those responsible for the unjust convictions of the men. In particular, she pointed out that there had been no inquiry into how such a 'horrendous' miscarriage of justice could have been perpetrated and no effort had been made to find the real killer. She regarded this state of affairs as a terrible indictment of the law, the judicial system and the Home Office. She further asserted that the men and the public deserve to see immediate action by the Home Office, Crown Prosecution System (CPS) and the police. She concluded that no doubt the authorities hoped that, following the successful appeals, the problem would go away. This, she said, will not happen. 'In acquitting these innocent men they have completed only half the task and must be reminded of this in no uncertain terms' (Whelan, 1998). In October 2002, Whelan (2002) reported that she was also experiencing socio-psychological harm because of her son's continuing mental health problems. Such narratives of the social consequences of wrongful convictions to the lives of families and/or friends of victims are also a common theme of other campaigns against miscarriages of justice (see, for instance, Hale, 2002 for an account of the social costs *to* Stephen Downing's family; Birnberg, 1998 for an account of the campaigning efforts of Derek Bentley's sister Iris Bentley.

A zemiological approach would also highlight that there are wider ranging socio-psychological harms arising from miscarriages of justice. The very legitimacy of the criminal justice system ultimately rests on its ability to deliver on its stated aims to be 'just', 'fair' and 'efficient' (Criminal Justice System, 2006). Miscarriages of justice highlight the failure of the system to meet those objectives and may have a profound and troubling effect upon each and every member of society. Simon Regan (1997a) articulated this position as follows: 'If a person is wrongly convicted it not only strikes at his or her personal liberty – serious enough by any standards – but at every last one of us. For, ultimately, it is we who have created the system and we who must live or die by it.' From such a perspective, the broader social harm of the scale of miscarriages of justice that can be inferred from the statistics on successful appeals have profound and troubling effects upon each and every member of society, signalling a failure of criminal justice system legitimacy that must urgently be addressed.

Finally, the overturn of wrongful convictions also raises questions about the real perpetrators of the crimes. The approach that I have adopted would point out that there are significant forms of social harm to the *families and friends of the victims of crime*. For example, the release of the three surviving members of the Bridgewater Four (Pat Molloy, the 'fourth' member, died in Prison in 1981) gave rise to the awkward question: 'Who, then, did murder Carl Bridgewater?' (Graves, 1997a–d). This question had long since been regarded as closed in the public's mind. There had been a general belief and conviction, particularly among Carl Bridgewater's former community, that justice had been done. Even after a *Rough Justice* television programme, that was helpful in the final referral of the case back to the CACD, Carl Bridgewater's father had asserted: 'I am firmly convinced that those men killed our son and are serving just sentences' (Brian Bridgewater cited Editorial, 1996). With the quashing of the Bridgewater Four's convictions, however, this position was called into question and it raised the possibility that someone else might have been responsible for Carl's murder. As yet, the case of who killed Carl Bridgewater remains officially unsolved. However, as Tongue (cited in Weaver, 1997) said, 'memories of the killing will fester like an open wound unless the case of who killed Carl is solved'.

Such examples are commonplace in the literature on successful appeals. They emphasise both the general *fear of crime* and the re-emergence of forms of social harm to the families and friends of the victims of criminal offences in consequence to the public knowledge of exceptional miscarriages of justice (see, for example, Leonard, 1997; Editorial, 2000b; Buncombe, 1999; Steele, 1995; Shaw, 1998; Roberts, 1999; Hale, 2002; Graves, 1997a–d). This indicates an important consequence of the zemiological approach: the failure to convict those persons guilty of serious offences can be conceived as of as much concern from the perspective of harm reduction as the conviction of the innocent. When an innocent person is wrongly convicted, if a perpetrator of a serious crime is *not* convicted and they remain at liberty, then there is the potential for them to commit more serious crime, and, hence, cause more harm.

Psychological harm

The profound psychological consequences to direct victims of miscarriages of justice were highlighted when Adrian Grounds (2004), a psychiatrist at the Institute of Criminology at Cambridge, examined 18 victims of long-term wrongful imprisonment over a 12-year period.

These included assessment of Gerry Conlon of the Guildford Four and four of the Birmingham Six in the mid-1990s when they were released. He found that they were all suffering from irreversible, persistent and disabling Post-Traumatic Stress Syndrome. He compared their mental state with that of brain damaged accident victims or people who had suffered war crimes. He concluded that it often made them impossible to live with.

In a newspaper article that appeared in June 2000, 11 years after his release, Gerry Conlon (one of the Guildford Four) claimed that he was 'still going through a terrible time, getting dreadful flashbacks' (Pallister, 2000). Adding support to Grounds's earlier findings he asserted that his 'psychiatrist (had told him) that he has never experienced a worse case of post-traumatic stress syndrome, worse even than the soldiers in the Falklands war' (Pallister, 2000).

Paul Hill (another member of the Guildford Four), stated in a BBC television programme, also broadcast in June 2000, that he did not think there was 'anybody alive who (could) come out of that experience and not be scarred' (Pallister, 2000). He continued that the most poignant thing about his case for him was that the judge had 'expressed regret that the death penalty was not an option' (Pallister, 2000).

This pattern is repeated for the surviving members of the Bridgewater Four. Michael Hickey, for example, suffered three nervous breakdowns (see Campbell, 1997) during his 19 years of wrongful imprisonment and has continued mental health problems since his release (see Ann Whelan talking about her son's continued mental health problems cited Carter, 1998). As for the costs to Vincent Hickey, five of his close family died during his wrongful imprisonment and his psychological despair resulted in a failed suicide attempt (see Campbell, 1997). As for the label 'child killers' attached to the Bridgewater case, the following quotation from the remaining surviving member, James Robinson, sums up well its agonising socio-psychological cost: 'For long, lonely years we have cried and been racked with despair. People have looked at us with hate in their eyes and called us child killers. We are not child killers' (James Robinson cited Graves, 1997b).

Physical harm

Victims of miscarriages of justice can also be subjected to a variety of forms of physical harm by the state as a consequence of their wrongful convictions and/or wrongful imprisonment. The case of Keith Twitchell provides a pertinent illustration. For his alleged part in an armed raid on a local factory in which a security guard was killed and £11,500 stolen, eight or nine police officers handcuffed Twitchell's wrists to the back legs of the chair upon which he was sitting. Next a plastic bag was placed over his head and pressed against his nose and mouth. This suffocation procedure was repeated until finally his resolve was broken and he agreed to sign the statement put in front of him. For his 'confession', Twitchell served 13 years of wrongful imprisonment. Quashing his conviction in the CACD, Lord Justice Rose emphasised that the case was: '...yet another appeal...[in which]...a significant number of police officers...some of whom rose to very senior rank, behaved outrageously, and in particular extracted confessions by grossly improper means, amounting in some cases to *torture*' (R v Twitchell [2000] 1 Cr App R 373).

In George Lewis's successful appeal case it was revealed that he was head-butted, punched in the head and threatened with a syringe as police officers questioned him after his arrest in 1987 for two armed robberies and a burglary that he did not commit. The officer who assaulted him was said to be the late John Perkins, a detective constable with the West Midlands Serious Crime Squad, which has since been disbanded. It subsequently emerged that the Squad secured at least 49 prosecutions on the basis of false confessions or other forms of fabricated evidence (Ford, 1998b; Pallister, 1999a).

An analysis of the Bridgewater case reveals a similar story. Most disturbingly, no forensic evidence of any kind against the four was ever submitted to any court. No fingerprints of the men were found. No murder weapon was ever found. And there were no witnesses. On the contrary, the only forensic evidence and witnesses known to the police clearly indicated that it was someone else who might be guilty. The police suppressed this and the entire prosecution case was based almost solely on the 'confession' of Patrick Molloy that occurred after days of violent interrogation, during which his teeth were broken and he was consistently hit around the face and head. For the first ten days he was denied access to a solicitor. During this time his food was heavily salted and he was denied liquids. In desperation he drank from the toilet. His sleep was interrupted regularly during the night. In the end, when he was traumatised and weakened by the experience, he was offered immediate bail if he signed a confession linking the other three to the murder. This he signed as DC John Perkins held him by the hair and read his 'confession' in his ear whilst DC Graham Leeke wrote it down (Regan, 1997b). When Patrick Molloy was allowed access to a solicitor he immediately retracted any statement that he had made, but to no avail. When the Bridgewater Three were freed on bail by the CACD in 1997 Lord Justice Roch (cited Graves, 1997c) made the assertion that: 'It now seems that Mr Molloy was interviewed by officers who were prepared to deceive him into making confessions.'

Financial harm

Whether measured directly or indirectly, the financial costs of the current scale of successful appeals are both significant and substantial. For my purposes here, 'direct' costs relate to all those expenditures that are normally considered as such costs including compensation paid out for miscarriages of justice, judicial costs for court hearings and appeals and defence lawyers and barristers' costs. But, there are also a whole host of possible secondary or 'indirect' economic costs of miscarriages of justice, described as such only because they are not normally considered. For example, there are the expert psychological or social services' assessments, probation reports, and so on necessary in court hearings. There are the costs to the penal system of containing the wrongfully convicted in prison. There are also the potential costs to the benefit system in terms of support provided by the state that was previously provided by the wrongly convicted person. And, there are all manner of other 'indirect' medical costs incurred, such as the socio-psychological counselling that was evident in many of the high profile exceptional miscarriage of justice cases in helping to reintroduce those wrongly imprisoned into society, sometimes after decades of incarceration.

Other 'indirect' financial costs of miscarriages of justice (in the sense that they are not normally considered) can also, arguably, include the costs of establishing and maintaining such governmental institutions as the CACD, the roots of which were a direct response to public pressure that was asserted by the case of Adolf Beck. They can include the costs of such governmental bodies as the CCRC, which, like the CACD was also created as a direct consequence of public knowledge of exceptional successful appeal cases. They can include the costs of establishing and maintaining extra-judicial governmental inquiries such as royal commissions into problematic aspects of the criminal justice system. They can include the costs of the Independent Police Complaints Commission (IPCC), which replaced the Police Complaints Authority (PCA) in April 2004. Moreover, they can, conceivably, include the costs of government policies designed at managing miscarriages of justice and all of their strategic implementations.

Additional financial costs of miscarriages of justice spoken about from a zemiological voice would also include the costs in overturning the criminal convictions in exceptional cases of successful appeal. For example, there were six separate police inquires into the Bridgewater Four case, three CACD appeals, one of which, an eight-week appeal that was dismissed in 1989, was the longest in British legal history (see Graves, 1997d; North and Wilson, 1996; Wilson, 1996). Similarly, the case of the Birmingham Six was referred back to the CACD three times.

More recently there was the case of the M25 Three. Previous CACD appeals also figured in this case that were dismissed in July 1993, with Lord Watkins stating that there was not 'even a lurking doubt' about the safety of their convictions (Lord Watkins cited Editorial, 2000a). Accordingly, Michael Davis, Randolph Johnson and Raphael Rowe – the M25 Three – spent a further seven years wrongfully convicted of a murder that at least two of them could not have committed. Witnesses had claimed that two of the gang were white – but the above named are all black – and forensic evidence and fingerprints found at the murder scene did not match any of the convicted men. This demonstrates a profound financial *inefficiency* in the ability of the criminal justice process to overturn meritorious post-appeal cases.

But, the question of the financial efficiency of justice does not only relate to exceptional cases of successful appeal that retrospectively show a failure to overturn wrongful convictions. The sheer number of successful appeals each year, both in the CACD and the Crown Court, further undermines the notion of the efficiency of the present system. If the system were efficient it would not make as many mundane and/or routine 'mistakes' as it does.

Any attempt to calculate such financial costs, however, can only be partial, as much of the information on such matters is not available. Indeed, the Home Office Statistical Bulletin collects statistical data only of 'notifiable' criminal offences. As miscarriages of justice are not regarded as notifiable *criminal* offences (to do so would be to define them under a general rubric of 'state crime') statistics on such matters are not collected. In addition, details of Home Office compensation in cases of miscarriages of justice is regarded as 'confidential' (see Editorial, 1998a) information, which only further obscures and obstructs any attempt at economic cost calculation. Despite these methodological problems, rough estimations can, however, be determined from a variety of sources. For example, Home Office Research Studies (HORS) reports on research undertaken by or on behalf of the Home Office and published by Research Development Statistics (RDS) can prove a very fruitful source. Similarly, Home Office sponsored research on the comparative merits of public versus private prisons divulges much statistical information on the relative costs of the prisons compared and assessed. Other useful sources published by RDS include Research Findings, the Research Bulletin, Statistical Bulletins and Statistical Papers. They can provide official statistics that are produced as by-products of other inquiries that are applicable here. Investigative newspaper journalism and biographical accounts of some of the high profile exceptional miscarriages of justice are a rich source of information. From these sources a trickle of information pieced together can present some indication of the 'bigger picture'. In an attempt to demonstrate, at least in part, the existence of the bigger picture of the financial costs of miscarriages of justice that are not normally taken into account, the remainder of this section will consider some of these costs in relation to four areas – compensation, legal fees, penal costs and the CCRC.

Popular perceptions of miscarriage of justice *compensation*, in line with popular perceptions of miscarriages generally, tend to think only about compensation paid out to exceptional high profile victims of wrongful imprisonment. From such a viewpoint, attention is focused upon individual cases such as the £1 million that was recently reported to have been offered to Paddy Hill of the Birmingham Six for his 17 years of wrongful imprisonment (see Bright and Hill, 2002). These costs seem significant enough, but they tend to give the impression that such compensation is uncommon. Indeed, Paddy Hill's offer comes over a quarter of a century after his wrongful conviction, and 11 years after his conviction was quashed by the CACD in 1991.

But, compensation to victims of miscarriages of justice is not an exceptional event, it is a routine feature of the criminal justice system if the miscarriage of justice derived from 'judicial error'. Over the last decade, for example, there have been over 150 successful applications for compensation for wrongful conviction or charge under the statutory or *ex-gratia* schemes. As this translates into economic terms, the Home Office paid out a record £6.65 million in compensation in 1997–1998, compared with £1.54 million in 1994–1995 (see Ford, 1998b).

In addition, according to a newspaper article published in December 1998, the Government faces the prospect of a future bill of up to £50 million in costs and compensation for miscarriages of justice uncovered by corruption investigators as part of an anti-corruption drive in the Metropolitan Police. The Metropolitan Police Commissioner is said to have given the Home Secretary this figure after a confidential review of 'Operation Stain' into the problems of tackling corruption among London's police force. The figures were said to be based on the possibility that 200 cases being investigated will all result in quashed convictions. The article concluded that whilst details of Home Office compensation in miscarriages of justice are 'confidential', they are believed to include awards of up to £20,000 for each year wrongly spent in jail (see Editorial, 1998a).

This figure for Home Office compensation awards of £20,000 for every year of wrongful imprisonment appears conservative in the context of a previous article that appeared in the same newspaper almost 12 months earlier. In that article it was revealed that in January 1998 George Lewis was awarded £40,000 compensation (£200,000 in total) for each of the five years that he had spent imprisoned for crimes that he did not commit (see Ford, 1998c). Further support for the current compensatory sum of £40,000 for each year spent wrongfully imprisoned stems from the Andrew Evans case. In June 2000, it was reported that Andrew Evans – a routine miscarriage of justice victim – received £1 million for the 25 years that he spent wrongfully convicted of a murder that he did not commit – which also averages out at around £40,000 for each year he spent wrongly imprisoned (see Weir, 2000).

More recently, it was estimated that Stephen Downing is expected to receive an £8 million Government 'apology' for his 27 years of wrongful imprisonment (see Hill, 2001b). If this estimation is achieved it will significantly increase the current estimate of between £20,000–£40,000 compensation for every year of wrongful imprisonment to almost £300,000 per year. Consequently, the estimated £50 million future bill for miscarriage of justice compensation would seem to be in need of a significant revision.

To gain a purchase upon the likely financial costs of mundane and routine successful appeals, it is interesting to consider how *legal fees* for legally-aided defence work relates to Publicly Funded Legal Services.[55] In 2001, for example, over 103,000 applications were made in magistrates' courts for publicly funded defence representation in the Crown Court, almost all of which were granted. This resulted in a total net expenditure on criminal legal aid in 2001 of £1,750 million (see Lord Chancellor's Department, 2001: 101–104). If these costs are set against the average number of cases that were successful in appeal against criminal conviction each and every year over the last decade (represented in Table 2.1 above), we can reasonably assume that possibly 5 per cent of legal aid spending in 2001 was spent wrongly convicting and then successfully overturning those wrongful convictions. This is based on the annual average of 237 cases that were successfully appealed in the CACD against criminal convictions given in the Crown Court and the annual average of 4,496 successful appeals in the Crown Court against criminal convictions given in the magistrates' court (see Table 2.1 above) would have been funded twice. This amounts to a sum in excess of £87 million in 2001 alone.

In addition to the financial costs of miscarriages of justice so far calculated, the total costs are increased still further if the *costs to the penal system* of containing the wrongfully imprisoned are also included. For instance, the average cost per prisoner in England and Wales between 2002–2003 was £36,268 (Home Office, 2002c: 189). Assuming that successful appellants who are convicted in the Crown Court were convicted for serious crimes and received a custodial sentence, then a further £8.6 million can be added to the annual expenditure on miscarriages of justice – annual average of 237 successful appellants in the CACD over the last 20 years multiplied by £36,268. This brings the likely annual running total of compensation, public legal assistance and prison costs to over £100 million.

The financial costs of establishing and running the *Criminal Cases Review Commission* are also directly attributable to exceptional successful appeals, the cases of the Guildford Four, the Maguire Seven, the Birmingham Six, and so on, back to the CACD. The CCRC, like the CACD and the royal commissions on miscarriages of justice exists only because miscarriages can and do occur. As the 'Management Statement' of the CCRC states it 'will come to play a key role in enhancing public confidence in the integrity and effectiveness of the criminal justice system as a whole, as Parliament intended' (Criminal Cases Review Commission, 2002). Moreover, one of the CCRC's five primary objectives also states that it will 'enhance public confidence in the criminal justice system' (Criminal Cases Review Commission, 2000). This renders any notion of the theoretical 'independence' of the CCRC is difficult to sustain. Indeed, the economic costs of the CCRC can be conceived as political governmental expenditure to domesticate identified failings in the legislative framework of the criminal justice system and, simultaneously, promote confidence in the rule of law. Accordingly the costs of the CCRC come into play, currently standing at around £8 million running costs per annum (Criminal Cases Review Commission, 2006), increasing the running annual total of miscarriages of justice to over £110 a year. When the costs of establishing and running such things as the CACD, the IPCC, (which replaced the PCA in April 2004), governmental inquiries and/or the royal commissions into problematic aspects of the criminal justice system are also added, the economic costs of miscarriages of justice over the last decade probably run into many hundreds of millions of pounds.

This analysis could be accused of stretching the argument too far. As no human system can be perfect, it is inevitable that *some* miscarriages of justice will occur. Accordingly, it is also inevitable that the provision of safeguards to attempt to prevent and remedy miscarriages of justice when they occur is a necessary requirement in a liberal democratic society and it will incur a financial cost. The problem with this argument is that the system doesn't *sometimes* get it wrong. As shown above, contrary to public perceptions and the stated aims of the criminal justice, over the last two decades there have been almost 95,000 successful appeals against criminal conviction in England and Wales, over 4,700 per year. This expenditure on miscarriages of justice is not only wasteful, but it is money which could be spent on essential social services. The excessive amount of money spent on wrongful imprisonment could be spent on deprived school children. The excessive amount spent on compensation to victims of wrongful criminal charges/convictions could be spent on the countless scores of people that are denied necessary hospital treatments. The excessive amount spent on legal fees could be used to improve the criminal justice system so that miscarriages of justice do not occur in the future.

Critical remarks

A zemiological voice on miscarriages of justice both enhances and extends the qualified human rights voice constructed in the previous chapter that invoked the limits and/or prohibitions of the lawful restriction and/or abuse of the HRA. It enhances the voice of the governed by contributing further insights of the extensive range of forms of harm that miscarriages of justice engender: a zemiological voice on forms of social and psychological harm further emphasises the effects of miscarriages of justice on the enjoyment and/or fulfilment of the lives of victims, thus further illustrating the contravention of Article 2 of the HRA (Right to Life); a zemiological voice on the physical harm of miscarriages of justice further enhances a human rights critique of the contravention of Article 3 of the HRA (Freedom from Torture); a zemiological voice on the financial harm of the current public expenditure on miscarriages of justice extends all existing voices into an important area of harm which contains significant human rights issues for all members of the population. In addition, a zemiological voice can serve to extend notions of miscarriages of justice still further by bringing to light an extra dimension of harm when successful appeals are achieved, i.e. the broader harm that accompanies the knowledge that justice 'failed' and that the real perpetrator remains at liberty to cause more harm. In this sense, zemiology can, indeed, be constructed as a 'defender of human rights', extending the critical gaze of the governed, contributing to *requalifying* a variety of forms of anti-discourse about miscarriages of justice that are currently an extremely marginalised or even hidden aspect of the overall potential of counter-discourse against miscarriages of justice.

There are, however, core questions and difficulties that need to be raised in appraising the promise of the zemiological project. Not least, there is a central vagueness or all-purposeness in the adoption of the 'harm' perspective. For instance, it is not obvious whether the locus of harm lies at the level of the individual or more indirectly, in some aspect of the social collectivity. The clarification of this issue, however, is of major importance, in addressing, for example, issues around the ubiquitous, but contested, idea of 'victimless crimes'. On the one hand, zemiology would seem to indicate that the only way to decide and assess the occurrence of injustice or 'crime' is to demonstrate some definite form of 'harm' or injury to an individual victim. On the other hand, and possibly with no reference to any particular complaints of individual harm, zemiology displays an inherent util-itarianism, insisting on highlighting *indirect* harms that may have an impact on other aspects of society more collectively conceived. To date, zemiological writings have not properly specified this kind of distinction.

There are also a range of issues relating to the inherent subjectivity and relativism of zemiological analyses in the sense that 'harm' is an irreducibly value-laden norm. Clearly, and most basically, some indi-viduals will tend to get more easily upset (psychological harm), or more easily hurt (physical harm), than others in the event of experi-encing very similar wrongdoings against them. This could play out to the effect that the treatment of individuals by state agencies such as the police and prison service, for example, that upset or hurt those individuals that are predisposed to psychological anxiety or more vul-nerable to physical harm would be defined as harmful and, hence, 'criminal'. By the same token, however, similar, or even the same treat-ment during police interviews and/or imprisonment would *not* be defined as harmful and, hence, not 'criminal', if they occurred to indi-viduals not so predisposed. To give an almost caricatured sense of the problem, would the wrongful imprisonment of someone prone to claustrophobia represent a worse 'crime' or harm than the wrongful imprisonment of someone who did *not* have that condition?

The serious point behind such a near-absurd scenario concerns the relationship between harm and *injustice*, a complex connection, which the logic of zemiology seems to oversimplify. This is an issue because the injustice of a miscarriage of justice might have little to do with the exact amount of harm experienced. An individual would be no less unfairly treated because he/she did not complain about their psychological deterioration in prison whilst hoping for the repeal of their sentence. This emphasises an inevitable subjectivity/relativism in calculations of harm. To take a case of economic harm, a £50 parking fine to a millionaire would cause little bother to that individual's daily life. However, the same penalty dealt out to a person on state benefits would probably account for a week's groceries, thus constituting a disproportionate amount of harm to the latter individual in relation to the same treatment. Whilst there would undoubtedly be some additional 'justice' in a kind of sliding scale of penalties according to harm, the effectiveness of the resulting system and the intrusive contestability of case-by-case relativities would be unlikely to create consistency of expectation, a prerequisite of *any* system of law/justice.

A further set of questions that could be levelled at zemiology relates to the conception of human nature that lies behind zemiological declarations of harm. What if it was thought, for example, that international human rights were actually themselves harmful to either individual freedom or group subcultures? It could be argued that we cannot simply assume that the notions of 'human rights' as they were constructed in the Universal Declaration of Human Rights in the aftermath of the Second World War (see United Nations, 2006; Franklin and Eleanor Roosevelt Institute, 2006), and generally and unproblematically incorporated by the ECHR and the HRA, always serve in the best interests of all human beings, in all places, and for all time. It could even be argued that forms of human rights legislation, by advocating certain forms of human behaviour and conduct and restricting and actively sanctioning others, can be regarded as a form of *social control* that limits the ability of individuals to act in self-determining ways. This is not necessarily to criticise or argue against signed-up-for human rights in England and Wales. Rather, it is to point up difficult matters such as the possible *eurocentricity* of their origins and question their applicability to states and societies that are not signatories to such legislation. A pertinent example of the difficulties faced by the universal and/or inalienable export of Western human rights ideals was the recent conflict in Afghanistan by the 'international community' that was sanctioned by the United Nations (see, for example, Woollacott, 2001).[56] In particular, that conflict was partly legitimated in the name of human rights and the liberation of Muslim women who, it was argued, were being oppressed, as they were not being afforded the rights and freedoms that are aspired to/signed-up-for in the West (see, for example, Viner, 2002). This took little, if any, account of the harm caused to the tens of thousands of human beings caught-up in the conflict that were defined as 'against us', as they were not in compliance with Western notions of 'proper' human conduct (see, for example, Scraton, 2002, 2002b; Chomsky, 2002; Green, 2002b; Mathiesen, 2002). A key conundrum for zemiology, then, is: isn't one person's (group's) injury another person's justice?

More generally, what is the basis of zemiology's implicitly assumed vantage point of moral superiority – something of which must be assumed if the adjudication of harm is to lead to real progressive change? A zemiological analysis of the psychological harm to a victim of a miscarriage of justice, for example, is not necessarily superior to a more legally grounded analysis of the harm caused by the denial of legal rights and freedoms. Following the same example, psychological harm can manifest itself precisely because legal rights and freedoms have been transgressed, and psychological equilibrium can possibly be restored once the denial of rights has been acknowledged by the state and remedied. As indicated, psychological harm can also be completely unrelated to external factors and could be a purely subjective mental state. Zemiological framing seems to take it for granted that there is an obvious and 'progressive' way of accounting for and dealing with harms, and that somehow those subscribing to zemiology will, in fact, be singing from the same moral hymn sheet. Not only is this very questionable in itself, the zemiological literature fails almost entirely to openly discuss such obvious lacunae.

Finally, there are a number of issues around the attitude of zemiology and the status of the existing criminal justice system. If the primary object of zemiology is the reduction of harm, then, in the context of miscarriages of justice, for example, zemiology could not reasonably be conceived as being entirely 'against' the criminal justice system as such. On the contrary, a strict zemiological approach would be just as concerned with the harm caused by perpetrators of serious crimes as they are already conceived by the criminal justice system, such as murder, rape, serious physical assault, and theft, for the harm that such occurrences cause to victims. From such a standpoint, zemiology would, logically, seek to ensure that such 'criminals' or 'harm producers', or whatever form of semantics one would care to use, were not at liberty to continue to produce harm/commit 'crime', and this, perhaps, could be thought to leave existing arguments for working in or against the criminal justice system pretty much in the place they were prior to the zemiological 'intervention'.

And, yet, it is manifestly the case that one of the key self-images of zemiology is that it does, precisely, intervene in such a way as to pro-mote the 'longer-term' abandonment of conventional notions of 'crime', 'law' and 'criminal justice' altogether in favour of analyses of 'harm' (Hillyard and Tombs, 2001: 23). Where this is the implication, a critical counter can be made, for example, with the recent introduction of the HRA, that renders the actions of state agencies and the employees of state agencies 'unlawful' if they are incompatible with the letter and/or the 'spirit' of the Act. This, I believe, significantly improves the opportunities for successful legal challenge against the criminal justice system for violations of the Act. Moreover, if zemiologists in the guise of 'defenders of human rights' can persuasively demon-strate violations of the HRA, then, the cause of such violation can be labelled as crime within a general rubric of definitions of state crime and legal redress can be effectively obtained. As Penny Green's (2002b: 76) definition of state crime asserted: 'If a state's own actions depart from that state's own rules or is unjustifiable in terms of the values the rules purport to serve, then those actions objectively are illegitimate.'

Accordingly, I do not see zemiology as necessarily different or dis-tinct from the 'state crime' perspective that attempts to highlight the violation or contravention from signed-up-for human rights. On the contrary, the critical modes of thinking behind zemiology and the state crime approach 'share a common appreciation of contradictory affairs in human affairs, a negative assessment of the status quo, and a belief in the need for fundamental change in productive and social relations' (Barak, 1991: 11); they can both be conceived as logical extensions of the call by criminologists such as Sutherland (1940, 1983) in the 1930s to include the behaviours of 'white-collar' and cor-porate offenders – behaviours which may or may not be legally defined as against the criminal law, but which nevertheless, cause harm, injury and violence – into what was then emerging as the precursor to the study of 'the crimes of the powerful'; and, they are both direct out-growths of the program outlined by Schwendinger & Schwendinger (1975). As Barak (1991b: 273) asserted in his call for an expanded definition of crime to incorporate state criminality: [My call is a response to] 'the call in the 1970s by two radical criminologists [Schwendinger and Schwendinger 1975] for the study of systems of exploitation and state crimogenic institutions [that] has not been seriously pursued by criminology.' In this sense, I believe that zemiology should continue to proceed within the 'short' to 'medium' term view presented by the main advocates of zemiology that:

> ...whether or not a new discipline of zemiology is to emerge, we must accept that raising issues of social harm does not [necessarily] entail making a simple, once-and-for-all choice between representing these as *either* crimes *or* harms; each may form part of an effective political strategy (Hillyard and Tombs, 2001: 22 original emphasis).

As Tombs (1999: 6) elsewhere noted:

> It is difficult to conceive of over-riding advantages to organising our work around 'social harm' [i.e. zemiology]. A focus on law through the category crime may be more productive: law provides a site of struggle, and facilitates the development of focused political action in a way that it is not necessarily the case with reference to social harm. That we should *restrict* our work and political activity to law does not, of course, follow from this observation (original emphasis).

This, undoubtedly, creates a paradox for the architects of the zemiological paradigm, for how can you have an alternative based in zemiology, and yet say, we can retain a notion of crime/law in the present term? Despite this, I see the utility of the short to medium zemiological lens to critical analyses of miscarriages of justice as having the potential to contribute to, not detract from, the forms of critical criminology from within which the 'frustrated' notion of zemiology derives. It can contribute to the attempt to reorientate definitions of miscarriages of justice to include all successful appeals precisely because it helps to illuminate, in a very persuasive way, the comparable forms of harm that occur in all successful appeals, whether they be exceptionally, routinely or mundanely determined. The human rights approach of zemiology can contribute to the incorporation of such events and behaviours that can be conceived to violate (contravene) domestic or international signed-up-for human rights legislation within the rubric of state crime in the struggle against forms of social injustice.

Moreover, as Carlen, (1991: 54–62) drawing from Bachelard (1940) and Derrida (1976) has noted:

> Radical theorists can diminish their perennial fear of the discursive power of the empirical referent by adopting 'the methodological protocol…that systems of thought must say "No" to their own conventions and conditions of existence…there is no reason why they should not *both* take seriously (that is, recognise) *and* deny the empirical referent's material and [discursive] effects…[for] the very task of theory is to engage in a struggle for power over the "meaning of things"…to produce new meanings which will empower' (original emphasis).

For me, zemiology and the state crime perspectives are complementary expressions of the long tradition within critical criminology of saying 'No' to power; to dominant definitions and categories of 'crime' and 'victim'; they are essentially a struggle for power over the 'meanings' of 'crime' and 'victim'. In this sense, I do not think that one has to be an out-and-out zemiologist to find a utility with the approach. Nor does one have to be an out-and-out critic. In the same way that Foucault can be used as a resource to picture aspects of existing forms of social reality without the need to be a 'Foucauldian' (see Gane, 1986: 111; Osborne, 1994: 493–499), zemiology, too, notwithstanding its difficulties/limitations, can be used as a resource, as a tool of analysis, a platform that can aid in the reorientation of popular perceptions of social ills such as miscarriages of justice. As Hillyard and Tombs (2001: 10, 2004: 20–26) stated, 'defining what constitutes harm is a productive… process…zemiology is partially to be defined in its very operationalisation, in its efforts to measure social harms.' Defining what constitutes 'crime' and 'victim' is equally a productive process. Definitions of 'crime' and 'victim' change over time, in part, precisely because certain events and/or forms of behaviour that cause harm are promoted and demoted in the discursive struggle between the defenders of the existing criminal justice system arrangements and critics who want to change them. It is within such a context that this book sees the utility of a fusion of Foucauldian insights of the operations and exercise of prevailing forms of criminal justice system knowledge-power with the perspectives of zemiology and state crime. They are *tools* to *picture* the *real* scale and the harmful effects of miscarriages of justice and to assess the possibilities of resistance. The motivation being, that it will initiate a more fruitful debate about conventional 'meanings' of miscarriages of justice in such a way as to question the management of the criminal justice system, change public perceptions and contribute to struggles for change.

Conclusion

In an attempt to extend still further the voice of the governed on the harmful consequences of miscarriages of justice, this chapter constructed a new voice from the emerging zemiological approach. In essence, zemiology works within the general agenda of human rights discourse but extends forms of human rights critique into a more morally grounded domain. To this end, a qualified zemiological voice was constructed that did not stray too far outside of a focus on the categories of 'lawfulness' and 'unlawfulness' as contained in the HRA. Notwithstanding significant theoretical and methodological challenges that lie at the heart of the zemiological perspective, it was shown to both enhance the extended human rights voice on the harmful consequences of miscarriages of justice that was reorientated in the previous chapter, and take the analysis into even newer territory. This provided a more detailed depiction than is available from other perspectives of a range of forms of harm that are likely to be experienced by the direct victims of miscarriages of justice.

It provided an insight into a more appropriate depiction of some of the wider harmful consequences to others caught-up in justice in 'error' and the broader society. It built on, and enhanced, critiques about the contravention of Article 2 of the HRA, that were constructed in the previous chapter, by emphasising forms of social and psychological harm of wrongful convictions. It strengthened the notion of the contravention of Article 3 of the HRA, also constructed in the previous chapter, through the provision of insights into the details of forms of physical harm experienced by victims in cases of successful appeal. Furthermore, a zemiological voice was applied to extend existing analyses still further by indicating the staggering costs to the public purse of miscarriages of justice that have profound socio-economic and human rights impacts upon society as a whole. A further consequence of a zemiological voice on successful appeals from a symmetrical perspective, is that the failure to convict those persons guilty of serious offences is of as much concern as the conviction of the innocent. When an innocent person is wrongly convicted, perpetrator of serious crimes remain at liberty with the potential for them to commit more crime, and, hence, cause more harm. A zemiological analysis, then, calls for the urgent need to significantly rethink how the harm of miscarriages of justice is conceived and acted upon, contributing to the production of more appropriate forms of counter-discourse in the interests of evoking more adequate governmental responses.

Conclusion

Overall, this book has been trying to shift analyses of miscarriages of justice along four lines: to make clear the *distinction* between popular (public and political) discourses on miscarriages of and what the criminal justice system deems to be a miscarriage of justice; to map a new terrain for miscarriages of justice as a *field of empirical enquiry*; to provide a more adequate *depiction* of both the scale of miscarriages of justice that are currently occurring and the possible harmful consequences of those miscarriages of justice; and, to critically review the activity of *counter-discourse*, highlighting the limits of all previous changes to the criminal justice system to prevent miscarriages of justice from occurring.

A clear understanding of what, precisely, constitutes a miscarriage of justice is important to the understanding of the limits of previous attempts to affect changes to the criminal justice system to prevent their occurrence. Put simply, in the mediation of miscarriages of justice, the term 'miscarriage of justice' has been deployed in the discursive dialogue between public/political and legal discourses, but has meant very different things: as popularly understood they relate to beliefs that innocent people have been wrongly convicted or imprisoned; for the criminal justice system they relate to technical breaches of the rules and procedures of due process, notwithstanding if the appellant is innocent or guilty. From this perspective, the criminal justice system does not respond to speculative critiques of 'errors' or 'failings' with the criminal justice process, no matter how accurate or valid those critiques may be. On the contrary, it requires those 'errors' to be proven in successful appeals. This transforms general critiques into powerful forms of counter-discourse that can act as prompts to legitimate governmental intervention with the aim of correcting the apparent 'errors' at hand. This is because changes to societal systems under governmentality forbids governmental intervention without such a mandate.

In an attempt to unearth a more appropriate depiction of the scale of the miscarriage of justice problem, existing definitions were shifted from a sole concern with exceptional cases overturned through post-appeal processes to include all successful appeals. This increases the number of official miscarriages of justice that can be calculated from 18 cases a year over the last decade to almost 5,000 cases a year. Moreover, it was shown that even if all of the cases that appear in the official statistics of successful appeals were defined as miscarriages they would still not capture the total number of miscarriages of justice in England and Wales as they would not include a whole variety of causes of miscarriages that will never feature in the official statistics. Accordingly, the scale of the victims of miscarriages of justice and the harmful consequences that they experience is also potentially in excess of that which can be inferred from the official statistics of successful appeals.

The analysis then turned to the most significant existing voices on miscarriages of justice and pointed up both their strengths and their pitfalls. Whilst the existing voices against miscarriages of justice routinely assert that they are widespread, they are grounded in a definition from which they can only be conceived as rare occurrences and quantified as small in number. In consequence, attempted changes of the system to remedy or avert miscarriages of justice have attempted to impact only within the very limited scope of procedural problematics that are exemplified by specific post-appeal cases. As this relates to the harmful consequences of miscarriages of justice, existing analyses have also been restricted to the denial of legal rights and freedoms and have only been conceived as rare occurrences involving a relatively small number of individual victims.

In response, I attempted to revise critical academic theory about the production and deployment of counter-discourse against miscarriages of justice and the processes of governmentality through which competing discourse is dealt with. In particular, the relevance of public crises of confidence that accompany successful appeals that exemplify previously unacknowledged 'errors' of the criminal justice system was emphasised. Such events should not be viewed entirely 'negatively'. On the contrary, they represent moments when the *conditions* for changes to the criminal justice system are right, and can be utilised to force through more effective changes. This has tended to be missed by critical academic analyses against miscarriages of justice, which have rather tended to gloat at the public crisis as if it were somehow evidence of a corresponding crisis in government. This indicates a deep theoretical misconception at the heart of the forms of critical academic counter-discourse that responded to the RCCJ. Governmentality, is precisely about the management of opposing discourses at critical moments and in response to problematic events. It is an on-going venture to purge society of lingering aspects of sovereign forms of rule. It is best seen as a relationship between government and governed with each playing a vital role in the transformation of the structures of society. As such, a primary task of critical counter-discourse to the way things are should be to attempt to invoke as many public crises of confidence as possible, which should then be viewed as opportunities to be exploited and to force more effective changes which may work to truly prevent miscarriages of justice from occurring rather than just introducing new ways for them to be overturned.

Historically, however, the changes that have followed public crises of confidence in specific aspects of the criminal justice system, such as the establishment of the CCRC as recommended by the RCCJ, have not met the expectations of the critical academic community. This has served to further the general misconceived conspiratorial tendency that government is no more than an authoritarian abuse of power, which dominates a citizenry or a population – the governed. If viewed differently, however, at least part of the problem can be attributed to the kinds of misconceived notions of power, resistance and government that were collectively expressed in the counter-discourse contained in *Criminal Justice in Crisis*. The RCCJ did not fail in the public's eyes, for it resolved the public crisis of confidence that it was established to address. Rather, the critical academic discourse that responded to the RCCJ can be conceived to have 'failed' to properly understand both the conditions for its establishment and to exploit the real opportunities that it provided.

In essence, then, this book represents a concerted attempt to move away from exceptionalist understandings of miscarriages of justice towards a much more inclusive depiction of the miscarriage of justice terrain. Extending existing analyses in this way, the domain of human rights and the moral promise of the HRA were explored. Although the HRA does allow for the lawful transgression from the rights and freedoms it provides, it does so only within the context of certain limits and prohibitions against the abuse of rights. From such a standpoint, a closer analysis of the various Articles of the HRA and the current scale of successful appeals revealed that almost all were conceivably being contravened by a judiciary that produces too many miscarriages of justice. This reconfigured human rights voice, however, also displayed insurmountable limitations in terms of depictions of the harmful consequences of miscarriages of justice, because human rights discourses are entirely grounded in notions of legally constructed *individual* subjects.

In an attempt to provide a voice that might be better able to depict the full range of harm, both to individuals other than the direct victims of miscarriages of justice and the collectivity (governed) as a whole, the fledgling zemiological approach was considered. This took the human rights analysis further into the territory of moral critique and onto a more collective plane. Even so, once again reservations were lodged. In its most extreme, but quite logical, guise the zemiological voice requires that critical discourse takes place completely outside of the legal agenda because 'crime' must be substituted in toto by 'harm'. This was argued to be a mistake as it would inevitably diminish the contribution of zemiology to struggles for change and more focused forms of political action against existing legal regimes. There is also an almost constitutive risk of subjectivism and incommensurability at the heart of zemiology, because of the experiential relativity of 'harm' across immeasurable social situations. Suitably qualified, the zemiological voice was put to work in the terrain of successful appeals whereupon it called up depictions and calculations of the consequences of miscarriage of justice that are not available from other perspectives.

Perhaps most significantly, the analyses offered here have illuminated a general need for a more appropriate understanding of the relations of power between governed and government in the realm of criminal justice. The governed are not passive in relation to government in the processes of the governmentality of the criminal justice system. On the contrary, progressive changes to the criminal justice system come, precisely, from the governed in the form of claims of miscarriage of justice which cause harm to victims that are officially acknowledged if they achieve a successful appeal. In this sense, power in governmentality society can be understood as the negotiated interplay of discourse and its counter-discursive opposition. The form of this negotiated outcome then constitutes (*produces*) a new regime of truth, and new forms of social reality. It has been shown that there is an apparent myopia on the problem of miscarriages of justice with eyes fixed firmly on successful appeals that derive from just one possible route, as opposed to wider analyses that take account, also, of the various other courts that determine criminal appeals. Consequently, the thousands of successful appeals that are overturned each year in England and Wales by routine and mundane criminal appeal mechanisms and the corresponding number of victims that are affected by 'justice in error' have been, equally, severely neglected. These subjugated voices need to be heard for what they have to say about the limitations of the existing criminal justice system and, by implication, the limitations of governmentality to protect us from 'errors of justice' and the harm that they cause.

The book, then, has sought to contribute towards the articulation of a new critical voice in several ways and at different, but related, levels. The existing definitions, calculations, conceptions of causality and understandings of changes to the criminal justice system around miscarriages of justice have been persistently questioned and cumulatively, at least to an extent, replaced by more inclusive horizons. This involved a series of *conceptual* 'interventions' derived from a particular reading of, and extension to, Foucault's insights, and it also required considerable reworking of both empirical cases and evaluative standpoints. When first embarking on this book I was struck by the fact that the 'terrain' or 'field' of miscarriage of justice analysis appeared rather incoherent and, even, morally arbitrary. Whilst it is hardly likely that the much needed task of remapping the entire field could be accomplished by any one study or another, the different aspects of argument and enquiry contained in this book contribute to something of a new agenda in this area.

Notes

1 For my purposes here, I have omitted from this quotation the reference to guilty acquittals and the inference by the RCCJ that they also constitute miscarriages of justice. This matter will be considered in some detail in the following chapter.

2 The Royal Commission on Criminal Justice (1993) was announced on the day that the Birmingham Six had their convictions overturned by the CACD (see Royal Commission on Criminal Justice, 1993: 1).

3 The RCCJ was also established, in part, to a line of other less well-publicised miscarriage of justice cases. See, for example, Woffinden (1987).

4 See, for example, McConville and Bridges (1994); Walker and Starmer (1993).

5 As will become apparent, this analysis, then, differs somewhat from Collini (1991) who did not invoke the abbreviations of 'discourse'/'counter-discourse' due to the specific assumptions about 'power' that they conjure up. Alternatively, this book grounds notions of voice within a Foucauldian inspired reading of the interplay of discourse and its counter-discursive opposition precisely in an attempt to show the processes of power within the terrain of miscarriages of justice and the reform of the criminal justice system.

6 Moreover, it was precisely in recognition of the dynamic link between public concerns about the possible wrongful conviction of the innocent and how this can prompt reforms to improve the criminal justice system that the Innocence Network UK (INUK) was founded. The INUK exists because innocent people can be wrongly convicted and the existing appeal system, despite the CCRC, cannot guarantee that all innocent victims of wrongful conviction will overturn their convictions (for details see Innocence Network UK, 2006). As will become evident below, the INUK is intended as a key 'watchdog for the governed' in this crucial arena.

7 There are, of course, exceptions to this 'general rule' such as if the guilty plea can later be shown to have derived from some form of vulnerability as, for example, in the case of Andrew Evans who spent 25 years in prison following his confession and guilty plea to the murder of Judith Roberts until fresh psychiatric evidence rendered his conviction unsafe (Duce, 1997; R v Evans [1997] EWCA Crim 3145). It is also possible that convictions from guilty pleas can be overturned if they are 'vitiated by the lack of true consent on the part of the applicant brought about by misapprehension stemming from, for example, the magistrate's discussion with counsel' (R v Turner [1970] 2 QB 321, 326).

8 The converse of this situation being the innocent who plead guilty at trial (for a number of possible reasons such as charge, plea and sentence bargaining) who then 'maintain guilt' in prison because they have no real hope of using the appeal procedures and maintaining guilt provides the fastest route back out of prison.

9   On the other hand, the inherent risk in abuse of process cases is that those who want to challenge proceedings (and subsequent convictions) on this basis should maintain a plea of not guilty throughout. This puts them in an invidious position of course, because if their appellate challenge is unsuccessful they will end up having to serve an undiscounted sentence.

10 This situation is only compounded by the on-going attempts by the Home Office to reform the compensation system for victims of miscarriages of justice who currently are eligible. In a speech by the Secretary of State for the Home Department (Charles Clarke) in April 2006 it was revealed that the plans include scrapping the discretionary scheme for compensation; the introduction of time limits for all applications; for the Assessor to take greater account of applicants' convictions when deciding the level of awards for non-pecuniary loss; for the Assessor to take greater account of conduct by applicants which contributed to the circumstances leading to the miscarriage of justice; to enable the Assessor to make deductions from the pecuniary element of the award because of criminal convictions of the applicant; to provide for an upper limit on the overall amount of compensation and as regards compensation for loss of earnings; and, to enable the Assessor to reduce an award of compensation to zero, in exceptional cases, on account of criminal convictions and/or contributory conduct of the applicant (see Home Office, 2006; for a critical evaluation see, BBC News, 2006).

11 In February 2005, for instance, 30 years after they were convicted, the Guildford Four received a public apology from the Prime Minister, Tony Blair, who said that they 'deserve to be completely and publicly exonerated' (see Editorial, 2005).

12 Explained in further detail below with relevant legislation and exceptions.

13 Prior to the establishment of the CCRC, post-appeal claims of miscarriage of justice were handled by C3 Division of the Home Office and referred back to the CACD if the Home Secretary saw fit.

14 Although, the statistics from the CACD will include convictions overturned following a referral by the CCRC.

15 An alternative critical view of official statistics which recognises their critical utility has been offered by a group of 'critical realists' who regarded them as problematic and in need of careful interpretation, but better than nothing, see Levitas and Guy (1996).

16 Walker (2002) also highlighted defective legal arguments and new evidence, categories which correspond, respectively, with the categories of inadequate defence and cases overturned by fresh evidence discussed as part of the critique of the limits of forensic science expert witness evidence.

17 This analysis of how individual actors may cause miscarriages of justice, then, can be said to reverse the methodology of previous accounts. Existing accounts analyse a data source of successful appeals and generate a range of categories by classifying the reasons for the successful appeal as the cause of the miscarriage of justice. Alternatively, this analysis works the other way around and starts with a list of categories and applies them to the recent literature of successful appeals. A potential methodological problem with the conventional approach is that the range of categories that can be discerned are determined by the range of cases that are analysed. Accordingly,

important causes might not be identified. Similarly, the potential method-ological problem with this analysis is that any categories that failed to be identified by the existing researches may also not be identified. The main point of this analysis, however, is not to provide a comprehensive analysis of *all* the current causes of miscarriages of justice. Rather, the attempt here is to update the attempt to chart the ways in which individual actors can cause miscarriages of justice with contemporary cases that acts as a litera-ture review and practical resource which illustrates that successful appeals are the products of a pragmatic approach to the procedures of the criminal justice system and the need to show some form of procedural transgression so that successful appeals can be achieved.

18 For details of the case of Shirley McKie that has undermined the reliability of fingerprint evidence in Scotland see Hannah (1999); also, ShirleyMcKie.Com (2006).

19 In their earlier account Brandon and Davies (1973: 49–65) also discerned three categories of false confession: (1) the 'mentally retarded', (2) the 'young', (3) 'people with a psychological predisposition that makes them prone to make false confessions to crimes with which they have no con-nection'. These categories can also be illustrated by the examples cited.

20 Against this perspective, Sanders and Young (1994) argued that PACE (1984) actually 'made matters worse'. See, also, Coleman et al (1983); Sanders and Bridges (1983). It is also interesting to note that since the claim was made that PACE (1984) would signal the end of miscarriages of justice there have been in excess of 90,000 successful appeals against criminal con-viction in England and Wales.

21 See, also, BBC News, 1999a–1999d, for details of how Darren Hall's coerced 'confession' contributed to the wrongful convictions of the Cardiff Newsagent Three post-Pace 1984 – Michael O' Brien, Ellis Sherwood and Darren Hall.

22 The possibility for miscarriages of justice under the CPIA (1996) will be discussed further below as a procedural cause.

23 Alleged victims of miscarriage of justice who have served 35 and 40 years in prison maintaining innocence were cited at a meeting that I attended between the organisation Progressing Prisoners Maintaining Innocence and key representatives from the agencies that comprise the post-conviction system in May 2004. As will be explained below, the meetings were con-ducted under 'Chatham House Rules' so the source of information and the cases cited must remain anonymous.

24 This is not to imply that the RCCJ only considered issues concerning the law on criminal appeals. On the contrary, the remit and terms of reference of the RRCJ extended well beyond such a narrow reading. It 'examine[d] the effectiveness of the criminal justice system in England and Wales in securing the conviction of those guilty of criminal offences and the acquittal of those who are innocent, having regard to the efficient use of resources' (Royal Commission on Criminal Justice, 1993: i). In so doing, a whole range of researches were conducted including police investigations, the right to silence and confession evidence, pre-trial procedures in the Crown Court, forensic science and other expert witnesses, the trial, the court of appeal and the correction of miscarriages of justice. The point I am

making here, however, is that as far as the public were concerned the RCCJ was *primarily* established in response to the cases of the Guildford Four and the Birmingham Six and the reluctance of politicians to return potentially meritorious cases back to the CACD. From this perspective, once the authority of the Home Secretary to refer cases back to the Court of Appeal had been removed and the establishment of the CCRC had been announced, the public crisis of confidence in the limits of post-appeal remedies for alleged miscarriages of justice was, apparently, resolved.

25 On the face of it, this seems an entirely functionalist analysis of legislative changes to the criminal justice system in response to the perceived problem of miscarriages of justice which resonates with what Nobles and Schiff's researches have shown to be the 'autopietic' internal logic and 'self-referential communications' of the criminal justice system (Nobles and Schiff, 1995: 300, 1997, 2001). This form of *systems* analysis, however, is not the conservative analysis normally attributed to such analyses which operate almost exclusively on a descriptive plane and are devoid of overt values or notions of power relations. On the contrary, this analysis is grounded in the critical and material realities of the processes of governmentality in the disposal of continual conflict or struggle. It is a form of critical analysis that attempts to understand such processes in the interests of an understanding that can contribute to the production and deployment of more effective counter-discursive tactics and strategies and the prevention of miscarriages of justice and the forms of harm that they cause.

26 It could, conceivably, be argued that PACE (1984) has prevented certain types of miscarriages of justice in that beaten confessions appear to be a thing of the past. However, new forms of false confessions have emerged in the shape of 'third-party' or 'prison-grass' confessions (discussed further in chapter 3 above), whereby claims are made that suspects of crimes confessed their crimes to others. Often, bargains lie at the bottom of such confessions such as deals to reduce charges and/or sentences in return. Moreover, with the lack of an accountability clause for breaches of PACE (1984) which cause miscarriages of justice, it is difficult to sustain an argument that they have prevented the continuation of forms of police mal and bad practice (also illustrated in chapter 3) to which they were supposed to redress.

27 Campaigning voices refer here to all those groups and organisations that exist to provide forms of support to alleged victims of miscarriages of justice and their families (usually comprised of groups of the families and friends of alleged victims) and/or provide information and/or lobby parliament on behalf of alleged victims and/or successful appellants.

28 These organisations differ from conventional miscarriage of justice organisations in the sense that they campaign on behalf of alleged victims of false allegations, even if these allegations do not lead to charges and/or criminal convictions. The majority of their members, however, are the families and friends of alleged victims of miscarriage of justice who claim that they were falsely accused and are charged and convicted, bringing them firmly within the miscarriage of justice campaign lexicon and this analysis.

29 It is important to note, also, that campaigns against miscarriages of justice often emerge from localised direct action. For instance, the 'Tottenham 3

Are Innocent Campaign', formed in the wake of the 1985 civil conflict between residents of Tottenham and the Metropolitan Police arose directly out of the Broadwater Farm Defence Campaign (see Rose, 2004).

30 Prior to the establishment of the CCRC in January 1997, although it did not start handling cases until 31 May, JUSTICE was the main organisation for investigating alleged miscarriages of justice in England and Wales (JUSTICE, 1989: 2). Since its inception in 1957, JUSTICE began receiving requests for help by, and on behalf of, hundreds of prisoners alleging miscarriages of justice in their cases. Initially, because of the voluntary nature of the organisation, and the lack of staff and resources, it was decided that JUSTICE would operate a policy of not investigating individual cases. However, the sheer volume of allegations soon persuaded Tom Sargant, the organisation's secretary for its first 25 years, that there was a real need to investigate where he could and assist with appeals and petitions to the Secretary of State (JUSTICE, 1989: 1). Since that time, and until the establishment of the CCRC in 1997 (almost exactly 40 years) JUSTICE, in line with public and political discourse, assisted victims of miscarriages of justice if 'the allegation [was] of actual, rather than technical, innocence' (JUSTICE, 1989: 1–2), and sought reform of the criminal justice system in order to protect the human rights of such individuals and uphold the rule of law (JUSTICE, 1994). When the CCRC was established, though, there was a general belief that the Commission was the solution to the problem of the wrongful conviction of the innocent, a belief shared by JUSTICE who ceased their concern with the plight of wrongly convicted innocents. This is not surprising as it was JUSTICE who provided the blueprint for the CCRC to the Royal Commission on Criminal Justice (1993) that was brought into effect under the Criminal Appeal Act 1995 (see Royal Commission Criminal Justice, 1993). A significant problem with this, as already shown above, is that the CCRC does not, specifically, address the plight of innocent victims of wrongful convictions. Rather, it is subordinate to the CACD and must apply the 'real possibility test' in its decisions about whether to refer an application or, as is more often, whether not to refer an application. As such the perennial problem of the wrongful conviction of the innocent remains, and JUSTICE's withdrawal from the plight of the factually innocent who are unable to overturn their convictions seems, at the very least, premature. It is in response to the continuing problem of the wrongful conviction of the innocent, despite the establishment of the CCRC, that the Innocence Network UK was established to resurrect the JUSTICE agenda (see Naughton, 2006).

31 Although there are examples of victim support/campaigning organisations supporting cases which blur the distinction between factual innocence and legal 'innocence' (see Naughton, 2006).

32 As discussed above, the case of the Cardiff Three, the first miscarriage of justice case to be resolved by the conviction of the real perpetrator of the crime, may appear to undermine such a claim. However, the Cardiff Three did not overturn their convictions because they were innocent. Rather, it was on the technical grounds of a breach of process in the questioning of Steven Miller.

33 In saying this it must be noted that many alleged miscarriage of justice victims do not contact a campaign organisation until after their mundane and/or routine appeal has been unsuccessful.

34 Of course, these are not objective facts, as such. Rather, they are, essentially, widespread beliefs that lead to official acknowledgement.

35 The campaign to abolish capital punishment can be traced to the 1770s. For a discussion see Capital Punishment UK (2006).

36 In the summer of 2006, following a directive from the governing organisation Liberty, South Wales Liberty stopped supporting and/or campaigning for alleged miscarriage of justice victims. In its place a new organisation, South Wales Against Wrongful Convictions, was formed out of the members of South Wales Liberty who wanted to continue their support/campaigning efforts for alleged innocent victims of wrongful convictions.

37 His position as a Patron of the Innocence Network UK, for instance, served to enhance the credibility of the venture.

38 Of the 24 cases taken up by *Rough Justice* between 1982 and 1997, 13 were referred back to the CACD with 8 of those being quashed after appeal (see Rough Justice, 1997). Between 1993 and 1999, 4 of the 15 cases in the Trial and Error series resulted in successful appeals and the others were in the appeals process (see Gibson, 1999).

39 Another Patron of the Innocence Network UK.

40 The notable exception to this general rule is a series of analyses offered by Nobles and Schiff (1995, 1997, 2000) from an 'autopietic' or 'systems theory' approach, which, as discussed above, serve to enhance understanding of the processes of change to the criminal justice system on a descriptive plane of analysis. They are not really relevant to this discussion, however, as they are neither a contribution to procedural reform or to structural critiques of the system.

41 The RCCP also led to the establishment of the Crown Prosecution Service.

42 It is acknowledged that both 'Justice in Error' and 'Criminal Justice in Crisis' also contained contributions from practitioners and activists, working in collaboration with academic colleagues.

43 Against this, it has been argued that 'making submissions which are not strictly the concern of governmental reviews, such as the RCCJ, can itself amount to a meaningful act of resistance. In particular, submissions outside of the terms of reference tend to highlight the fact that even relatively flexible reviews like the RCCJ are closed off to certain questions or issues.' Moreover, it has been said that 'this may have been the intention of some of the pressure groups that submitted evidence to the RCCJ. Its effect is to illustrate the closed nature of debate and, therefore, can be an important political strategy.' I acknowledge the theoretical relevance of such critique. Indeed, I believe that the operational remit of critical counter-discourses is to play their role on behalf of the governed, highlighting the narrow confines of the political debate and the policy agenda; it is to criticise the way things are and force the establishment of committees of inquiry and royal commission to address systemic problems and recommend corrective reforms. I would, however, maintain that my point here is to question the specific value of a 'political strategy' that chose not to offer more practical

changes to a royal commission that may have improved the criminal justice system and reduced the possibility of miscarriages of justice in the future. Such opportunities for change do not occur all that often and might be more fruitfully exploited by submitting evidence that will not be deemed as outside of the terms of reference and, therefore, irrelevant (see Naughton, 2005d: fn 4: 227).

44   Under the 'Chatham House Rules', participants are free to use the information received. But neither the identity nor the affiliation of the speaker(s), nor that of any other participant may be revealed.

45   Here I must declare an interest. I am one of the founders of PPMI and I am a Steering Group Member.

46   This challenge predates the introduction of the HRA in October 2000 and, hence, was made under Article 10 of the ECHR, which provided exactly the same rights and freedoms that are currently provided by Article 10 of the HRA.

47   At the time of writing, the prison population in England and Wales stands at almost 80,000, an all time high.

48   This combined total for these four high profile cases of wrongful imprisonment would have been substantially greater had Patrick Molloy of the Bridgewater Four and Guiseppe Conlon of the Maguire Seven had served their full sentences and not died in prison in 1981 and 1980 respectively.

49   For a critical analysis of the CPT see Evans and Morgan (1999).

50   This figure also includes privately operated prison establishments in England and Wales.

51   See, also, The Prison (Amendment) Rules 2005 London: HMSO: ISBN 0110726448; The Prison (Amendment) (No. 2) Rules 2005 London: HMSO: ISBN 011073792X.

52   See, also, The Prison (Amendment) Rules 2005 London: HMSO: ISBN 0110726448; The Prison (Amendment) (No. 2) Rules 2005 London: HMSO: ISBN 011073792X.

53   For details of punishments see also Prisoners' Information Book, 2002: 81–82; Prisoners' Information Book, 2003: 81–83.

54   The only Article of the HRA that this chapter did not assess was Article 16: Restriction on Political Activity of Aliens. However, a case that was reported in July 2002 would indicate that even this was being routinely contravened in England and Wales when the special immigration appeals commission ruled that the government had acted unlawfully by discriminating against foreign nationals when it arrested 11 terrorist suspects and imprisoned them in high security jails without charge (for details see Gillan, 2002).

55   The Legal Services Commission replaced the Legal Aid Board in April 2001.

56   For a detailed history and chronology of the United Nations see United Nations (1997).

References

Ahmed, K. (2000) 'Move to ban plea bargains after molester walks free'. *The Observer* October, 22.

Allan v The United Kingdom European Court of Human Rights Application Number 48539/99, 5 November 2002.

Amnesty International (2007) 'Working to protect human rights worldwide'. <http://www.amnesty.org>, 8 March 2007.

Arkinstall, J. (2003) 'Criminal Justice Bill House of Lords: Briefing in support of amendments proposed by Legal Action Group In relation to Part 11, Chapter 2 on Hearsay evidence'. London: JUSTICE.

Aron, R. (1965) *Main Currents of Sociological Thought 1*. London: Weidenfield & Nicolson.

Arthur, C. (2002) 'Paediatrician on discipline charges over parental abuse allegations'. *The Independent*, January 31.

Auld, R. (2001) 'Review of the Criminal Courts of England and Wales'. <http://www.criminal-courts-review.org.uk>, 29 November 2006.

Bachelard, G. (1940) *The Philosophy of No*. London: Orion Press.

Baldwin, J. & McConville, M. (1977) *Negotiated Justice: Pressures to plead guilty*. London: Martin Robertson.

Baldwin, J. & McConville, M. (1980) 'Confessions in Crown Court trials' (Royal Commission on Criminal Procedure – Research study 5). London: HMSO.

Barak, G. (1991a) 'Toward a Criminology of State Criminality', in Barak, G. (1991) (ed.) *Crimes by the Capitalist State: An Introduction to State Criminality*. Albany: State University of New York Press.

Barak, G. (1991b) 'Resisting State Criminality and the Struggle for Justice', in Barak, G. (1991) (ed.) *Crimes by the Capitalist State: An Introduction to State Criminality*. Albany: State University of New York Press.

Batt, J. (2005) *Stolen Innocence: The Sally Clark Story – A Mother's Fight for Justice*. London: Ebury Press

BBC News (1999a) 'Murder suspect "handcuffed to radiator"', December 7. <http://www.innocent.org.uk/cases/cardiff3/index.html#7decbbc>, 3 January 2007.

BBC News (1999b) 'Murder convictions "at risk" of being unreliable', December 10. <http://www.innocent.org.uk/cases/cardiff3/index.html#7decbbc>, 3 January 2007.

BBC News (1999c) 'Murder suspect's evidence "unsafe"', December 16. <http://www.innocent.org.uk/cases/cardiff3/index.html#7decbbc>, 3 January 2007.

BBC News (1999d) 'Court of Appeal clears Newsagent Three', December 17. <http://www.innocent.org.uk/cases/cardiff3/index.html#7decbbc>, 3 January 2007.

BBC News (2000) '"Murderer" freed after 20 years', March 30. <http://news.bbc.co.uk/1/hi/uk/696214.stm>, 29 November 2006.

BBC News (2003) 'Mysteries unlocked by DNA', <http://news.bbc.co.uk/1/hi/wales/3039618.stm>, 28 October 2006.

BBC News (2005) Q&A: 'UK Prisoners' right to vote', October 6, <http://news.bbc.co.uk/1/hi/uk/4316148.stm> 14 September 2006.

BBC News (2006) 'Crime appeal pay-outs cut by £5m', <http://news.bbc.co.uk/1/hi/uk/4921230.stm>, 9 March 2007.

Benn, M. (2000) 'Sisters of mercy'. *The Guardian*, July 27.

Bennathon, J. (2000) 'Made for miscarriages'. *The Times*, July 25.

Berlins, M. (2000) 'Weller's call for rape trial rights'. *The Guardian*, November 6.

Berlins, M. (2002) 'When innocence and death don't count'. *The Guardian*, June 18.

Berlins, M. (2002a) 'Turning a blind eye'. *The Guardian*, July 16.

Birch, D.J. (1985) 'The Police And Criminal Evidence Act 1984: (2) Powers of Arrest and Detention'. *Criminal Law Review*. London: Sweet and Maxwell.

Bird, S. (2000) 'Three jailed for M25 robberies are freed'. *The Times*, July 18.

Bird, S. (2002) 'Man cleared of murder after 26 years in jail'. *The Times*, June 27.

Birnberg, B. (1998) 'Why the law failed Derek Bentley'. *The Times*, August 4.

Black, D.J. (1972) 'The Boundaries of Legal Sociology'. *The Yale Law Journal*, 81, 1086–1100.

Blair, T. (2002) 'Prime Minister's speech on 'Re-balancing of criminal justice system'. <http://www.pm.gov.uk/output/Page1717.asp>, 30 October 2006.

Block, B.P. & Hostettler, J. (1997) *Hanging in the Balance: A History of the Abolition of Capital Punishment in Britain*. Winchester, England: Waterside Press.

Blyth, E.K. (1889) 'Letter to the editor of The Times'. *The Times*, August 19, 4.

Boothman, C. (1994) 'Race and Racism – the Missing Dimension in the Royal Commission on Criminal Justice', in McConville, M. & Bridges, L. (1994) (eds) *Criminal Justice in Crisis*. Aldershot: Edward Elgar.

Bowcott, O. (2003) 'Pair win appeal against murder conviction after 14 years in jail'. *The Guardian*, June 18.

Box, S. (1971) *Deviance, Reality and Society*. London: Holt, Rinehart & Winston.

Box, S. (1983) *Power, Crime and Mystification*. London: Routledge.

Brandon, R. & Davies, C. (1973) *Wrongful Imprisonment: Mistaken Convictions and their Consequences*. London: George Allen & Unwin.

Bridges, L. & McConville, M. (1994) 'Keeping Faith with their Own Convictions: The Royal Commission on Criminal Justice', in McConville, M. & Bridges, L. (1994) (eds) *Criminal Justice in Crisis*. Aldershot: Edward Elgar.

Bright, M. & Hill, A. (2002) 'Birmingham Six man wins £1m payout'. *The Guardian*, June 9.

Bright, M. & Nicklin, M. (2002) 'New magistrates for old'. *The Observer*, September 15.

Broadbridge, S. (2002) 'The Criminal Justice Bill: Double jeopardy and prosecution appeals', Bill 8 of 2002–03 Research Paper 02/74. London: House of Commons Library.

Brogden, M. (1994) 'Gatekeeping and the Seamless Web of the Criminal Justice Process', in McConville, M. & Bridges, L. (1994) (eds) *Criminal Justice in Crisis*. Aldershot: Edward Elgar.

Buncombe, A. (1999) 'Court frees three over killing of newsagent'. *The Independent*, December 18.

Bunyan, N. (1995) 'Prisoner studied neurology in fight for murder appeal'. *The Daily Telegraph*, March 30.

Burchell, G., Gordon, C. & Miller, P. (1991) (eds) *The Foucault Effect: Studies in Governmentality*. London: Harvester Wheatsheaf.

Burrell, I. (2000) 'Police expert questions the reliability of fingerprint evidence'. *The Independent*, October 23.

Burrell, I. & Bennetto, J. (1999) 'Miscarriages of justice emerge 10 years after break-up of group that tortured suspects'. *The Independent*, November 1.

Cain, M. (1993) 'Foucault, feminism and feeling: what Foucault can and cannot contribute to feminist epistemology', in Ramazanoglu, C. (1993) (ed.) *Up Against Foucault: Explorations of some tensions between Foucault and Feminism*. London: Routledge.

Callaghan, J. (1997) 'Foreword', in Block, B.P. & Hostettler, J. (1997) *Hanging in the Balance: A History of the Abolition of Capital Punishment in Britain*. Winchester, England: Waterside Press.

Callaghan, H. & Mulready, S. (1995) *Cruel fate: one man's triumph over injustice*. Amhurst: University of Massachusetts Press.

Campaign Against Racism and Fascism (2007). <http://www.carf.demon.co.uk>, 8 March 2007.

Campbell, D. (1997) 'How Bridgewater defendants are coping with being free'. *The Guardian*, July 31.

Campbell, D. (1998) 'Justice at last, 45 years too late'. *The Guardian*, July 31.

Campbell, D. (2002) 'Fall Guys'. *The Guardian*, July 10.

Campbell, D. & Hartley-Brewer, J. (2000) 'Torso murders case goes to appeal court'. *The Guardian*, June 23.

Campbell, C.M. & Wiles, P. (1977) 'Introductory note', in Baldwin, J. & McConville, M. (1977) *Negotiated Justice: Pressures to plead guilty*. London: Martin Robertson.

Cannings, A. & Davies, M.L. (2006) *Against All Odds The Angela Cannings Story: A mother's fight to prove her innocence*. London: Time Warner Books.

Cape, E. (1994) 'Defence Services: What Should Defence Lawyers do at Police Stations', in McConville, M. & Bridges, L. (1994) (eds) *Criminal Justice in Crisis*. Aldershot: Edward Elgar.

Capital Punishment UK (2006) 'The Abolition of hanging in Britain'. <http://www.richard.clark32.btinternet.co.uk/contents.html>, 30 November 2006.

Carlen, P. (1991) 'Criminal women and criminal justice: the limits to, and potential of, feminist and left realist perspectives', in Matthews, R. & Young, J. (1991) (eds) *Issues in Realist Criminology*. London: SAGE Publications.

Carroll, R. (1998) 'Cardiff Three released on bail pending murder appeal'. *The Guardian*, December 23.

Carter, H. (1998) 'Police in miscarriage of justice will not be prosecuted'. *The Guardian*, December 24.

Carter, H. & Bowers, S. (2000) 'Verdict quashed after 19 years'. *The Guardian*, March 31.

Carvel, J. (1999) 'The risks faced in the classroom'. *The Guardian*, November 11.

Carvel, J. (1999b) 'School trickery dupes Ofsted'. *The Guardian*, March 4.

Carvel, J. (2000) 'Teacher's agony at pupil's abuse lie'. *The Guardian*, April 21.

Chapman, B. & Niven, S. (2000) *A guide to the criminal justice system in England and Wales*. London: Crown Copyright.

Chibnall, S. (1979) 'The Metropolitan Police and The News Media', in Holdaway, S. (1979) *The British Police*. London: Edward Arnold.

Chomsky, N. (2002) 'September 11 Aftermath: Where is the World Heading?', in Scraton, P. (2002) (ed.) *Beyond September 11: An Anthology of Dissent*. London: Pluto Press.

Chrisafis, A. (2000) 'Trawling for abuse victims defended'. *The Guardian*, December 7.

Christoph, J.B. (1962) *Capital Punishment and British Politics: The British Movement to Abolish the Death Penalty 1945–57*. London: George Allen & Unwin Ltd.

Coates, T. (2001) *The Strange Case of Adolph Beck*. London: Stationery Office Books.

Coleman, C., Dixon, D. & Bottomley, K. (1993) 'Police Investigative Procedures: Researching the Impact of PACE', in Walker, C. & Starmer, K. (1993) (eds) *Justice in Error*. London: Blackstone Press Limited.

Collini, S. (1991) *Public Moralists: Political Thought and Intellectual Life in Britain 1850–1930*. Oxford: Clarendon Press.

Collins Concise Dictionary (2000). London: Collins ISBN 0-00-433070-6.

Colvin, M. (1994) 'Miscarriages of Justice: The Appeal Process', in McConville, M. & Bridges, L. (1994) (eds) *Criminal Justice in Crisis*. Aldershot: Edward Elgar.

Conlon, G. (1990) *Proved Innocent*. London: Hamish Hamilton.

Coser, L.A. (1956) *The Functions of Social Conflict*. London: Routledge & Kegan Paul Ltd.

Coulter, H.L. (1996) 'SIDS and Seizures'. <http://www.pnc.com.au/~cafmr/coulter/sids.html>, 30 November 2006.

Criminal Appeal Act 1907. London: HMSO.

Criminal Appeal Act 1968. London: HMSO.

Criminal Appeal Act 1995 (c35). London: HMSO.

Criminal Appeal Rules 1968. London: HMSO.

Criminal Cases Review Commission (2000) 'Criminal Cases review Commission Annual Report 1999–2000'. Birmingham: CCRC ISBN 1-84082-480-8.

Criminal Cases Review Commission (2002) 'Background to the Commission'. <http://www.ccrc.gov.uk>, 3 May 2002.

Criminal Cases Review Commission (2002b) 'Results of cases referred to the Court of Appeal'. <http://www.ccrc.gov.uk>, 3 May 2002.

Criminal Cases Review Commission (2006) 'Can we help'. <http://www.ccrc.gov.uk/canwe.htm>, 23 August 2006.

Criminal Cases Review Commission (2006b) 'Annual Report and Accounts: Criminal Cases Review Commission HC 1290'. London: The Stationery Office.

Criminal Cases Review Commission (2006c) 'Examples of cases we have referred'. <http://www.ccrc.gov.uk/canwe/canwe_87.htm>, 14 December 2006.

Criminal Justice System (2006) <http://www.cjsonline.gov.uk>, 14 December 2006.

Criminal Justice Act (1988) (c33). London: HMSO.

Criminal Justice Act (2003) (c44). London: The Stationery Office Limited.

Criminal Procedure and Investigations Act (1996). London: HMSO.

Davies, M., Croall, H. & Tyrer, J. (1998) *Criminal Justice: An introduction to the Criminal Justice System in England and Wales.* London; New York: Longman.

Davey, G.W. (2000) 'Plea-bargaining'. *The Times*, December 6.

Department for Constitutional Affairs (2003) Judicial statistics England and Wales for the year 2004. The Stationery Office (TSO): Cm 6251.

Department for Constitutional Affairs (2004) Judicial statistics England and Wales for the year 2004. The Stationery Office (TSO): Cm 6565.

Department for Constitutional Affairs (2005) Judicial statistics (revised) England and Wales for the year 2005. The Stationery Office (TSO): Cm 6903.

Department of Constitutional Affairs (2006) *Judicial statistics (revised) England and Wales for the year 2005.* London: The Stationery Office (TSO): Cm 6903.

Derrida, J. (1976) *Of Grammatology.* London: Johns Hopkins University Press.

Devlin, A. & Devlin, T. (2000) *Anybody's Nightmare: The Sheila Bowler Story.* London: Waterside Press.

Director of Public Prosecutions v. Shannon [1974] 59. Cr.App.R.250.

Dodd, V. (2000) 'Innocents suffer when law of the lynch-mob takes hold'. *The Guardian*, July 24.

Dodd, V. (2002) 'Torso murder convictions quashed'. *The Guardian*, July 17.

Dodd, V. & Milne, L. (2001) 'Move to lift prison voting ban foils'. *The Guardian*, April 5.

Douglas, J.D. (1967) *The Social Meanings of Suicide.* Princeton: Princeton University Press.

Doyal, L. (1979) 'A Matter of Life and Death: Medicine, Health and Statistics', in Irvine, J. Miles, I. & Evans, J. (1979) (eds) *Demystifying Social Statistics.* London: Pluto Press.

Duce, R. (1997) 'Murder nightmare ends after 25 years'. *The Times*, December 4.

Dudley, R. (2002) 'We were victims too'. *The Observer*, July 7.

Dunne, M. (1997) 'Women fight back: Southall Black sisters raise a fist', *Third World Network* June 8. <http://www.hartford-hwp.com/archives/61/061.html>, 8 March 2007.

Durkheim, E. (1952) *Suicide: A study in sociology.* London: Routledge & Kegan Paul.

Dyer, C. (1997) 'Birmingham Six to sue Tory MP'. *The Guardian*, March 19.

Dyer, C. (1999a) 'Appeal quashes murder conviction'. *The Guardian*, December 11.

Dyer, C. (1999b) 'Prosecutors breaking law over evidence'. *The Guardian*, July 15.

Dyer, C. (1999d) 'Lord Denning, controversial "people's judge", dies aged 100'. *The Guardian*, March 6.

Dyer, C. (2000a) 'Prosecutors forbidden to make secret plea bargains'. *The Guardian*, December 8.

Dyer, C. (2000b) 'Making a pact with the devil'. *The Guardian*, October 30.

Dyer, C. (2000c) 'Legal "safeguard" risks injustice'. *The Guardian*, March 3.

Dyer, C. (2001) 'Woolf proposes jury compromise'. *The Guardian*, October 10.

Dyer, C. (2004) 'Prisoners must get right to vote, says court'. *The Guardian*, March 31.

Eden, R. (2002) 'Welsh police "assaults" condemned'. *The Telegraph*, April 22.

Editorial (1996) 'Parents: No Error'. *Daily Mirror*, July 27.

Editorial (1998a) 'Corruption may cost £50 million'. *The Times*, December 22.

Editorial (1998b) 'Former MP apologises to the Birmingham Six'. *The Times*, July 10.

Editorial (1998c) 'QC sued for libel over IRA claims'. *The Times*, December 1.

Editorial (2000a) 'The M25 three'. *The Guardian*, July 17.

Editorial (2000b) 'Police must now find out the truth'. *Liverpool Echo*, March 31.

Editorial (2000c) 'Man freed after wrongful rape conviction'. *The Guardian*, April 7.

Editorial (2001) 'Real risk is posed by Tory far right'. *The Observer*, August 26.

Editorial (2002a) 'Justice on parole'. *The Observer*, January 20.

Editorial (2005) 'Blair apologises to Guildford Four family'. *The Guardian*, February 9.

Elias, N. (1978) *The Civilizing Process: Volume One*. Oxford: Blackwell.

Emmerson, B. (1999) 'Prosecution in the dock'. *The Guardian*, November 14.

Erzinclioglu, Z. (1998) 'Science and the law: A cause for concern'. *Contemporary Review*, August.

Erzinclioglu, Z. (2000) *Maggots, Murder and Men: Memories and reflections of a forensic entomologist*. Colchester: Harley Books.

Erzinclioglu, Z. (2001) 'How forensic scientists are fiddling with the truth'. *The Mail on Sunday*, January 14.

European Committee for the Prevention of Torture and Inhuman or Degrading Treatment or Punishment, (2002) 'European Anti-Torture Committee Publishes United Kingdom report'. <http://www.cpt.coe>, 25 April 2002.

Evans, M.D. & Morgan, R. (1999) *Preventing Torture: A Study of the European Convention for the Prevention of Torture and Inhuman or Degrading Treatment or Punishment*. Oxford: Clarendon Press.

Ezeh & Conners v The United Kingdom, 2003 European Court of Human Rights Application Number 39665/98;40086/98, 9 October 2003.

False Allegations Support Organisation (2002) 'About Us'. <http://www.false-allegations.org.uk/page4.html>, 22 July 2002.

False Allegations Support Organisation (2002b) 'Yes it might'. <http://www.false-allegations.org.uk/page2.html>, 30 July 2002.

False Allegations Support Organisation (2006) <http://www.false-allegations.org.uk/faso-disclaimer.html>, November 21 2006.

Falsely Accused Carers and Teachers (2002) 'Aims and Objectives'. <http://www.factnotfiction.org.uk>, 2 July 2002.

Falsely Accused Carers and Teachers (2006) <http://www.factuk.org>, November 21 2006.

Feeley, M.M. (1976) 'The Concept of Laws in Social Science: A Critique and Notes on an Expanded View'. *Law and Society Review*, 10, 497–523.

Festenstein, M. (1997) *Pragmatism & Political Theory*. Oxford: Polity Press.

Feyerabend, P. (1981) 'How To Defend Society Against Science', in Hacking, I. (1981) (ed.) *Scientific Revolutions*. Oxford, Toronto: Oxford University Press.

Fisher, H. (1977) Report of an Inquiry by the Honourable Sir Henry Fisher into the circumstances leading to the trial of three persons on charges arising out of the death of Maxwell Confait and the fire at 27 Doggett Road, London SE6, London: HMSO.

Fitzgerald, M. & Sim, J. (1982) *British Prisons* 2nd Edition. Oxford: Blackwell.

Foot, P. (1986) *Murder at the Farm: Who Killed Carl Bridgewater?*. London: Sidgewick and Jackson.

Foot, P. (2002) 'Hanratty's appeal is over, but justice is yet to be done'. *The Guardian*, May 13.

Ford, R. (1998a) 'Motorists awarded conviction payouts'. *The Times*, June 25.

Ford, R. (1998b) 'Damages for rough justice top £6m'. *The Times*, July 30.

Ford, R. (1998c) '£200,000 for man beaten by police into confession'. *The Times*, January 20.

Forst, B. (2004) *Errors of Justice: Nature, Sources and Remedies*. Cambridge: Cambridge University Press.

Foucault, M. (1977) *Discipline And Punish: The Birth of the Prison*. London: Allen Lane.

Foucault, M. (1979a) 'Governmentality', *Ideology & Consciousness* 6, Autumn.

Foucault, M. (1979b) *The History of Sexuality: Volume 1 An Introduction*. London: Allen Lane.

Foucault, M. (1980) *Power/Knowledge: Selected interviews and other writings 1972–1977* edited by Colin Gordon. London: Harvester Wheatsheaf.

Foucault, M. (1980a) 'Truth and Power', in Foucault, M. (1980) *Power/Knowledge: Selected interviews and other writings 1972–1977* edited by Colin Gordon. London: Harvester Wheatsheaf.

Foucault, M. (1980b) 'Two Lectures', in Foucault, M. (1980) *Power/Knowledge: Selected interviews and other writings 1972–1977* edited by Colin Gordon. London: Harvester Wheatsheaf.

Foucault, M. (1980c) 'Prison Talk', in Foucault, M. (1980) *Power/Knowledge: Selected interviews and other writings 1972–1977* edited by Colin Gordon. London: Harvester Wheatsheaf.

Foucault, M. (1986) 'Kant on Enlightenment and Revolution', *Economy and Society*, 15, 1, 88–96.

Foucault, M. (1991) 'Governmentality', in Burchell, G., Gordon, C. & Miller, P. (1991) (eds) *The Foucault Effect: Studies in Governmentality*. London: Harvester Wheatsheaf.

Franklin and Eleanor Roosevelt Institute (2006) 'Universal Declaration of Human Rights'. <http://www.udhr.org/index.htm>, 30 November 2006.

Fraser, N. (1989) 'Foucault on modern power: empirical insights and normative confusions', in *Unruly Practices: Power, Discourse and Gender in Contemporary Social Theory*. Cambridge: Polity Press.

Gane, M. (1986) 'The Form of Foucault'. *Economy and Society*, Volume 15, Number 1, February.

Geffen, I. (1999) 'Costing injustice'. *The Guardian*, June 29.

George, A. (1991) 'The Discipline of Terrorology', in George, A. (1991) (ed.) *Western State Terrorism*. Cambridge: Polity Press.

Gibb, F. (2000) 'Trial bargaining to be outlawed'. *The Times*, December 4.

Gibb, F. (2002) 'Lawyers claim police bugging is widespread'. *The Times*, January 30.

Gibbons, T. (1985) 'The Police And Criminal Evidence Act 1984: (3) The Conditions of Detention and Questioning'. *Criminal Law Review*. London: Sweet and Maxwell.

Gibson, J. (1999) 'Channel 4 to drop programme'. *The Guardian*, July 17.

Gillard, S.M. & Flynn, L. (2000) 'DPP inquiry into collapse of drugs case'. *The Guardian*, November 6.

Gillan, A. (2001) 'Innocent "dumped like sacks of garbage"'. *The Guardian*, March 14.

Gillan, A. (2002) 'Detention of 11 foreign terror suspects unlawful, judges rule'. *The Guardian*, July 31.

Goodman, J. (1999) 'Is Michael Stone Innocent of the Two Russell Murders?'. *The Daily Mail*, March 13.

Gordon, C. (1980) 'Afterword', in Foucault, M. (1980) *Power/Knowledge: Selected interviews and other writings 1972–1977* edited by Colin Gordon. London: Harvester Wheatsheaf.

Gordon, C. (1986) 'Question, ethos, event: Foucault on Kant and Enlightenment'. *Economy and Society*, 15(1), 71–87.

Gordon, C. (1991) 'Governmental Rationality: An Introduction', in Burchell, G., Gordon, C. & Miller, P. (1991) (eds) *The Foucault Effect: Studies in Governmentality*. London: Harvester Wheatsheaf.

Gordon, D., Hillyard, P. & Pantazis, C. (1999) 'Introduction to Zemia and Zemiology'. Paper presented at the 'Zemiology Beyond Criminology' conference, Dartington, England (February).

Government Statistician's Collective (1979) 'How Official Statistics are Produced: Views from the Inside', in Irvine, J., Miles, I. & Evans, J. (1979) (eds) *Demystifying Social Statistics*. London: Pluto Press.

Graves, D. (1997a) 'Spotlight turns on farm killer'. *Electronic Telegraph* Issue 638. <http://www.telegraph.co.uk>, 2 February 2000.

Graves, D. (1997b) 'Bridgewater Three walk free'. *Electronic Telegraph* Issue 638. <http://www.telegraph.co.uk>, 2 February 2000.

Graves, D. (1997c) 'Crucial evidence of fabrication was overlooked'. *Electronic Telegraph* Issue 638. <http://www.telegraph.co.uk>, 2 February 2000.

Graves, D. (1997d) 'Bridgewater three set to be released'. *Electronic Telegraph* Issue 637 <http://www.telegraph.co.uk>, 2 February 2000.

Green, A. (1995) 'Fitting up: an analysis of the manufacture of wrongful convictions' unpublished Phd thesis, Keele University.

Green, A. (1997) 'How the Criminal Justice System knows'. *Social and Legal Studies*. Volume 6, Number 1, 4–22.

Green, A. (2000a) 'Cover up – or opportunity?: the Criminal Procedure and Investigations Act 1996 (CPIA)'. <http://www.fitting-up.org.uk/index.html>, 14 September 2006.

Green, A. (2000b) 'The Missing Twin'. <http://www.innocent.org.uk/cases/chrisdanks/indexhtml>, 14 September 2006.

Green, P. (2002) 'A Question of State Crime?', in Scraton, P. (2002) (ed.) *Beyond September 11: An Anthology of Dissent*. London: Pluto Press.

Green, P.J. & Ward, T. (2000) 'State Crime, Human Rights, And the Limits of Criminology'. *Social Justice*, 27(1).

Greenhill, S. (2006) 'Man freed but serial rape accuser remains anonymous'. *The Mail on Sunday*, September 10.

Greenslade, R. (1998) 'The wrong arm of the law'. *The Guardian*, November 4.

Greer, S. (1994) 'Miscarriages of Criminal Justice Reconsidered'. *The Modern Law Review*, 57: 1.

Gregory, W.L., Mowen, J.C. & Linder, D.E. (1978) 'Social psychology and plea bargaining: Applications, methodology and theory'. *Journal of Personality and Social Psychology*, 36, 1521–1530.

Griffiths, C. (2002) 'Counsel for the defence'. *The Observer*, July 21.

Grounds, A. (2004) 'Psychological consequences of wrongful conviction and imprisonment'. *Canadian Journal of Criminology and Criminal Justice*, 46(2): 165–182.

Guardian Unlimited (2006) 'Special Report: The Stephen Lawrence Case'. <http://www.guardian.co.uk/lawrence/0,,179674,00.html>, 1 December 2006.

Guidorizzi, D.D. (1998) 'Should We Really "Ban" Plea Bargaining? The Core Concerns of Plea Bargaining Critics'. *Emory Law Journal*, Vol. 47.

Hacking, I. (1990) *The taming of chance*. Cambridge: Cambridge University Press.

Hale, D. (2002) *A Town Without Pity*. London: Century.

Hall, S., Critcher, C., Jefferson, T., Clarke, J. & Robert, B. (1977) *Policing the Crisis: mugging, the state, and law and order*. London: Macmillan.

Hall, S. (1980) *Drifting into a law and order society: the Cobden Trust Human Rights Day lecture*. London: Cobden Trust.

Hancock, R. (1963) *Ruth Ellis: the last woman to be hanged*. London: Weidenfeld & Nicolson.

Hannah, V. (1999) 'Jury clears policewoman of lying about fingerprint; Murder scene evidence of four experts from Scottish Criminal Records Office rejected'. *The Herald*, May 15.

Hardy, J. (1999) 'Guilty, until the judge thinks otherwise'. *The Guardian*, July 22.

Hattenstone, S. (2002) 'I'm dead inside'. *The Guardian*, June 17.

Henry, S. (1983) *Private Justice*. London: Routledge.

Heumann, M. (1978) *Plea bargaining: the experiences of prosecutors, judges and defense attorneys*. Chicago, London: University of Chicago Press.

Hickey & Ors, R v [1997] EWCA Crim 2028.

Hill, A. (2001a) 'I won my freedom, but those years in jail smashed my life to bit'. *The Observer*, March 18.

Hill, A. (2001b) 'Freed man set for £8m apology'. *The Observer*, February 18.

Hill, A. (2002) 'Robert Brown won't get parole – because he maintains his innocence of murder'. *The Guardian*, March 3.

Hill, A. (2002a) '25 years in jail for denying that he's a killer'. *The Guardian*, March 3.

Hill, A. (2002b) 'I thought it was love. Now I know that I was wrong'. *The Observer*, June 2.

Hill, A. (2002c) 'They set me free but left my life in ruins'. *The Guardian*, June 30.

Hill, P. (2001) 'The Parole Deal'. *Inside Time*, Autumn. London: The New Bridge.

Hill, P.J. & Hunt, G. (1995) *Forever Lost, Forever Gone*. London: Bloomsbury Publishing Plc.

Hill, P., Young, M. & Sargant, T. (1985) *More Rough Justice*. Harmondsworth: Penguin.

Hillyard, P. (1993) *Suspect Community: people's experience of the Prevention of Terrorism Acts in Britain*. London: Pluto.

Hillyard, P. (1994) 'The Politics of Criminal Injustice: the Irish Dimension', in McConville, M. & Bridges, L. (1994) (eds) *Criminal Justice in Crisis*. Aldershot: Edward Elgar.

Hillyard, P. (1996) 'Policing the Streets: Stop and Search Powers in 1995'. *Statewatch*, July–August.

Hillyard, P. (1998) 'New Labour and ethnic monitoring in policing'. *Radical Statistics*, Number 70, Winter.

Hillyard, P. & Tombs, S. (1999) 'From Crime to Harm?'. Paper presented to the Zemiology: Beyond Criminology? Conference, Dartington Hall, 12–13 February.

Hillyard, P. & Tombs, S. (2001) 'Criminology, Zemiology, and Justice'. Paper presented at the Socio-Legal Studies Association Annual Conference, University of Bristol, 4–6 April.

Hillyard, P. & Tombs, S. (2004) 'Beyond Criminology?', in Hillyard, P., Pantazis, C., Tombs, S. & Gordon, D. (2004) (eds) Beyond Criminology: Taking Harm Seriously. London: Pluto Press.

Hillyard, P. & Watson, S. (1996) 'Postmodern Social Policy: A Contradiction in Terms?'. *Journal of Social Policy*, 25, 3, 321–346.

Hindess, B. (1973) *The Use of Official Statistics in Sociology*. London: Macmillan.

Hinsliff, G. & Bright, M. (2000) 'Irish all suspects, police are told'. *The Observer*, December 10.

Hird, C. & Irvine, J. (1979) 'The Poverty of Wealth Statistics', in Irvine, J., Miles, I. & Evans, J. (1979) (eds) *Demystifying Social Statistics*. London: Pluto Press.

Hirst v Secretary of State for the Home Department [2002] 1 WLR 2929.

HM Prison Service (2002) 'Prison establishments in England and Wales'. <http://www.hmprisonservice.gov.uk>, 29 April 2002.

Hodgson, J. (1994) 'No Defence for the Royal Commission', in McConville, M. & Bridges, L. (1994) (eds) *Criminal Justice in Crisis*. Aldershot: Edward Elgar.

Holt, J.C. (1992) Magna Carta (2nd edition). Cambridge: Cambridge University Press.

Home Office (2002) 'Justice for All'. London: Crown Copyright Cm 5563.

Home Office (2002b) 'Criminal Statistics England and Wales 2002: Statistics relating to Criminal Proceedings for the year 2002'. *Cm 6054*. London: The Stationery Office.

Home Office (2002c) 'Prison Statistics: England and Wales 2002'. London: HMSO. Cm 5996.

Home Office (2006) 'Compensation for Miscarriages of Justice'. Home Office <http://press.homeoffice.gov.uk/Speeches/compensation-miscarriage-justice>, 9 March 2007.

Hopkins, N. (1999) 'Man in jail for 23 years wins right to murder appeal'. *The Guardian*, July 22.

Hopkins, N. (2000) 'Corrupt police framed three for robbery'. *The Guardian*, July 13.

Hopkins, N. (2001) 'Presumed guilty'. *The Guardian*, February 14.

Hopkins, N. (2002) 'Victim's evidence may free man in jail since 1976'. *The Guardian*, June 24.

Hopkins, N. (2002b) 'Man wrongly convicted of murder freed after 25 years', 14 November.

Hopkins, N. & Dodd, V. (1999) 'Police corruption leads to collapse of arms plot trial'. *The Guardian*, May 27.

House of Lords Select Committee on Science and Technology (1993). London: HMSO.

Hoy, D.C. (1998) 'Foucault: Modern or Postmodern?', in Arac, J. (1988) (ed.) *After Foucault: Humanistic Knowledge, Postmodern Challenges*. London: Rutgers University Press.

Huff, R.C., Rattner, A. & Sagarin, E. (1996) *Convicted But Innocent: Wrongful Conviction and Public Policy*. California; London: Sage.

Hui Chi-Ming v R [1992] 1 A.C. 34.

Human Rights Act (1998). London: HMSO.

Hunt, A. & Wickham, G. (1994) *Foucault and Law: Towards a Sociology of Law as Governance*. London: Pluto Press.

Hyman, R. & Price, B. (1979) 'Labour Statistics', in Irvine, J., Miles, I. & Evans, J. (1979) (eds) *Demystifying Social Statistics*. London: Pluto Press.

Ingrams, R. (2001) 'Tory hopeful would have let them swing'. *The Observer*, August 19.

Ingrams, R. (2002) 'Blinded by science'. *The Observer*, May 12.

Innocence Network UK (2006) 'About Innocence Network UK'. <http://www.innocencenetwork.org.uk>, 31 October 2006.

INNOCENT (2006) 'Fighting miscarriages of justice since 1993'. <http://www.innocent.org>, 30 November 2006.

Institute of Race Relations (2007) 'Educating for Racial Justice'. <http://www.irr.org.uk>, 8 March 2007.

Irving, B. & Hilgendorf, L. (1980) 'Police interrogation' (Royal Commission on Criminal Procedure – Research study; no. 1 & 2). London: HMSO.

James, A. (2002a) 'Miscarriages of Justice in the 21st Century'. Paper presented at the Socio-Legal Studies Association Annual Conference at the University of Wales, Aberystwyth 3–5 April.

James, E. (2002) 'Neither bitter nor broken'. *The Guardian*, January 17.

James, W. (1992) 'What Pragmatism Means', in Olin, D. (1992) *Pragmatism in Focus*. London; New York: Routledge.

James, A., Taylor, N. & Walker, C. (2000) 'The Criminal Cases Review Commission: Economy, Effectiveness and Justice'. *Criminal Law Review*, March, 140–153.

James, A., Taylor, N. & Walker, C. (2000b) 'The Reform of Double Jeopardy'. *Web Journal of Current Legal Issues* (5).

Jefferson, T. & Grimshaw, R. (1984) *Controlling the Constable: Police Accountability in England and Wales*. London: Frederick Muller/The Cobden Trust.

Jefferson, T. & Grimshaw, R. (1987) *Interpreting Policework*. London: Unwin Hyman.

Jessel, D. (1994) *Trial and Error*. London: Headline.

Jones, T.L. (2001) *Ruth Ellis: The Last to Hang*. <http://crimelibrary.com/classics2/ellis>, 30 November 2006.

JUSTICE (1989) *Miscarriages of Justice*. London: JUSTICE.

JUSTICE (1994) *Remedying Miscarriages of Justice*. London: JUSTICE.

JUSTICE (2007) 'About Us'. <http://www.justice.org.uk/enterb/enterb.html>, 8 March 2007.

Justice For Women (2007) <http://www.jfw.org.uk/index.htm>, 8 March 2007.

K.B. & Ors, R. (on the applications of) v Mental Health Review Tribunal [2002], EWHC 639 (Admin).

Kee, R. (1986) *Trial and error: the Maguires, the Guildford pub bombings and British justice*. London: Hamish Hamilton.

Kennedy, H. (2004) *Just Law: The changing face of justice – and why it matters to us all*. London: Chatto & Windus.

Kennedy, L. (1961) *Ten Rillington Place*. London: Gollancz.

Kennedy, L. (2002) *Thirty-Six Murders & Two Immoral Earnings*. London: Profile Books.

Kettle, M. (1979) 'Trying to make the Verdicts Fit the Evidence'. *New Society*.

Kincaid, J. (1979) 'Poverty in the Welfare State', in Irvine, J., Miles, I. & Evans, J. (1979) (eds) *Demystifying Social Statistics*. London: Pluto Press.

Kituse, J. & Cicourel, A. (1963) 'A note on the use of official statistics'. *Social Problems*, Volume 11, Number 31.

Koestler, A. (1956) *Reflections on Hanging*. London: Gollancz.

Lacey, N. (1994) 'Missing the Wood...Pragmatism versus Theory in the Royal Commission', in McConville, M. & Bridges, L. (1994) (eds) *Criminal Justice in Crisis*. Aldershot: Edward Elgar.

Lahiri, S. (2000) 'Uncovering Britain's South Asian past: the case of George Edalji'. *Violence and Abuse*, Volume 6, Number 1, January.

Langdon-Down, G. (1999) 'The whole truth and nothing but?'. *The Independent*, December 7.

Latour, B. (1986) 'Visualisation And Cognition: Thinking With Eyes And Hands', in *Knowledge and Society: Studies in the Sociology of Culture Past and Present*, Volume 6: Jai Press.

Latour, B. (1987) *Science In Action*. Cambridge, Massachusetts: Harvard University Press.

Lee, A. (1998) 'Widow wins fight to clear hanged husband'. *The Times*, February 25.

Leigh, L.H. (1985) 'The Police And Criminal Evidence Act 1984: (1) Search, Entry and Seizure'. *Criminal Law Review*. London: Sweet and Maxwell.

Lemke, T. (2000) 'Foucault, Governmentality and Critique'. Paper presented at the Rethinking Marxism Conference, University of Amherst, 21–24 September 2000.

Leonard, T. (1997) 'Euphoria gives way to anger over lost years'. *Electronic Telegraph*, Issue 638: <http://www.telegraph.co.uk>, 30 November 2006.

Leppard, D. (2002) 'Blunkett faces challenge on "brutal" child prisons'. *The Times*, July 28.

Letwin, O. (2002) 'Mr Blunkett and the threat to freedom'. *The Observer*, November 17.

Levitas, R. (1996) 'Fiddling While Britain Burns?', in Levitas, R. & Guy, W. (1996) (eds) *Interpreting Official Statistics*. London; New York: Routledge.

Levitas, R. & Guy, W. (1996) 'Introduction', in Levitas, R. & Guy, W. (1996) (eds) *Interpreting Official Statistics*. London; New York: Routledge.

Lewis, G. (1999) 'Judges overturn convictions for newsagent killing'. *South Wales Echo*, December 17.

Lewis, G. (2004) 'Counting the cost of injustice'. *Wales on Sunday*, September 19.

Liberty (1998) 'Human Rights Act 1998'. <http://www.liberty-human-rights.org.uk/mpolic1.html>, 2 July 2002.

Liberty (2001) 'Paul Wright – death in custody: judge orders investigation'. <http://www.liberty-human-rights.org.uk/news-and-events/1-press-releases/2001/paul-wright-death-in-custody-judge-orders-in.shtml>, 14 March 2007.

Liberty (2007) 'Protecting Civil Liberties Promoting Human Rights'. <http://www.liberty-human-rights.org.uk>, 8 March 2007.

Lilley, P. (2002) *Taking Liberties*. London: Adam Smith Institute.

Linder, S. (1997) 'From jail to...what?'. *New Statesman*, February 28.

Liverpool Echo (2000) 'Police must find out the truth'. March 31 <http://www.innocent.org.uk/cases/johnkamara/index.html>, 30 November 2006.

Lord Chancellor's Department (1986) *Judicial Statistics: England and Wales for the year 1986*. London: HMSO Cm 173.

Lord Chancellor's Department (1987) *Judicial Statistics: England and Wales for the year 1987*. London: HMSO Cm 428.

Lord Chancellor's Department (1988) *Judicial Statistics: England and Wales for the year 1988*. London: HMSO Cm 745.

Lord Chancellor's Department (1989) *Judicial Statistics: England and Wales for the year 1989*. London: HMSO Cm 1154.

Lord Chancellor's Department (1991) *Judicial Statistics Annual Report*. London: HMSO Cm 1990.

Lord Chancellor's Department (1992) *Judicial Statistics Annual Report*. London: HMSO Cm 2268.

Lord Chancellor's Department (1993) *Judicial Statistics Annual Report*. London: HMSO Cm 2623.

Lord Chancellor's Department (1994) *Judicial Statistics Annual Report*. London: HMSO Cm 2891.

Lord Chancellor's Department (1995) *Judicial Statistics Annual Report*. London: HMSO Cm 3290.

Lord Chancellor's Department (1996) *Judicial Statistics Annual Report*. London: HMSO Cm 3716.

Lord Chancellor's Department (1997) *Judicial Statistics Annual Report*. London: HMSO Cm 3980.

Lord Chancellor's Department (1998) *Judicial Statistics Annual Report*. London: HMSO Cm 4371.

Lord Chancellor's Department (1999) *Judicial Statistics Annual Report*. London: HMSO Cm 4786.

Lord Chancellor's Department (2000) *Judicial Statistics Annual Report*. London: HMSO Cm 5223.

Lord Chancellor's Department (2001) *Judicial Statistics Annual Report*. London: HMSO Cm 5551.

Lord Chancellor's Department (2002) *Judicial Statistics Annual Report*. London: HMSO Cm 5863.

Macpherson (1999) The Stephen Lawrence Inquiry: report of an inquiry by Sir William Macpherson of Cluny. Presented to Parliament by the Secretary of State for the Home Department by Command of Her Majesty, February 1999: Cm 4262-I.

Magistrates' Court Act (1980) (c43). London: HMSO.

Maguire, A. (1994) *Miscarriage of Justice: An Irish Family's Story of Wrongful Conviction*. London: Roberts Rinehart Publishers.

Maher, G. (1994) 'Reforming the Criminal Process: A Scottish Perspective', in McConville, M. & Bridges, L. (1994) (eds) *Criminal Justice in Crisis*. Aldershot: Edward Elgar.

Major-Poetzl, P. (1983) *Michel Foucault's Archaeology of Western Culture: Toward a New Science of History*. Brighton, Sussex: The Harvester Press.

Manning, P.K. (1979) 'The Social Control of Police Work', in Holdaway, S. (1979) *The British Police*. London: Edward Arnold.

Mansfield, M. (1993) *Presumed Guilty: The British Legal System Exposed*. London: Heinmann.

Mansfield, M. & Taylor, T. (1993) 'Post-Conviction Procedures', in Walker, C. & Starmer, K. (1993) (eds) *Justice in Error*. London: Blackstone Press Limited.

Mark, R. (1977) *Policing a Perplexed Society*. London: Allen and Unwin.

Mark, R. (1978) *In the Office of Constable*. London: Collins.

Mathiesen, T. (1974) *The Politics of Abolition: essays in political action theory*. London: Martin Robertson.

Mathiesen, T. (2002) 'Expanding the concept of terrorism?', in Scraton, P. (2002) (ed.) *Beyond September 11: An Anthology of Dissent*. London: Pluto Press.

Mather, L.M. (1979) *Plea bargaining or trial? The process of criminal-case disposition*. Lexington, Mass D.C.: Heath.

May, J.D. (1994) *The Guildford and Woolwich Inquiry*. London: HMSO HC 449.

McBarnet, D.J. (1981) *Conviction: Law, the State and the Construction of Justice*. London: The MacMillan Press Ltd.

McConville, M. (1989) 'Weaknesses in the British Judicial System'. *Times Higher Education Supplement*, November 3.

McConville, M. & Bridges, L. (1994) (eds) *Criminal Justice in Crisis*. Aldershot: Edward Elgar.

McConville, M. & Bridges, L. (1994a) 'Foreword', in McConville, M. & Bridges, L. (1994) (eds) *Criminal Justice in Crisis*. Aldershot: Edward Elgar.

McConville, M., Sanders, A. & Leng, R. (1991) *The case for the prosecution*. London: Routledge.

McElree, F. & Starmer, K. (1993) 'The Right to Silence', in Walker, C. & Starmer, K. (1993) (eds) *Justice in Error*. London: Blackstone Press Limited.

McGraw, E. (2006) 'Lock them up or let them out'. *Inside Time: The National Monthly Newspaper for Prisoners*, November.

McNay, L. (1994) *Foucault: A Critical Introduction*. Oxford: Polity Press.

Mega, M. & Syal, R. (2001) 'Errors put wrong men in jail, says fingerprint specialist'. *Daily Telegraph*, August 26.

Mental Health Act (1983). London: HMSO.

Merritt, S. (2000) 'Cry rape, not wolf'. *The Observer*, September 10.

Merseyside Against Injustice (2002) 'About us'. <http://website.lineone.net/~mai5>, 14 July 2002.

Miles, I. & Irvine, J. (1979) 'The Critique of Official Statistics', in Irvine, J., Miles, I. & Evans, J. (1979) (eds) *Demystifying Social Statistics*. London: Pluto Press.

Miller, W.R. (1979) 'Police Tradition in a Changing Society', in Holdaway, S. (1979) *The British Police*. London: Edward Arnold.

Miller, P. & Rose, N. (1990) 'Programming the Poor: Poverty, Calculation and Expertise'. Paper presented at the International Expert Meeting on Deprivation, Social Welfare and Expertise, Helsinki, August 27–29.

Mirfield, P. (1985) 'The Police And Criminal Evidence Act 1984: (4) The Evidence Provisions'. *Criminal Law Review*. London: Sweet and Maxwell.

Misak, C.J. (1999) 'Introduction', in Misak, C.J. (1999) (ed.) *Pragmatism*. Calgary: Canada University of Calgary Press.

Miscarriage of Justice Organisation UK (2000) 'Miscarriages of Justice Organisation'. <http://home.beseen.com/belief/mojouk>, 24 July 2000.

Miscarriages of Justice Organisation, Scotland (2006) 'Bringing hope to the innocent'. <http://www.mojoscotland.com>, 21 November 2006.

Miscarriages of Justice UK (2006) <http://www.mojuk.org.uk>, 15 December 2006.

Miscarriages of Justice UK (2002a) 'Gary Mills' *Miscarriages of justice UK Bulletins*. /eddie/tonygary.html>, 30 July 2002.

Morgan, B. (1992) 'Parents of sick children "being falsely accused"'. *The Independent*, August 21.

Morris, N. (2002) 'Conditions in jails "close to breaching Human Rights Act"'. *The Independent*, August 8.

Morton J. (1994) *Bent Coppers*. London: Warner.

Mullin, C. (1986) *Error Of Judgement: The Truth About The Birmingham Bombs*. London: Chatto & Windus Ltd.

Munro, C. (1985) 'The Police And Criminal Evidence Act 1984: (5) The Accountability of the Police'. *Criminal Law Review*. London: Sweet and Maxwell.

Murder (Abolition of Death Penalty) Act 1965. London: HMSO.

Murphy, J.P. (1990) *Pragmatism: From Peirce to Davidson*. Boulder, Colorado: Westview Press.

National Civil Rights Movement (2007) <http://www.ncrm.org.uk/index.html>, 8 March 2007.

Naughton, M. (2001) 'Wrongful convictions: towards a zemiological analysis of the tradition of criminal justice system reform'. *Radical Statistics*, 76, 50–65.

Naughton, M. (2002) 'Is the criminal justice system really ineffectual in obtaining conviction?'. *Inside Out*, July.

Naughton, M. (2003) 'How big is the "iceberg?": A zemiological approach to quantifying miscarriages of justice'. *Radical Statistics*, 81, 5–17.

Naughton, M. (2004a) 'Reorientating miscarriages of justice', in Hillyard, P., Pantazis, C., Gordon, D. & Tombs, S. (2004) (eds) *Beyond Criminology: Taking Harm Seriously*. London: Pluto Press.

Naughton, M. (2004b) 'The parole deal is not a "myth"'. *Inside Time: The National Monthly Newspaper for Prisoners*, 59, May.

Naughton, M. (2005) 'Why the Failure of the Prison Service and the Parole Board to Acknowledge Wrongful Imprisonment is Untenable'. *Howard Journal of Criminal Justice*, 44(1), 1–11.

Naughton, M. (2005b) 'Evidence-based-policy' and the government of the criminal justice system – only if the evidence fits!'. *Critical Social Policy*, 25(1), 47–69.

Naughton, M. (2005c) 'Redefining miscarriages of justice: a revived human rights approach to unearth subjugated discourses of wrongful criminal conviction'. *British Journal of Criminology*, 45(2), 165–182.

Naughton, M. (2005d) 'Miscarriages of justice and the government of the criminal justice system: an alternative perspective on the production and deployment of counter-discourse'. *Critical Criminology: An International Journal*, 13(2), 211–231.

Naughton, M. (2005e) 'The Parole Deal Does Exist'. *Inside Time: The National Monthly Newspaper for Prisoners*, 77, November, 18–19.

Naughton, M. (2006) 'Wrongful Convictions and Innocence Projects in the UK: Help, Hope and Education'. *Web Journal of Current Legal Issues*, 3.

Naughton, M. (2006b) 'The Parole Deal – Discredited?'. *Inside Time: The National Monthly Newspaper*, 81, 21.

Naughton, M. (2006c) 'Giving "voice" to prisoners maintaining innocence who may be innocent: excavating counter-discourses subjugated by the Parole Deal'. Paper presented at the Socio-Legal Studies Association Annual Conference, University of Stirling, 28–30 March 2006.

Naylor, L. (2004) *Judge for yourself how many are innocent*. London: Roots Books.

Nichols, T. (1996) 'Social Class: Official, Sociological and Marxist', in Levitas, R. & Guy, W. (1996) (eds) *Interpreting Official Statistics*. London; New York: Routledge.

Nobles, R. & Schiff, D. (1997) 'The Never Ending Story: Disguising Tragic Choices in Criminal Justice'. *The Modern Law Review*, 60, 2 March.

Nobles, R. & Schiff, D. (1995) 'Miscarriages of Justice: A Systems Approach'. *The Modern Law Review*, 58, 3 May.

Nobles, R. & Schiff, D. (2000) *Understanding Miscarriages of Justice: Law, the Media, and the Inevitability of Crisis*. Oxford: Oxford University Press.

Nobles, R. & Schiff, D. (2001) The Criminal Cases Review Commission: Reporting Success?. *Modern Law Review*, Vol. 64, No. 2, 280–299.

Norman, K. (2000) 'The causes of cot death'. <http://www.portia.org/chapter05/frame5.html>, 20 July 2002.

Norman, K. (2001) *Lynch – Mob Syndrome*. Elton, Cheshire: Infinity Junction.

Norman, K. (2001a) 'Meadow and MSbP', The Portia Campaign. <http://www.portia.org>, 8 November 2001.

Norman, K. (2001b) 'Guilty or Innocent: They do not care!'. <http://www.portia.org/chapter09/frame9.html>, 7 September 2001.

Norman, K. & Fryer, J. (2002) 'Angela Joyce Cannings: Another miscarriage of justice', The Portia Campaign. <http://www.portia.org>, 18 April 2002.

North, N. & Wilson, E. (1996) 'I'm Coming Home Mum: Bridgewater Four man's joy'. *Daily Mirror*, July 27.

Norton-Taylor, R. (2001) 'Guilty until proven innocent'. *The Guardian*, February 19.

Oakley, A. & Oakley, R. (1979) 'Sexism in Official Statistics' in Marxist', in Irvine, J., Miles, I. & Evans, J. (1979) (eds) *Demystifying Social Statistics*. London: Pluto Press.

O' Connor, P. (1993) 'Prosecution Disclosure: Principle, Practice and Justice', in Walker, C. & Starmer, K. (1993) (eds) *Justice in Error*. London: Blackstone Press Limited.

Osborne, T. (1994) 'Sociology, liberalism and the historicity of conduct'. *Economy and Society*, 23(4), 484–501.

Osborne, T. (1996) 'Security and Vitality: drains, liberalism and power in the nineteenth century', in Barry, A., Osborne, T. & Rose, N. (eds) (1996) *Foucault and Political Reason: Liberalism, neo-liberalism and rationalities of government*. London: UCL Press.

Osborne, T. (1998) *Aspects of Enlightenment: Social theory and the ethics of truth*. London: UCL Press.

Osoba, M.M. (1988) 'Obtaining the views of the people'. *The Police Journal: A Quarterly Review for the Police of the World*. Chichester, Sussex: Barry Rose Law Periodicals Ltd.

Owers, A. (2006) Annual Report of HM Inspector of Prisons for England and Wales 2004–2005. London: The Stationery Office.

Pallister, D. (1999) 'Appeal court clears police torture victim'. *The Guardian*, October 27.

Pallister, D. (1999a) 'An injustice that still reverberates'. *The Guardian*, October 19.

Pallister, D. (2000) 'Blair's apology to Guildford four'. *The Guardian*, June 6.

Panorama (2001) 'Finger of Suspicion'. *Broadcast Sunday*, 8 July 2001, 22:15 p.m. BBC1.

Pantazis, C. (1998) 'Inequalities in crime and criminal justice'. *Radical Statistics*, Number 68, Spring.

Parris, J. (1991) *Scapegoat: the inside story of the trial of Derek Bentley*. London: Duckworth.

Pattenden, R. (1996) *English Criminal Appeals 1884–1994: Appeals against conviction and sentence in England and Wales*. Oxford: Clarendon Press.

Patton, P. (1994) 'Foucault's Subject of Power'. *Political Theory Newsletter*, 6, 60–71.

Pearce, F. & Tombs, S. (1992) 'Realism and corporate crime', in Matthews, R. & Young, J. (1992) (eds) *Issues in Realist Criminology*. London: SAGE Publications.

Peek, L. (2001) 'Prisoner cleared after girl admits rape lie'. *The Times*, December 15.

Police and Criminal Evidence Act 1984 (1985) (s. 66) 'Codes of Practice'. London: HMSO.

Porter, S. (1996) 'Contra-Foucault: Soldiers, Nurses and Power'. *Sociology*, Vol. 30, No. 1, 59–78.

Prasad, R. (2002) 'Paralysed prisoner to sue over loss of dignity'. *The Guardian*, August 15.

Price, C. & Caplan, J. (1976) *The Confait Confessions*. London: Marion Boyars.

Price, C. (1985) 'Confession Evidence, the Police and Criminal Evidence Act and the Confait Case', in Baxter, J. & Koffman, L. (1985) (eds) *Police: The Constitution and the Community: A collection of original essays on issues raised by The Police and Criminal Evidence Act 1984*. Abingdon: Professional Books Limited.

Prison Reform Trust (2006) 'Disabled Prisoners'. <http://www.prisonreformtrust.org.uk>, 14 September 2006.

Prison Service Standards Manual (2000). London: HMSO.

Prisoners Information Book (2002) *Male Prisoners and Young Offenders*. London: Prison Reform Trust and HM Prison Service ISBN 0-946209-53-7.

Prisoners Information Book (2003) *Women Prisoners and Female Young Offenders*. London: Prison Reform Trust and HM Prison Service ISBN 0-946209-55-3.

Punch, M. (1985) *Conduct Unbecoming: The Social Construction of Police Deviance and Control*. London; New York: Tavistock Publication.

R v Dallagher [2002], EWCA Crim 1903.

R v Evans [1997], EWCA Crim 3145.

R v Davis, Johnson and Rowe, *The Times*, July 25, 2000; (2001) 1 Cr App R 115.

R v Mullen [1999], EWCA Crim 278.

R (Mullen) v Secretary of State for the Home Department [2002], EWCA Civ 1882.

R v Paris, Abdullahi and Miller (1993) 97, Cr App R99.

R v Secretary of State for the Home Department Ex parte Mellor [2001], EWCA Civ 472.

R v Treadway [1996], EWCA Crim 1457.

R v Turner [1970] 2, QB 321, 326.

R v Twitchell [2000] 1, Cr App R 373.

Rabinow, P. (1984) (ed.) *The Foucault Reader: An introduction to Foucault's thought.* London: Penguin.

Ramazanoglu, C. (1993) 'Introduction', in Ramazanoglu, C. (1993) (ed.) *Up Against Foucault: Explorations of some tensions between Foucault and Feminism.* London: Routledge.

Randall, C. (1997) 'Ex-soldier wins appeal after serving 25 years for murder'. *The Daily Telegraph*, December 4.

Regan, S. (1997a) 'Miscarriage....Ultimate Scenario for a Nightmare' *Scandals in Justice* 27 May 1997 <http://www.scandals.org/articles/sr970527c.html>, 30 November 2006.

Regan, S. (1997b) 'The Bridgewater Catastrophe'. *Scandals in Justice*, 27 May 1997. <http://www.scandals.org/articles/sr970527c.html>, 30 November 2006.

Regina v. Secretary of State for the Home Department Ex Parte Simms (A.P.) Secretary of State for the Home Department Ex Parte O'Brien (Consolidated Appeals).

Reiman, J. (1995) *The Rich Get Richer and the Poor Get Prison: Ideology, Class and Criminal Justice* (Fourth Edition). Boston; London: Allyn & Bacon.

Reiner, R. (1985) *The Politics of the Police.* London: Wheatsheaf Books Ltd.

Reiner, R. (1996) 'The Case of the Missing Crimes', in Levitas, R. & Guy, W. (1996) (eds) *Interpreting Official Statistics.* London; New York: Routledge.

'Report of the Committee of Inquiry into the Beck Case'. *The Times*, 1904, November 26, 6–7.

Roberts, S. (2003) 'Unsafe Convictions: Defining and Compensating Miscarriages of Justice'. *Modern Law Review*, 3: 441–451.

Roberts, Y. (1999) 'Freedom fighter'. *The Guardian*, September 30.

Robins, J. (2000) 'Fingerprints system that needs a helping hand'. *The Times*, November 7.

Rose, D. (2002) '"Abuser" was netted in police trawl. But is he innocent'. *The Guardian*, January 6.

Rose, D. (2004) 'They created Winston Silcott, the beast of Broadwater Farm. And they won't let this creation lie down and die'. *The Observer*, January 18.

Rose, G. (1994) *Dialectic of Nihilism: Post-Structuralism and the Law.* Oxford: Blackwell.

Rose, J., Panter, S. & Wilkinson, T. (1997) *Innocents: How Justice Failed Stefan Kiszko and Lesley Molseed.* London: Fourth Estate.

Rose, N. (1990) *Governing The Soul: The Shaping of the Private Self.* London: Routledge.

Rose, N. (1991) 'Governing By Numbers: Figuring Out Democracy'. *Accounting, Organisations and Society*, Vol. 16, No. 7, 673–692.

Rose, N. (1993) *Towards a critical sociology of freedom.* Inaugural Lecture delivered 5 May 1992 at Goldsmiths College, University of London: Goldsmiths College Occasional Paper.

Rose, N. (1999) *Powers of Freedom: Reframing Political Thought.* Cambridge: Cambridge University Press.

Rose, N. (1996) 'Governing "advanced" liberal democracies', in Barry, A., Osborne, T. & Rose, N. (1996) (eds) *Foucault and political reason: liberalism, neo-liberalism and rationalities of government*. London: UCL Press.

Rose, N. & Miller, P. (1992) 'Political power beyond the State: problematics of government'. *The British Journal of Sociology*, 43(2).

Rowe, R. (2000) 'Not fair'. *The Guardian*, March 17.

Royal Commission on Capital Punishment (1953) *Report* (Cmd. 8932), London: HMSO.

Royal Commission on Criminal Procedure (1981) *Report* (Cmnd 8092), London: HMSO.

Royal Commission on Criminal Justice (1993) *Report* (Cm. 2263), London HMSO.

Rozenberg, J. (2001) 'Man who served 27 years for murder freed on bail'. *The Telegraph*, February 8.

Rozenberg, J. (2002) 'Man walks free after ruling on 1973 killing'. *The Telegraph*, January 16.

Ruggiero, V., Ryan, M. & Sim, J. (1995) (eds) *Western European Penal Systems: A Critical Anatomy*. London: SAGE Publications.

Ryan, B. (1977) *The poisoned life of Mrs Maybrick*. London: Penguin.

Ryan, M. (1978) *The acceptable pressure group: Inequality in the penal lobby: a case study of the Howard League and RAP*. Farnborough: Saxon House.

Ryan, M. (1983) *The Politics of Penal Reform*. London: Longman.

Sanders, A. (1999) 'Responding to Harm – Integrating the Rights of Victims and Perpetrators'. Paper presented at the 'Zemiology Beyond Criminology' Conference, Dartington, England (February).

Sanders, A. & Bridges, L. (1983) 'The Right to Legal Advice', in Walker, C. & Starmer, K. (1993) (eds) *Justice in Error*. London: Blackstone Press Limited.

Sanders, A. & Young, R. (1994) 'The Legal Wilderness of Police Interrogation'. The Tom Sargant Memorial Lecture <http://www.btinternet.com/~peter.hill34/sander.htm>, 24 October 2006.

Schwendinger, H. & Schwendinger, J. (1975) 'Defenders of order or guardians of human rights?', in Taylor, I., Walton, P. & Young, J. (1975) *Critical Criminology*. London: Routledge & Kegan Paul.

Scraton, P. and Gordon, P. (1984) (eds) *Causes for concern: British Criminal Justice on Trial*. Harmondsworth: Penguin.

Scraton, P. (2002) 'The Politics of Morality', in Scraton, P. (2002) (ed.) *Beyond September 11: An Anthology of Dissent*. London: Pluto Press.

Scraton, P. (2002b) 'In the name of a "Just War"', in Scraton, P. (2002) (ed.) *Beyond September 11: An Anthology of Dissent*. London: Pluto Press.

Scraton, P., Sim, J. & Skidmore, P. (1991) *Prisons under protest*. Milton Keynes: Open University Press.

Sedley, S. (1999) 'A benchmark of British justice'. *The Guardian*, March 5.

Shaw, T. (1998) 'Woman twice jailed for murder is freed'. *The Daily Telegraph*, April 8.

Sheck, B., Neufeld, P. & Dwyer, J. (2001) *Actual Innocence: Five Days to Execution and other Dispatches from the Wrongly Convicted*. New York: Signet Publications.

Sheridan, A. (1980) *Michel Foucault: The Will To Truth*. London: Tavistock Publications.

ShirleyMcKie.Com (2006) <http://www.shirleymckie.com>, 14 December 2006.

Singh, S. (1994) 'Understanding the Long-Term Relationship between the Police and the Policed', in McConville, M. & Bridges, L. (1994) (eds) *Criminal Justice in Crisis*. Aldershot: Edward Elgar.

Simmel, G. (1955) *Conflict*. London: Collier-Macmillan.

Smart, B. (1988) *Michel Foucault*. London: Routledge.

Southall Black Sisters (2007) <http://www.southallblacksisters.org.uk>, 8 March 2007.

South Wales Liberty (2002) 'What South Wales Liberty do'. <http://www.south-wales-liberty.org.uk/whatwedo.htm>, 2 July 2002.

Statewatch (2007) 'Monitoring the state and civil liberties in Europe'. <http://www.statewatch.org>, 8 March 2007.

Steele, J. (1995) 'Ex-soldier jailed for killing is free after 16 years'. *The Daily Telegraph*, July 14.

Steele, J. (1997) 'Police errors "could not be repeated"'. *Electronic Telegraph* Issue 638: <http://www.telegraph.co.ukm>, 22 March 2000.

Support Organisation for Falsely Accused People (2006) <http://www.crime-line.info/sofap.htm>, 25 November 2006.

Supporting All Falsely Accused with Resources Information (2006) <http://home.vicnet.net.au/~safari>, 20 November 2006.

Supreme Court Act (1981) London: HMSO.

Sutherland, E.H. (1940) 'White-Collar Criminality'. *American Sociological Review*, 5 (February), 1–12.

Sutherland, E.H. (1983) *White collar crime: Uncut version*. London: Yale University Press.

Sweeney, J., Ahmed, K. & Bright, M. (2000) 'Elite police squad in graft probe'. *The Guardian*, May 14.

Sweeney, J. & Law, B. (2001) 'Gene find casts doubt on double "cot death" murders'. *The Guardian*, July 15.

Taylor, C. (2001) 'Advance Disclosure: reflections on the criminal Procedure and Investigations Act 1996'. *The Howard Journal*, 40(2).

Tempest, M. (2002) 'Criminal justice bill under fire'. *The Guardian*, November 21.

Tendler, S. (1998) 'Man of 70 to be cleared of murder after 23 years in jail'. *The Times*, June 10.

The Citizen's Commission on Scandals in Justice (2006) 'Mission Statement'. <http://www.scandals.org/mission.html>, 12 September 2006.

The Five Percenters (2002) 'Home'. <http://www.sbs5.dircon.co.uk/five.htm>, July 4.

The Five Percenters (2006) '3 things we'd like to see happen'. <http://www.sbs5.dircon.co.uk/five.htm>, 4 October 2006.

The Law Commission (2001) 'Double Jeopardy and Prosecution Appeals: Report on two references under section 3(1)(e) of the Law Commissions Act 1965'. LAW COM Number 267, Cm 5048.

The Portia Campaign (2006) 'The Portia Campaign'. <http://www.portia.org>, 24 October 2006.

The Portia Campaign (2002) 'Portia History'. <http://www.portia.org/History.html>, 21 February 2002.

The Prison (Amendment) Rules 2005. London: HMSO, ISBN 0-11-072644-8.

The Prison (Amendment) (No. 2) Rules 2005. London: HMSO, ISBN 0-11-073792-X.

The Prison Rules (1999) Norwich: HMSO, ISBN 0-11-082248-X.

Thompson, T. (2000) 'Corrupt police split reward cash with fake informants'. *The Guardian*, December 17.

Times Parliamentary Proceedings (1889) August 9, 5.

Times Law Report (1998) 'Bentley trial unfair through flawed summing-up'. *The Times*, July 31.

Times Law Report (2000) 'Court of Appeal bound by plea bargain'. *The Times*, October 25.

Tombs, S. (1999) 'The Politics of Crime and Harm: the case of occupational health and safety'. Paper presented to the Zemiology: Beyond Criminology? Conference Dartington Hall, 12–13 February.

Tombs, S. & Whyte, D. (2003) (eds) *Unmasking the crimes of the powerful: Scutinizing states and corporations*. New York: Peter Lang.

Trasler, G. (1976) Letter to *The Times*, February 28.

Travis, A. (2001) 'Ministers to make selective response'. *The Guardian*, October 9.

Travis, A. & Hopkins, N. (2002) 'Criminal justice system ineffectual, says Blair'. *The Guardian*, June 19.

Trow, M.J. (1990) *'Let him have it Chris': the murder of Derek Bentley*. London: Constable.

United Against Injustice (2006) 'The National Federation of Miscarriage of Justice Campaign and Support Organisations'. <http://www.unitedagainstinjustice.org.uk>, 25 November 2006.

United Campaign Against False Allegations of Abuse (2000) 'Groups Unite in National Campaign' Action Against False Allegations of Abuse. Newsletter 5 Autumn–Winter 2000. <http://www.aafaa.org.uk>, 30 July 2002.

United Nations (1997) 'Milestones in United Nations History'. <http://www.un.org/Overview/milesto4.htm>, 16 September 2006.

United Nations (2006) 'The Universal Declaration of Human Rights'. <http://www.un.org/Overview/rights.html>, 30 November 2006.

Vasagar, J. (2000) 'The modest crusader'. *The Guardian*, November 20.

Vasagar, J. (2000a) 'Wrongly convicted soldier gets £1m'. *The Guardian*, June 9.

Vasagar, J. (2002) 'End of a nightmare'. *The Guardian*, January 16.

Vasagar, J. & Ward, D. (2001) 'After 27 years, Downing is freed'. *The Guardian*, February 8.

Viner, K. (2002) 'Feminism as imperialism'. *The Guardian*, 21 September.

Wadham, J. (2001) 'Innocents are going to be locked up'. *The Guardian*, November 21.

Walker, C. (1993) 'Introduction', in Walker, C. & Starmer, K. (1993) (eds) *Justice in Error*. London: Blackstone Press Limited.

Walker, C. (2002) 'Miscarriages of justice: An inside job?'. Paper presented at the Annual Lecture of the Institute for Criminology and Criminal Justice, University of Hull, May 2001. <http://www.leeds.ac.uk/law/ccjs/an_reps/13rep07f.doc>, 1 September 2006.

Ward, D. (2002) 'Prisoner's 27 long years of defiance'. *The Guardian*, January 16.

Ward, T. (1999) 'Contested Harms: Law, Science and Zemiology'. Paper presented at the 'Zemiology Beyond Criminology' Conference. Dartington, England (February).

Ward, J. (1993) *Ambushed: My Story*. London: Vermilion.

Watkins, T. (2001) 'Miscarriage Statistics', E-mail correspondence in reply to my enquiry about the reliability of the Portia Campaign's statement that there are currently 3000 innocent people wrongfully imprisoned in England and Wales, 19 September 2001.

Weale, S. (2000) 'This ex-head teacher abused these women when they were his pupils. So why didn't he go to prison?', *The Guardian*, June 22.

Weaver, M. (1997) 'Justice provides no comfort for Carl's parents'. *Electronic Telegraph* Issue 638. <http://www.telegraph.co.uk>, 12 August 2001.

Weaver, M. (1998) 'Man "fitted up" by police gets £200,000'. *Daily Telegraph*, January 20.

Weaver, M. (2000) 'Appeal for lifer who has spent 27 years in jail'. *Daily Telegraph*, November 15.

Webster, R. (2005) *The Secret of Bryn Estyn: The Making of a Modern Witch Hunt*. Oxford: The Orwell Press.

Weir, P. (2000) 'What price 25 years'. *The Guardian*, June 20.

Wells, C. (1994) 'The Royal Commission on Criminal Justice: A Room Without a View', in McConville, M. & Bridges, L. (1994) (eds) *Criminal Justice in Crisis*. Aldershot: Edward Elgar.

Whelan, A. (1998) 'Bridgewater Four'. *The Times*, July 30.

Whelan, A. (2002) 'Miscarriages of Justice'. Paper presented United Against Injustice Official Launch Blackburne House, Hope Street, Liverpool, October 12.

White, M. (1997) 'David Evans: "In the gutter"'. *The Guardian*, March 5.

Williams, G. (1976) Letter to *The Times*, February 25.

Wilson, E. (1996) 'Agony of 17-year battle for justice'. *Daily Mirror*, July 27.

Wilson, J. (2001) '£1.4 award for family of wrongfully hanged man'. *The Guardian*, May 14.

Wilson, D. (2001a) 'The guilt trap'. *The Guardian*, February 1.

Winter, J. (1994) 'Criminally Unjust: The Royal Commission and Northern Ireland', in McConville, M. & Bridges, L. (1994) (eds) *Criminal Justice in Crisis*. Aldershot: Edward Elgar.

Woffinden, B. (1987) *Miscarriages of Justice*. London; Toronto; Sydney: Hodder & Stoughton.

Woffinden, B. (1998) 'Evidence of innocence'. *The Times*, June 2.

Woffinden, B. (1998a) 'Wrong again: Sion Jenkins is innocent'. *New Statesman*, July 10.

Woffinden, B. (1999) 'No, you can't see. It might help your client'. *The Guardian*, May 4.

Woffinden, B. (1999b) 'Thumbs down'. *The Guardian*, January 12.

Woffinden, B. (1999c) 'The case of the missing thumbprint'. *The New Statesman*, January.

Woffinden, B. (2000) 'No judge or jury will ever believe those officers fitted you up. You've just got to serve your sentence'. *The Guardian*, July 13.

Woffinden, B. (2000a) 'Guilty until proven innocent'. *The Guardian*, May 22.

Woffinden, B. (2000b) 'Extra time for being "in denial"'. *The Guardian*, October 16.

Woffinden, B. (2001) 'Justice in jeopardy'. *The Guardian*, March 8.

Woffinden, B. (2001a) 'There are probably 20 convictions that I now consider unsafe'. *The Guardian*, November 7.

Woffinden, B. (2001b) 'Case for the defence'. *The Guardian*, December 12.

Woffinden, B. (2001c) 'Prisoners win right to challenge governor'. *The Guardian*, August 6.

Woffinden, B. (2004) 'Earprint landed innocent man in jail for murder'. *The Guardian*, January 23.

Wolin, S.S. (1988) 'On the Theory and Practice of Power', in Arac, J. (1988) (ed.) *After Foucault: Humanistic Knowledge, Postmodern Challenges*. London: Rutgers University Press.

Woollacott, M. (2001) 'The United Nations faces an Afghan nightmare'. *The Guardian*, October 26.

Younge, G. (2000) 'The day of reckoning'. *The Guardian*, July 3.

Index